Hybrid Threats, Cyberterrorism and Cyberwarfare

Nowadays in cyberspace, there is a burst of information to which everyone has access. However, apart from the advantages the internet offers, it also hides numerous dangers for both people and nations. Cyberspace has a dark side, including terrorism, bullying, and other types of violence. Cyberwarfare is a kind of virtual war that causes the same destruction that a physical war would also do.

A hybrid threat is an umbrella term encompassing a wide variety of existing adverse circumstances and actions, such as terrorism, migration, piracy, corruption, ethnic conflict, etc., and is not exclusively a tool of asymmetric or non-state actors, but can be applied by state and non-state actors alike. 'Cyberconflict' and 'cyberwar' serve as examples of the use of new technologies within the scope of hybrid threats. Cyberwar basically refers to a sustained computer-based cyberattack by a state against the information technology (IT) infrastructure of a target state. On the other hand, cybersecurity is a major factor that shapes productivity and efficiency of the modern industry in both technical and economic terms.

The book discusses and analyses current posture of cyberterrorism, cyberwarfare, and hybrid threats—sector-specific cyberattacks that have the form of cyberterrorism and represents the recent actions that members of the European Union (EU), the United States, and other nations have taken in order to strengthen their systems against such attacks. There has never been a higher risk of a major catastrophe as a result of the rise in offensive cyberactivity, particularly the possibility of cyber–physical strikes against critical services. Recent cyberattacks against critical infrastructure, along with the continuous migration crisis, have been the main driving forces that led to the decision to publish this book.

Hybrid Threats, Cyberterrorism and Cyberwarfare

Edited by
Mohamed Amine Ferrag,
Ioanna Kantzavelou, Leandros Maglaras
and Helge Janicke

CRC Press
Taylor & Francis Group
Boca Raton London New York

CRC Press is an imprint of the
Taylor & Francis Group, an **informa** business

Designed cover image: Shutterstock Images

First edition published 2024
by CRC Press
2385 Executive Center Drive, Suite 320, Boca Raton, FL 33431

and by CRC Press
4 Park Square, Milton Park, Abingdon, Oxon, OX14 4RN

CRC Press is an imprint of Taylor & Francis Group, LLC

© 2024 selection and editorial matter, Mohamed Amine Ferrag, Ioanna Kantzavelou, Leandros Maglaras and Helge Janicke; individual chapters, the contributors

Library of Congress Cataloging-in-Publication Data
Names: Ferrag, Mohamed Amine, 1987–editor. | Kantzavelou, Ioanna, editor. |
   Maglaras, Leandros, editor. | Janicke, Helge, editor.
Title: Hybrid threats, cyberterrorism and cyberwarfare / edited by Mohamed
   Amine Ferrag, Ioanna Kantzavelou, Leandros Maglaras, Helge Janicke.
Description: Boca Raton, FL : CRC Press, 2024. | Includes bibliographical
   references and index.
Identifiers: LCCN 2023020284 (print) | LCCN 2023020285 (ebook) |
   ISBN 9781032323749 (hbk) | ISBN 9781032323763 (pbk) | ISBN
   9781003314721 (ebk)
Subjects: LCSH: Cyberterrorism. | Computer security.
Classification: LCC HV6773.15.C97 H93 2024 (print) | LCC HV6773.15.
   C97 (ebook) | DDC 363.325—dc23/eng/20230720
LC record available at https://lccn.loc.gov/2023020284
LC ebook record available at https://lccn.loc.gov/2023020285

ISBN: 978-1-032-32374-9 (hbk)
ISBN: 978-1-032-32376-3 (pbk)
ISBN: 978-1-003-31472-1 (ebk)

DOI: 10.1201/9781003314721

Typeset in Caslon
by Apex CoVantage, LLC

Contents

Foreword

Cybercrime consists of criminal activities committed online by using electronic means and information and communications technology (ICT) systems. All critical sectors (e.g., financial, governmental, health, transport, energy) have experienced various attacks in recent years. Cybercrime has become an increasing threat to European Union (EU) and international cyberspace. The rapid increase of digitalization is not accompanied by mitigation actions exposing our infrastructures, networks, and services, and provides cybercriminals with the opportunity to attack them. Motivations (e.g. political, terrorism, commercial, financial) and capabilities (e.g. computing power, skills, sophistication) of the cybercriminals increase the massive attack potential daily.

Collaboration, effective policies, certification, skills, competencies, interdisciplinary synergies, and ethical values are the main mitigation actions that will make out cyberspace resilient from attacks and security incidents. Strong collaboration between EU member states and international allies is necessary to shield cyberspace from upcoming attacks.

EU has already taken policy and legislative measures (e.g. NIS, NISII, eIDAS, GDPR, Cyber Resilience Act and proposed AI and Chip Acts) to stepping up EU capacity to respond to cybercrises. On the external front, the EU is implementing the 'cyberdiplomacy toolbox', its diplomatic response to malicious cyberactivities, which sets out the measures under the Common Foreign and Security Policy.

As digitization and automation across all domains progresses rapidly and decision-making at all levels becomes heavily dependent on Big Data, artificial intelligence (AI) systems, and emerging technologies (e.g. satellite, 5G/6G, robots), the safety of government, civilian, and military operations depend heavily on secure systems, services. and self-healing, dual-use cybersecurity technologies.

The increasing sophistication and complexity of the attacks require accelerated advances at all aspects of the cybersecurity process ranging from cybersecurity management to incident handling (to forecast, identify, analyze, and respond to incidents) to auditing to certifying.

Although it is difficult to capture all aspects and complexity of today's cybercriminal ecosystem, this book adopts an interesting view. The various chapters of the book address not only specific sectors where cyberwarfare can be used like 5G, smart grids and industrial productions, but also general questions related to the discernible difference between cyberwarfare and cyberterrorism, and the problem of attribution of cyberattacks, especially those targeting critical infrastructures.

The reader of the book will find major security issues faced by new technologies like 5G, smart grids, and industrial control systems. The various chapters discuss the main attack vectors that are used in order to perform cyberattacks against critical systems and ways of mitigating the impact of likely vulnerabilities on the systems.

Each chapter can be read independently, providing interesting case studies. The book contributes to the literature on the topics of hybrid threats, cyberwarfare, and cyberterrorism.

Professor Nineta Polemi
University of Piraeus (Greece)

Preface

The expansion of the digital world tends to be unlimited, and no authority or government might ever achieve to restrict its ability to cover nearly everything in the future. As a consequence of this broadness, threats and attacks transform into different evolutionary types, aiming for more targets, and attackers use advanced technology with intelligence—and the outcomes reveal a new world with enormous gaps compared to decades ago. This remodels real-world attacks and wars into hybrid attacks and virtual wars, named cyberwarfare. Terrorism likewise is advancing all the time, by incorporating cutting-edge technology and intelligent tools, generating corresponding cyberterrorism. All these new formations and structures eventually are well established nowadays, creating significant problems in securing computing systems and preventing attacks against infrastructures owned by countries, or against the safety and peace of people.

As we must strive to address this problem, we admit that in cyberspace, there is a burst of information to which everyone has access. However, apart from the advantages the internet offers, it also hides numerous dangers for both people and nations. Cyberspace has a dark side, including terrorism, bullying, and other types of violence. Cyberwarfare is a kind of virtual war that causes the same destruction as would a physical war. Hybrid threat is an umbrella term encompassing a wide variety of existing adverse circumstances and actions, such as terrorism, migration, piracy, corruption, ethnic conflict, etc., and is not exclusively a tool of asymmetric or non-state actors, but can be applied by state and non-state actors alike. 'Cyberconflict' and 'cyberwar' serve as examples of the use of new technologies within the scope of hybrid threats. Cyberwar mainly refers to a sustained computer-based cyberattack by a state against the information technology (IT) infrastructure of a target state.

In this book, we discuss cyberterrorism, cyberwarfare, and hybrid threats. We outline the different types, motivations, and countermeasures from a narrative point of view. With a strategic vision, we attempt to provide a comprehensive understanding of advanced critical issues in cybersecurity that directly affect people's lives. Recent cyberattacks against critical infrastructures in the United States, along with the continuous migration crisis, have been the main driving forces that led to the decision to produce this book.

The book consists of nine chapters with substantial coverage of cyberterrorism and cyberwarfare issues in an in-depth approach. These include the introduction and analysis of the current posture of cyberterrorism, cyberwarfare, and hybrid threats, then focusing on sector-specific cyberattacks that have the form of cyberterrorism (maritime, smart grids, Industry 4.0, etc.) and, in the end, present the recent actions that the European Union (EU), United States, and other nations have taken in order to strengthen their systems against such attacks.

Chapter 1 introduces the areas of cyberwarfare and cyberterrorism and establishes their different types, as well as the origins of motivations, which guide activities that fall within. Espionage, sabotage, and propaganda are among the types of cyberwarfare that initiate new paths of research interests through the digital world. A number of incidents present the size of the problem and the level of resilience that can be achieved.

Chapter 2 reveals significant security-related challenges imposed by globalization, and examines the EU policies connected to 5G technologies that address these challenges. Beyond this, 5G geopolitics games between the two giants, the United States and China, leave Europe embarrassed with no clear roles to play. Issues connected to the concepts of European sovereignty and strategic autonomy are examined and discussed to define whether the EU would take action and which actions.

Chapter 3 discusses the problem of attribution, explores legal issues and ethical concerns prompted by certain types of cyberattacks, and concludes on the likelihood that international cyberwar can be regulated via conventional means. Interesting conjectures about whether effective techniques will be developed to counteract cyberattacks on a global scale provide theoretical aspects of attributing and regulating cyberwars.

Chapter 4 presents the transformation of terrorism into cyberterrorism. This transformation has a theoretical background based on Rapoport's wave theory. Two separate cases, Al Qaeda and the Islamic State/ISIS, give the practical point of view necessary to reveal the 'Digital Jihad' model upon which cyberterrorism is being developed.

Chapter 5 explores vulnerabilities against communication and network technologies, such as advanced persistent threats (APT), and focuses on distributed denial of service (DDoS) attacks. A solution is presented to counteract DDoS attacks on smart grids which includes machine learning–based transmission control protocol (TCP) congestion control strategies. The proposed strategies aim for network performance optimization, and to adjust parameters and resource allocation in cases of DDoS attacks.

Chapter 6 delves into maritime cybersecurity challenges and examines potential solutions. An analysis of cyberattacks against cyber–physical systems onboard ships presents the diversity and the increasing sophistication problems that have to be addressed. The outcome of this survey is a complete cyberattack landscape specific to such systems and with proposed solutions to mitigate damage and loss.

Chapter 7 describes cyberwarfare in Ukraine and compares this new type against the old ones. By examining incidents, the targets, the tools, and the services are presented to identify new methods and tactics assisted by technology that cover a wide range of cyberattacks and victim systems. Misinformation and disinformation spread around are discussed as other significant problems that affect not only Ukrainian people but worldwide.

Chapter 8 examines the types and levels of exposure an industrial control system (ICT) encounters when different cyberthreats target it. The vulnerable points in different types of ICTs are presented, and then methods for theoretical estimations of cybersecurity risks are provided. The production process in Industry 4.0 environments is also considered as the way cost analysis could affect these estimations.

Chapter 9 initiates a debate on critical differences between cyberwarfare and cyberterrorism. Arguments are opposed about whether there is a line that no longer distinguishes one from the other. The interest is concentrated on the subject that is committing the act. Subjects are examined by state-driven motivations or by financial incentives, depending on the goals of the cyberactivities.

About the Editors

Mohamed Amine Ferrag received bachelor's, master's, Ph.D., and habilitation degrees in computer science from Badji Mokhtar—Annaba University, Annaba, Algeria, in June 2008, June 2010, June 2014, and April 2019, respectively. From 2014–2022, he was an associate professor at the Department of Computer Science, Guelma University, Algeria. From 2019–2022, he was a visiting senior researcher with the NAU-Lincoln Joint Research Center of Intelligent Engineering, Nanjing Agricultural University, China. Since 2022, he has been the lead researcher at Artificial Intelligence & Digital Science Research Center, Technology Innovation Institute, Abu Dhabi, United Arab Emirates. His research interests include wireless network security, network coding security, applied cryptography, blockchain technology, and Artificial Intelligence (AI) for cybersecurity. He has published over 120 papers in international journals and conferences in these areas. He has been conducting several research projects with international collaborations on these topics. He was a recipient of the 2021 Institute of Electrical & Electronic Engineers (IEEE) TEM Best Paper Award, as well as the 2022 Scopus Algeria Award. He is featured in Stanford University's list of the world's top 2% of scientists for the years 2020, 2021, and 2022. He is a senior member of the IEEE and a member of the Association for Computing Machinery (ACM).

Ioanna Kantzavelou is an assistant professor at the Department of Informatics and Computer Engineering at the School of Engineering of the University of West Attica. She received a B.Sc. in informatics from the Department of Informatics of the Technological Educational Institute of Athens, an M.Sc. by Research in computer security from the Department of Computer Science at the University College Dublin of the National University of Ireland, and a Ph.D. on 'Intrusion Detection in Information Technology Security' from the Department of Information and Communication Systems Engineering of the University of the Aegean. She has worked in research and development (R&D) projects funded by the Greek government, the Irish government, and the EU. Her published work includes chapters in books (IOS Press), conferences, and journals, recording remarkable citations in her research work. She has joint editorship of three IOS Press collections. She has been a repetitive reviewer in many international conferences, such as ACM SEC, IEEE TrustCom, IFIP SEC, ESORICS, and IEEE CIS, and she is currently a reviewer for high-ranking journals of IEEE, Elsevier, Springer, and Emerald. She is a member of the Greek Computer Society (GCS), the ACM, and the IEEE Computer Society.

Leandros A. Maglaras is a professor of cybersecurity in the School of Computing at Edinburgh Napier University. From September 2017–November 2019, he was the director of the National Cyber Security Authority of Greece. He obtained a B.Sc. (M.Sc. equivalent) in electrical and computer engineering from the Aristotle University of Thessaloniki, Greece in 1998, M.Sc. in industrial production and management from the University of Thessaly in 2004, and M.Sc. and Ph.D. degrees in electrical and computer engineering from the University of Thessaly, in 2008 and 2014, respectively. In 2018, he was awarded a Ph.D. in intrusion detection in supervisory control and data acquisition (SCADA) systems from the University of Huddersfield. He is featured in Stanford University's list of the world's top 2% of scientists. He is a senior member of the IEEE and is an author of more than 200 papers in scientific magazines and conferences.

Helge Janicke is the research director of the Cyber Security Cooperative Research Centre, Australia. He is affiliated with Edith Cowan University and holds a visiting professorship in cybersecurity at De Montfort University (DMU), UK. His research interests are in the area of cybersecurity, in particular with applications in critical infrastructures using cyber–physical systems, SCADA and industrial control systems. His current research investigates the application of agile techniques to cyberincident response in critical infrastructure, managing human errors that lead to cyberincidents, and research on cyberwarfare and cyberpeacekeeping. He established DMU's Cyber Technology Institute and its Airbus Centre of Excellence in SCADA Cyber Security and Forensics Research. He has been the Head of School of Computer Science at De Montfort University, UK before taking up his current position as research director for the Cyber Security Cooperative Research Centre. He founded the International Symposium on Industrial Control system cybersecurity research (ICS-CSR) and contributed over 150 peer-reviewed articles and conference papers to the field that resulted from his collaborative research with industry partners such as Airbus, BT, Deloitte, Rolls-Royce, QinetiQ, and General Dynamics.

Contributors

John M.A. Bothos
Department of Economics
University of Thessaly
Volos, Greece

Konstantinos Demertzis
School of Science & Technology
Informatics Studies
Hellenic Open University, Greece

Nathan Downes
School of Computing
Engineering and Media
De Montfort University, UK

Lazaros Iliadis
School of Engineering
Department of Civil
   Engineering
Democritus University of Thrace
Kimmeria, Xanthi, Greece

Ioanna Kantzavelou
Department of
   Informatics and Computer
   Engineering
University of West Attica
Athens, Greece

Eleni Kapsokoli
Department of International and
   European Studies
University of Piraeus,
   Greece

Georgios Kavallieratos
Department of Information
   Security and Communication
   Technology
Norwegian University of Science
   and Technology
Gjøvik, Norway

Sokratis Katsikas
Department of Information
    Security and Communication
    Technology
Norwegian University of
    Science and Technology
Gjøvik, Norway

Panayotis Kikiras
School of Science
Department of Computer Science
University of Thessaly
Galaneika, Lamia, Greece

Theodoros Komninos
Computer Technology Institute
    and Press "Diophantus"
    (CTI-Diophantus)
Athens, Greece

Andrew N. Liaropoulos
Department of International and
    European Studies
University of Piraeus, Greece

Leandros Maglaras
School of Computing
Edinburgh Napier University, UK

Spyridon Sampanis
Department of Informatics and
    Computer Engineering
University of West Attica
Athens, Greece

Dimitrios Serpanos
Computer Technology Institute
    and Press "Diophantus"
    (CTI-Diophantus)
Athens, Greece

Charalabos Skianis
Department of Information and
    Communication Systems
    Engineering
University of the Aegean
Karlovassi, Samos, Greece

Melina-Eleftheria Spiliopoulou
Department of Informatics and
    Computer Engineering
University of West Attica
Athens, Greece

Dimitrios Taketzis
Hellenic National Defence
    General Staff
Stratopedo Papagou
Athens, Greece

Vasileios Vlachos
Department of Economics
University of Thessaly
Volos, Greece

Pete Wilkinson
School of Computing,
    Engineering and Media
De Montfort University, UK

1

CYBERWARFARE IN THE MODERN WORLD

SPYRIDON SAMPANIS,
MELINA-ELEFTHERIA
SPILIOPOULOU,
IOANNA KANTZAVELOU, AND
LEANDROS MAGLARAS

1.1 Introduction

Many years ago, there was a fear that in the future wars would no longer be fought only by soldiers with guns or with planes dropping bombs, but that warfare would take other forms and be more frightening and comprehensive—and that it would also be waged with the click of a mouse on the other side of the world, triggering carefully weaponized computer programs that disrupt or destroy critical industries such as utilities, transportation, communications, and energy. Such attacks could also disable military networks that control the movement of troops, the paths of jet fighters, and the piloting of warships. This fear has now become a reality. Now two states can fight and cause serious damage to each other through computers. Also, terrorism can be conducted through computers. Therefore, a state or a terrorist organization can act through a network all over the world and immediately.

1.2 Methodology

In this chapter, we have gathered and selected information on the subject of cyberwarfare in the modern world from other research works that have published valuable and useful results and findings. The research work was based on the reliability and relevance of the information on the subject. The information we sought is targeted at

DOI: 10.1201/9781003314721-1

1

each subsection to delve as deeply as possible into each piece of work and address certain challenges.

1.3 Cyberwarfare

The first efforts to create the internet were made during the Cold War, in an attempt by the United States to protect itself from a possible nuclear attack by the then-Soviet Union. Consequently, the internet was created to serve military operations. Therefore, with such great technological development since 1969, when ARPANET (Advanced Research Projects Agency Network) was first installed, it is expected to be used as a means of war and terrorism.

Every state which is at war tries to inflict the greatest possible damage on its adversary at the lowest possible cost to itself. What is more effective than the internet? Through cyberattacks, a virtual war can be waged that causes the same disaster in a state that a natural war could inflict.

Cyberwarfare is any action that takes place in cyberspace and targets the power systems of a country, critical infrastructures [1], or other non-governmental entities—for example, companies and organizations. Cyberwarfare can cause physical disasters through computers. It completes military operations using virtual media. In this way, countries manage to achieve missions that would otherwise require the physical presence of troops. Of course, there is a huge possibility that an electronic war will lead to a natural one, causing even greater disaster. In short, we could say that cyberwarfare is the techniques and tactics that a country uses virtually and naturally, simultaneously or alternatively, over a long period against another state.

As for the exact definition of cyberwarfare, we have not come up with a widely accepted absolute definition. While most scholars, military, and governments use definitions that refer to government agencies, other definitions may include non-state actors such as terrorist groups, corporations, political or ideological extremist groups, hackers, and/or transnational criminal organizations.

1.3.1 Types of Cyberwarfare

There are several types of cyberwarfare. Among these types, one can be used at a time or several together in combination. Usually, such attacks are used to support traditional warfare, such as disrupting the air defense function through online media to facilitate an airstrike. However, it can also contribute to more "mild" threats, such as espionage and propaganda. Some of the most common types of cyberwarfare are described in what follows.

1.3.1.1 Espionage Espionage is one of the oldest methods used in war to obtain secret and confidential information about the enemy. The first report of espionage dates back to the 18th century BCE when a spy broke into the court of King Hammurabi disguised as a diplomatic envoy.

Cyberspying, or cyberespionage, is the act or practice of obtaining secrets and information without the permission and knowledge of the holder of the information from individuals, competitors, rivals, groups, governments, and enemies for personal, economic, political, or military advantage using methods on the internet.

The purpose of any spy is to get critical information without being perceived by the enemy. If this theft is detected, then the information obtained is useless to the spy. The attacker can take necessary measures to prevent any negative consequences from the leakage of this information, so this is what cyberspies tried to achieve.

Most commonly, Trojan horse programs and other related malware are used. One way to achieve this could be through emails. The attacker can use malware hidden in legitimate-looking email messages, infecting unsuspecting users' computers and exploiting the data on them by sending it to control servers.

More specifically, an email message can arrive in the target's inbox carrying the malware in an attachment or web link. The attackers' objective is to get the target to open the attachment or click the malicious link so that the malicious code can execute. The key to that is the carrier emails to become more sophisticated in their targeting and content to trick their recipients into believing that they are receiving legitimate messages. This is also known as "social engineering." It is common to see legitimate documents recycled for such attacks or the attacker injecting their messages into an ongoing group conversation. There are also cases when it appears that content stolen from previously infected machines was recycled to enhance the appearance of legitimacy.

The targeted user proceeds to open the attachment or click the malicious link. Once opened, the infected file or link exploits a vulnerability on the user's machine and installs the malware on the user's computer, along with a seemingly benign file. From the user's perspective, the infected document will often open normally, leaving the user unaware of the infection that just took place.

After infecting the target, the Trojan packed in the attachment or the malicious link performs a domain name system (DNS) lookup to find its control server and then connects to that server for the communication to continue [2].

1.3.1.2 Sabotage   Unlike espionage, sabotage is intended to harm the object of the attack, not just to seize the information. This damage can be data deletion, data replacement, the shutdown of a vital device, etc. Saboteurs are usually users with privileged access rights which were acquired either due to someone's location or due to a system breach.

Most sabotage attacks occur after the device was shut down, and privileged access is used to take technical action to configure the attack before quitting, which may include creating backdoor accounts, installing and running password crackers, deployment of a logic bomb, and exploiting security breaches in access controls.

Insider threats are often categorized by intent and considered either: 1) malicious, 2) nonmalicious and volitional or self-benefitting, or 3) nonmalicious and unintentional. Insider threats have also been classified by motive, with eight perpetrator subtypes: explorers, samaritans, hackers, Machiavellians, proprietors, avengers, career thieves, and moles.

The most common type of attack in this type of Cyberwarfare is a denial of service (DoS) attack. In this type of attack, the perpetrator seeks to make a machine or a website unavailable to its legitimate users. This is done by temporarily or indefinitely interrupting the services of a server that is connected to a network and achieves the flooding of the machine or the website we are attacking, with unnecessary requests in an attempt to overload the systems and prevent some or all of them from fulfilling of legal requests [3].

The most successful such attacks in recent years have been the Distributed Denial of Service (DDoS) attacks. The difference with the DoS attack is that in the latter case, the incoming traffic that floods the victim comes from many different sources, in a distributed way. In this attack, a programmer designs a malicious piece of software that integrates into hundreds or thousands of computers around the world. This turns other computers into remotely controlled slaves or botnets.

Then, either at a predetermined time or at the command of the developer, the built-in malware bombards a targeted website with emails or response requests. On the Internet, any information stream or information packet is identified by your ISP or IP address. In a simple denial of service (DoS) attack, this information will have the same IP address.

In direct DoS attacks, attacking message packets can be blocked by the server or even on gateways and nodes on the internet itself. In a DDoS attack, this technique will not work, as response requests will come from many different IP addresses, often in different parts of the world.

Such an attack can be countered by requiring a confirmatory dialogue between the source and the target, i.e. a "handshake" between them. But even this can exceed the computing power of the target computer. Websites like Google or those within the U.S. Department of Defense probably have the computing power to keep up with a huge number of such attacks in real time. A smaller business site running on a single server may not respond.

Concerning cyberwarfare, the most common and effective attack for sabotage is the interruption of the electronic network. Without electricity, a country can no longer function, there are huge financial losses, citizens cannot meet their daily needs, and of course, the military cannot prepare to protect the country.

This can be caused by data attacks and not by attacks on physical systems' computer controls. Of course, the most dangerous and important form of cyberdisruption is a DoS attack [4].

Some other common attacks are false data injection attacks (FDIA), energy theft, insertion of malware or worms, and physical damage to the power grid such as causing equipment to self-destruct.

FDIA scenarios are realized when an attacker injects false data with the intent to deceive the network operator. FDIAs may result in a wide variety of outcomes depending on the intruder's intention, some of which include energy theft, miscalculation of locational marginal prices (LMP) for illegal market profits, and physical damage to the network.

The insertion of malware or worms can range in different types from malicious software which runs in the background and slows down the operations of the electric utility computers, to the insertion of Trojan software to steal practical security certificates.

The electrical network does not only consist of the power system. Various systems often interact with the grid, such as electric vehicle procurement equipment. In some cases, attacks can be undetectable, such as malicious data injection attacks that change measurement values without being detected, which can have serious consequences [5].

1.3.1.3 Propaganda   In Latin, propaganda means "to propagate" or "to sow." Words frequently used as synonyms for propaganda are lies, distortion, deceit, manipulation, mind control, psychological warfare, brainwashing, and palaver. According to the Merriam-Webster online dictionary (www.merriam-webster.com), propaganda is defined as: "ideas, facts, or allegations spread deliberately to further one's cause or to damage an opposing cause; also: a public action having such an effect."

Thus, propaganda is generally the dissemination or promotion of specific ideas. Cybertechnology is perfect for completing such a task, as access to the internet has now become very easy for users around the world, who use social media daily. At the same time, propaganda is very much related to the media, such as the press, radio, television, movies, computers, etc. The media are the main propaganda tool.

In a war, each of the two opponents needs others for support. Each also seeks to revitalize the morale of its soldiers and civilians, and at the same time reduce the morale of its opponents. These days, the best way to achieve this is through cyberpropaganda.

Nevertheless, through cyberpropaganda, terrorist organizations can easily recruit new members, who do not have to be close to their area of action. Therefore, they can be extended to the whole world [6].

1.3.2 Motivation of Cyberwarfare

Cybercriminals are motivated by different perspectives, aspects, and targets. Personal recognition, financial gain, and political motivation are common triggers in a large number of cyberattacks. The most significant motivation points are described in the following.

1.3.2.1 Military Cyberattacks in war are often counter-force attacks and stand in contrast to the use of strategic cyberattacks in peacetime, to influence the decision calculus of adversaries.

Military theory divides war into three levels: strategic, operational, and tactical. These levels are interrelated and what happens on one level influences the others. The strategic level deals with issues of "how to win a war" [7]. The strategic level allocates national resources and instruments of power to achieve victory in war. Strategies ideally define how to use the various means of state power, including cyber-capabilities, toward the end of achieving peace.

Below the strategic level is the operational level, which is often concerned with the running of campaigns and the question of how to employ forces in various fields, such as a geographic region [8]. The goal on the operational level is to obtain advantages over the enemy in a series of battles. the tactical level is the realm of combat engagements between individual warfighters and units in a combat situation. Most traditional weapon systems operate at this level. The tactical level deals with the controlling and movement of troops in a given territory.

1.3.2.2 Civil Cyberwarfare cannot only hit a country's military systems, but it can also hit civilians. This is probably worse, because in many cases, the military can take some countermeasures, having prepared for a possible attack of this kind. But the citizens are not prepared, so they will not be able to react.

Potential targets in internet sabotage include all aspects of the internet from the backbones of the web to the ISPs, to the varying types of data communication mediums and network equipment. This would include web servers, enterprise information systems, client-server systems, communication links, network equipment, desktops, and laptops in businesses and homes. Electrical grids, financial networks, and telecommunication systems are also deemed vulnerable, especially due to current trends in computerization and automation.

1.3.2.3 Hacktivism Internet activism, or hacktivism (a combination of the words "hack" and "activism"), is the use of computer-based techniques, such as hacking, as a form of civil disobedience to promote a political agenda or social change. With roots in hacker culture and hacker ethics, its ends are often related to free speech, human rights, or freedom of information movements.

Hacktivism involves attacks through code. An example is Pretty Good Privacy (PGP) encryption software, which can be used for communication security, i.e., someone cannot gain access to a conversation in any way.

A second way to attack hacktivism is mirroring. Website mirroring is used as a bypass tool to foil various censorship blocks on websites. This technique copies the content of a censored website and distributes it to other non-censored domains and subdomains. Document mirroring, similar to web mirroring, is a technique that focuses on backing up various documents and other works. One such example is RECAP, which is software written to "release U.S. case law" and make it widely available online.

Another thing that characterizes hacktivism is anonymity. To achieve this, a method of speaking to a wide audience on human rights issues, government repression, etc., is used, which deploys various web tools, such as free and/or consumable email accounts, IP coverage software, and blogs, to maintain a high level of anonymity.

Also, a characteristic of hacktivism is doxxing, a practice in which private and/or confidential information, documents, and files are violated and made public. Hacktivists see this as a form of guaranteed transparency, while experts claim it is harassment.

Of course, hacktivists use DoS attacks, website defacement, website redirects, virtual sit-ins, protestware, and geo-bombing.

1.3.2.4 Income Generation   Cyberattacks, including ransomware, can be used to generate income. States can use these techniques to generate significant sources of income, which can evade sanctions, perhaps while simultaneously harming adversaries (depending on targets).

1.4 Cyberterrorism

In recent years, especially after the 9/11 attack on the World Trade Center twin towers in 2001, the term terrorism has entered our lives for good. It makes sense, then, that the internet also has a role to play in this. The current incarnation of terrorist organizations tends to be more networked and ad hoc. A network structure allows individuals, groups, and organizations to flatten their lines of authority and control through the use of a web of communication technologies, much in the same way that virtual corporations operate. As a result, organizations can be more flexible and resilient due to functional independence with operationally coordinated efforts. [9]

1.4.1 Types of Cyberterrorism

According to the U.S. Federal Bureau of Investigation (FBI), cyberterrorism is a "premeditated, politically motivated attack against information, computer systems, computer programs, and data, which results in violence against non-combatant targets by sub-national groups or clandestine agents." [10]

We can categorize cyberterrorism into five parts, apart from cyberwarfare, according to the way technology is used to cause harm:

1.4.1.1 Weapons of Mass Destruction   Such attacks can directly harm individuals on a massive scale or cause damage to natural and man-made structures and monuments. In addition, they can provoke indirect outcomes that will eventually lead to natural disasters, as the destruction of the earth's surface morphology or the biosphere.

1.4.1.2 Weapons of Mass Distraction   This kind of attack takes place when something happens that will make enough people open a specific website that may be a mirror of the real thing, for example, a news website. Users would then be reading fake news, which would be intended to further terrorize them and possibly trigger terrorist attacks and riots by making computers the real weapons of mass destruction.

1.4.1.3 Weapons of Mass Disruption   Weapons of mass disruption aim to make public infrastructure, such as public transport, health services, financial institutions, etc., unreliable for citizens. This time, cyberterrorists are trying to cause mental harm to people instead of physical harm.

1.4.1.4 Hybrid Warfare   Hybrid warfare combines the military with diplomats, hackers, journalists, and even civilians. All these forces together create an extremely strong group that can easily propagate people. The target of this kind of war is uninformed people.

1.4.1.5 Unlimited Warfare   This kind of war is an upcoming way to attack another nation without any barriers. It is said that the first rule of unlimited warfare is the absence of rules and limits—that "rule" violates any ethical border and leads people to act without any reservations. Unrestricted warfare can be extremely dangerous to modern society due to the lack of respect among developed countries. Undeniably, the sense of justice and safety is affected during a war. In the case of unlimited warfare, we are talking about a total demolition of what current societies have built [11].

1.5 Cyberincidents

1.5.1 State-Sponsored Attacks

1.5.1.1 Estonia 2007   In protest of the government's relocation of a Soviet military monument from downtown Tallinn, Russia-based attackers conducted a series of DoS assaults against Estonian public and commercial sector entities in April 2007 [12]. Threat actors targeted state and commercial websites for three weeks, overwhelming their bandwidth and flooding their servers with trash traffic, leaving them unreachable to the public. Estonia briefly closed its digital borders and barred all international web traffic to counter the onslaught. This series of DoS attacks in Estonia in 2007 was the first time a foreign actor used cyberoperations to endanger the security and political freedom of another country. Even though it has not publicly produced any conclusive evidence, Estonia's government continues to blame Moscow for these attacks. A tiny group of Russian activists linked to the pro-Kremlin youth movement Nashi claimed responsibility. Although the allegation has not been independently validated, many Estonian specialists consider it to be true. The strikes reverberated throughout Estonia and abroad. They spurred NATO to beef up its cyberwarfare capabilities and to open a cyberdefense research center in Tallinn in 2008. They also prompted Estonia to request that the European Union make initiation of cyberattacks a crime.

1.5.1.2 Stuxnet 2007–2010   Inspectors from the International Atomic Energy Agency visited the Natanz uranium enrichment plant in Iran in January 2010 [13], and observed that centrifuges used to enrich uranium gas were failing at an alarming pace. The cause was a complete mystery, according to both the Iranian technicians who were replacing the centrifuges and the inspectors who were watching them.

A seemingly unrelated event occurred five months later. A Belarusian computer security firm was hired to debug a series of PCs in Iran that kept crashing and rebooting. The cause of the problem was once again unknown. That is until the researchers uncovered the world's first digital weapon after discovering a handful of malicious files on one of the systems.

Stuxnet, as it was dubbed, was unlike any other virus or worm that had before existed. Rather than just hijacking or stealing information from targeted computers, it escaped the digital realm to destroy the devices the computers controlled.

The Stuxnet computer virus was created to attack the nuclear processing plant in Natanz. Stuxnet targeted Windows systems and employed well-known tactics to steal data and conceal from a victim's PC; nonetheless, it was specifically tailored to attack PCs running the Siemens SIMATIC Step 7 industrial control application. It was also the first time a virus has attacked programmable logic controllers (PLCs) using comparable approaches.

Stuxnet was designed to attack PLCs in nuclear fuel refining centrifuges. The valves on each centrifuge are unique. Additional auxiliary valves govern access to the stages and the cascade; sets of centrifuges are structured into stages that create a cascade. The Stuxnet code is designed to target specific centrifuges at that facility, as indicated by symbols in the PLC code; it also has features that take use of the system's interconnectedness of centrifuges. The system structure may have been learned from other sources, although early versions of Stuxnet may have stolen design documents.

The first known version of Stuxnet is Stuxnet 0.5. It may have started operating in November 2005 and was discovered by malware scanners in November 2007. On July 4, 2009, it was created to prevent computers from being compromised and infecting networks that were not connected to the internet. One machine on the target network could be infected with an infected device, such as a USB key. Stuxnet would subsequently use peer-to-peer mechanisms to pro-liferate throughout the network. It was created to function largely independently. It exclusively used external websites to get and update code. Stuxnet was controlled and commanded by four separate URLs, each of which presented the same home page for a fictitious internet marketing firm.

Many people assume that Stuxnet is the result of a state-sponsored attack because of its sophistication, and suspicion fell on the United States and Israel. Stuxnet is extremely tough to spot. The majority of existing security best practices cannot avoid or guarantee Stuxnet detection. Because Stuxnet exploited four zero-day vulnerabilities, even a properly patched system was insufficient to protect against it. Because antivirus software has difficulty dealing with low-volume threats, the attack could not have been prevented: the first antivirus signatures were published after the worm had been in circulation for more than six months.

1.5.2 Cyberterrorism Attacks

1.5.2.1 PlayStation Network Attack 2010 The Sony PlayStation Network (PSN) is a global online multiplayer gaming service with more than 100 million registered members. It is an important part of Sony's game division, which generated $9 billion in revenue in 2010 [14]. Owners of Sony' PlayStation 3 or later generation video game consoles can access and use the network. Users can obtain new games, system and game software upgrades, downloadable content, on-demand streaming movies, and a music store through the network. Users can also track their progress, earn rewards for completed activities, and communicate socially with other users using the network's in-game features. Sony uses the network to verify the operational integrity of PlayStation clients, preventing network tampering and user misbehavior. Users must give personal information, such as their name, birth date, residence address, and a valid email address, to create an account on the network. As part of the registration process, users can also enter their credit card information. After that, the personal identifying and financial data is encrypted and kept on a central server.

On April 20, 2011, the network became unreachable to users all around the world without warning or explanation, and PlayStation owners were unable to access any of the network's features [15]. Sony announced on its official blog a day later that the network might be unavailable for a day while they investigated the issue.

This network disruption lasted more than three weeks in total. Various news outlets eventually stated that the network had been hacked and that user credentials, email addresses, credit card numbers, and transaction history information had been stolen from 77 million user accounts, amid discussion regarding the cause. Sony began gradually restoring network connections across specific nation sites in May 2011. Sony compensated all network users with a "Welcome Back" package that included a selection of free games, temporary access to premium network features, and a free one-year subscription to a credit monitoring service in early June.

The culprits behind the attack, we came to know after all these years, are a hacking group called LulzSec. Jake Davis, Mustafa Al-Bassam Ryan Ackroyd, and Ryan Cleary have all pleaded guilty to many attacks, among them the great PSN hack.

1.5.2.2 WannaCry Ransomware Attack 2017   The WannaCry ransomware attack of 2017 was the worst in history. WannaCry ransomware is a type of malicious software that prevents users from accessing files or systems by encrypting them and holding them hostage until the victim pays a ransom in exchange for a decryption key that allows them to access the files or systems encrypted by the program.

The first ransomware attack took place in 1989, dubbed the AIDS Trojan, but it now appears rudimentary. It was disseminated via floppy disks, and the ransom was paid by paying $189 to a Panamanian post office box. Ransomware includes Reveton, CryptoLocker, CryptoLocker.F, TorrentLocker, CryptoWall, CryptoTear, Fusob, and WannaCry. Ransomware WannaCry infected more than 2,000,000 people in hospitals, businesses, universities, and government organizations spanning at least 150 universities. It wanted a ransom for all machines. WannaCry is a ransomware cryptoworm that encrypts (locks) data on machines running the Microsoft Windows operating system and demands ransom payments in the Bitcoin cryptocurrency.

Because it incorporates a transport mechanism to automatically distribute itself, it is classified as a network worm. This transport code checks for susceptible computers before gaining access and installing and executing a copy of itself using the EternalBlue vulnerability and the DoublePulsar tool [16].

The Shadow Brokers disclosed EternalBlue, an exploit of Microsoft's implementation of the server message block (SMB) protocol. The fact that the U.S. National Security Agency (NSA)—from whom the exploit was presumably stolen—had already found the vulnerability and utilized it to construct an exploit for its offensive activity, rather than reporting it to Microsoft, drew a lot of attention and debate. Microsoft finally found the bug, and on Tuesday, March 14, 2017, they released the security bulletin MS17–010, detailing the flaw and announcing that patches were available for all Windows versions supported at the time.

Initially, a security researcher tweeted about code similarities between WannaCry and prior attacks. Both Kaspersky Lab and Symantec have stated that the malware is identical to that used by the Lazarus Group, which is linked to North Korea and is suspected of carrying out the Sony Pictures cyberattack in 2014 and a Bangladesh bank heist in 2016. This may be a simple re-use of code by another party or an attempt to deflect blame—as in a cyber–false flag operation—but a leaked internal NSA letter is said to link the worm's development to North Korea. Microsoft President Brad Smith stated that he believes North Korea was behind the WannaCry attack.

On December 18, 2017, the U.S. government formally said that it believes North Korea was the primary perpetrator of the WannaCry attack. Tom Bossert, then-U.S. President Donald Trump's homeland security advisor, penned an op-ed in *The Wall Street Journal* regarding the allegation, saying: "This is not an accusation we make lightly. It is supported by evidence." [17]. The evidence shows that Kim Jong-un gave the command to conduct the malware attack, according to Bossert, who spoke at a press conference the next day. Canada, New Zealand, and Japan, according to Bossert, agree with the U.S. assessment of the evidence linking the attack to North Korea, while the Foreign and Commonwealth Office of the United Kingdom also supports the U.S. claim. North Korea, however, denied being responsible for the cyberattack.

1.5.3 Cyberpropaganda

1.5.3.1 ISIS/Islamic State   ISIS/Islamic State is a forerunner in the use of cyberterrorism. This is because this extremist group utilized cyberspace more extensively and systematically than any other in the past, taking advantage of the benefits it gives to instill fear or cause harm. After a period of rapid expansion in 2015, when ISIS reached its pinnacle by seizing and controlling large portions of Iraq and Syria, the group lost control of nearly all of this territory. ISIS has used physical tactics of attack since its inception, intending to cause physical pain and numerous fatalities. The majority of the attacks are carried out with homemade explosives.

Assassinations, beheadings, torture, kidnappings, and suicide strikes are all examples of terrorism. At the same time, ISIS engages in "new terrorism," in which a computer or the internet plays a key role in terrorism. It has expanded its activity in cyberspace, with the primary goal of instilling panic and instability in societies rather than causing death. ISIS uses social media and the internet extensively. "Some members are technically proficient enough to promote the message and culture by defacing websites, social media accounts, and other media outlets with text, photographs, and videos, glorifying the group's purpose," according to Scott and Spaniel [18].

ISIS jihadists are using cyberspace to recruit, radicalize, and instill their views and jihadist ideology in new members. Furthermore, ISIS actively promotes "lone wolf" assaults on social media, encouraging supporters to fight non-believers. However, cyberattack strategies, tools, and expertise are fast evolving, as is the network of hacker groups dedicated to committing cyberterrorism in the name of ISIS, particularly against the Western world.

Terrorists are increasingly exploiting not just their weapons and techniques on the ground, but also technologies and cyber-resources for propagating ideas and coordinating activities, thanks to technological breakthroughs.

ISIS has devised a clever strategy for utilizing cyberspace's resources to spread its propaganda, influence the media agenda, recruit new warriors, and organize and coordinate its attacks. The organization makes amazing use of the dark corners of the internet, its technological resources, and legal loopholes to elude law enforcement and armed forces [19].

As a result, a generation of young people, like the thousands who have already been identified as possible targets, have been exposed to its propaganda and have become prone to silent radicalization in the privacy of their homes. In this volatile climate, determining degrees of radicalization and distinguishing between what is merely rebellion or adolescent provocation and what reflects a true risk of action is challenging.

ISIS did not develop psychological warfare, but its very sophisticated use of the internet has elevated it to a new level—a new dimension that is neither virtual nor detached from a very real conflict. ISIS propaganda easily crosses borders, infiltrates the locations where young people connect online, and infiltrates their private spaces to control their minds more effectively.

1.6 Cyberterrorism vs. Cyberwarfare

1.6.1 Cyberterrorism

Based on the capabilities and motives of the offenders, cyberterrorism may necessitate a distinct set of responses. Motivation is the force that propels people to take specific actions. As a result, attempts to attain objectives and pick appropriate attack targets are more focused and determined. As a result, from a motivational standpoint, the precise agendas that underpin perpetrators' actions differ. This form of cyberattack is more specifically focused and intended at more essential systems or populations with a bigger impact, which might be described as fanaticism. However, to be called a cyberterrorist, an individual's assaults must be politically motivated. Although computer attacks do not result in physical harm or death, they do cause widespread fear and panic, and they therefore thus could be classified as cyberterrorism.

Other factions are also pursuing the economy as a means of undermining the country. Though economic reasons drive these dynamics, whether state-sponsored or not. They want to erode public trust in the political system and cause divisions within the political system. Many factors play roles, including economics, wars, politics, and trade. Terrorists have a high level of motivation within their organizations, which drives their ideology and, as a result, their cyberterrorism.

Cyberterrorism is a new way for countries to become unstable. Whether it is a nation-state or a terrorist organization, both use the current technology to improve their strategies and instruments for carrying out cyberattacks in a variety of ways.

Different interpretations of cyberattacks and the lack of a clear definition of cyberterrorism or act of war among policymakers and scholars make combating the crime challenging. Because a well-defined concept of cyberterrorism can serve as a guide and principle for opposing cyberwarfare, reaching such an understanding is critical. This section concludes that motivation is important in comprehending cyberterrorism. Continuous attempts to understand the motivations for cyberterrorism, as well as to establish and improve national rules and policy responses, will help combat this modern threat.

1.6.2 Cyberwarfare

War is distinct in that it is a battle between nation-states; it is carried out by individuals, as is all human activity, but those individuals are acting on behalf of a specific nation-state. Warfare, like terrorism, is characterized by the damage of property, typically on a large scale, as well as harm to and death of humans, also often on a massive scale. Unlike terrorism, war is supposed to be confined to battles between assemblages of persons (militaries) acting for opposing nation-states. Civilians—those who are not serving in any military of a combatant nation-state—are injured and killed, but this is considered to be a collateral occurrence, like most property damage/destruction. The basic goal of war, in general, and specific wars in particular, is to "win" over the hostile nation-state(s), whatever that implies in any given situation. The basic goal of warfare is not to injure or kill civilians or destroy civilian property.

It is essentially outside the purview of our research because combat is conducted between nation-states to maintain or restore external order. Our key issue is how those in charge of enacting and implementing domestic laws—intended to keep the peace—should deal with the connected phenomena of cybercrime and cyberterrorism.

There are international laws that govern warfare, but they only apply to nation-states, not to individual criminals or terrorists. As a result, those laws are distinct from the domestic laws that we are principally concerned with herewith. However, laws controlling warfare are not completely irrelevant to this discussion. At the very least, they are relevant in terms of the need to separate cyberwarfare from cybercrime and cyberterrorism [20].

Before we get into that topic, there is one last point to make: One area where the laws of warfare need to be updated is in the realm of cyberwarfare. Under existing legislation, it is unclear how a nation-state can retaliate against a cyberattack perpetrated by another nation-state. Can Taiwan respond with military force if the People's Republic of China (PRC) launches virtual strikes on Taiwan's infrastructure? Can Taiwan reply with cyberforce as an alternative or in addition? Is it capable of launching defensive cyberattacks against the aggressor? If that is the case, who can carry out these cyberattacks? Is cyberwarfare just conducted by military people, or may civilians also participate?

The last point is crucial because, in cyberwarfare, the attacking nation-state engages directly with civilian targets in a way that is impossible in the actual world. When the Allies bombarded Dresden during World War II, civilian commercial targets had no option of retaliating against their attackers since military might is monopolized by nation-states. However, if Taiwanese firms are attacked by cyberattacks launched by another country, the civilian organizations targeted by the assaults can directly reply with defensive and/or offensive countermeasures. This idea poses several concerns, including the possibility of private persons engaging in cyberwarfare against a hostile nation-state.

1.6.3 Cyberterrorism vs. Cyberwarfare

Aside from cyberterrorism and cyberwarfare, cybercrime might be considered a third category of cyberincidents. Creating conceptual categories is one thing; putting them into practice is quite another. The difficulty in putting the categories in place can take numerous shapes.

"The attackers were never identified" is a common term we hear nowadays when it comes to cyberattacks. Given the chances, cyberspace provides for the remote execution of assaults and the potential for an attacker to stay anonymous, cybercriminals are significantly more likely than not to remain unidentified and unapprehended [19].

But that assumes that we are dealing with cybercriminals, which leads to another conclusion of the preceding statement: Not only were the attackers not identified as persons, but neither was the nature of the attack. It seems that the attack originated in China, for example, but what type of attack was it?

- Was it cybercrime? Chinese hackers at large?
- Was it cyberterrorism? Terrorists with peculiar ideological objectives?
- Was it cyberwarfare? the People's Liberation Army launched a military assault?

This demonstrates the importance of attribution, which is far less difficult in practice. There are two aspects to attribution: Who was the perpetrator of the attack, and what type of assault was it? The first challenge is determining who is responsible for an attack. The second step is determining who is responsible for responding to an attack.

In the actual world, we know who is in charge of what. The police deal with crime and terrorism, while the military only deals with conflict, and all of these categories are easily distinguished.

Consider why determining the nature of a cyberattack is so challenging. We do not know who carried out the act, so we cannot use the crime-vs.-terrorism calculus, and we cannot tell if it was carried out by agents of a nation-state (military operatives). We believe we know where the attack originated, but even that may be in doubt; it is not difficult to route attacks through computers in other countries to hide the true source.

Consider the following attack scenario. At least initially, police would respond to each attack. Unless and until someone understood the attacks were more than unrelated cybercrimes, police would be the only government employees to respond. Because of the way we currently compartmentalize responsibility for responding to distinct kinds of threats, if they were something more than unrelated cybercrimes, they might go unreported for a long time. This raises the risk that a large-scale, complicated cyberterrorism or cyberwarfare event could go unnoticed by authorities until subsequent attacks revealed the true nature of the earlier strikes.

1.7 Conclusion

To conclude this chapter, let us assume that all protective systems are operational (technical-wise). To properly deal with cyberthreats, we need not just national rules that allow us to identify and prosecute cybercriminals and cyberterrorists, but also a clear international framework governing cyberwarfare. We must also develop and implement protocols that allow police and other government agents to distinguish between "routine" and "non-routine" cyberthreats.

References

[1] Leandros Maglaras, Ioanna Kantzavelou, Mohamed Amine Ferrag, Editors, Cybersecurity of Critical Infrastructures: Challenges and Solutions. *MDPI AG*, 2021, ISBN 978-3-0365-2726-0 (Hbk), www.mdpi.com/books/pdfdownload/book/4750.

[2] Nart Villeneuve, Greg Walton, SecDev Group, Munk Centre for International Studies. Citizen Lab. Tracking GhostNet: Investigating a Cyber Espionage Network (JR02-2009). Toronto, ON: Citizen Lab, Munk Centre for International Studies, University of Toronto, Information Warfare Monitor, pages 18–22, 2009.

[3] Michele Maasberg, Xiao Zhang, Myung Ko, Stewart R. Miller, Nicole Lang Beebe. An Analysis of Motive and Observable Behavioral Indicators Associated with Insider CyberSabotage and Other Attacks, IEEE Engineering Management Review, Vol. 48, No. 2, pages 1–2, 2020.

[4] Randall R. Dipert. The Ethics of Cyberwarfare, Journal of Military Ethics, Vol. 9, pages 386–392, 2010.

[5] Tien Nguyen, Mohannad Alhazmi, Mostafa Nazemi, Abouzar Estebsari, Payman Dehghanian. Electric Power Grid Resilience to Cyber Adversaries: State of the Art, IEEE Access, Vol. 8, pages 87595, 2020.

[6] J. Manzaria, J. Bruck. War & Peace: Media and War, Media's Use of Propaganda to Persuade People's Attitude, Beliefs and Behaviors, 1998. https://web.stanford.edu/class/e297c/war_peace/media/hpropaganda.html

[7] Robert Bateman. Understanding Military Strategy and the Four Levels of War: When 'Strategy' Gets Thrown Around by Politicians and the Media, You Can Bet It's Being Misused, 2015, www.esquire.com/news-politics/politics/news/a39985/four-levels-of-war/.

[8] Francis C. Domingo. Cyber War Versus Cyber Realities: Cyber Conflict in the International System by Brandon Valeriano and Ryan C. Maness, Journal of Information Technology & Politics, Vol. 12, No. 4, pages 399–401, 2015, DOI: 10.1080/19331681.2015.1101039

[9]   S. W. Brenner. "At Light Speed": Attribution and Response to Cybercrime/ Terrorism/Warfare, The Journal of Criminal Law and Criminology, pages 427–429, 2007.

[10] Centre of Excellence Defence Against Terrorism (ed.). Responses to Cyber Terrorism, NATO Science for Peace and Security Series, Sub-Series E: Human and societal Dynamics, Vol. 34. Amsterdam: IOS Press, page 119, 2008. ISSN 1874-6276, ISBN 9781586038366.

[11] Maria Papathanasaki, Leandros Maglaras. The Current Posture of Cyber Warfare and Cyber Terrorism, ResearchGate, pages 7–8, 2020.

[12] Scott J Shackelford. Estonia Two-and-a-Half Years Later: A Progress Report on Combating Cyber Attacks, November 4, 2009. *Journal of Internet Law*. Retrieved from http://dlc.dlib.indiana.edu/dlc/bitstream/ handle/10535/10242/SSRNid1499849.pdf?sequence=1&isAllowed=y

[13] David Kushner. The Real Story of Stuxnet, IEEE Spectrum, Vol. 50, No. 3, pages 48–53, 2013.

[14] Sony Annual Report, 2011, https://www.sony.com/en/SonyInfo/IR/ library/ar/report2011/SonyAR11-E.pdf, accessed 26/6/2023.

[15] Bolanle A. Olaniran, Andrew Potter, Katy A. Ross, Brad Johnson. A Gamer's Nightmare: An Analysis of the Sony PlayStation Hacking Crisis, Journal of Risk Analysis and Crisis Response, Vol. 4, No. 3, pages 151–159, 2014.

[16] S. Mohurle, M. Patil. A Brief Study of Wannacry Threat: Ransomware Attack 2017, International Journal of Advanced Research in Computer Science, Vol. 8, No. 5, pages 1938–1940, 2017.

[17] Homeland Security Briefing on WannaCry Malware Attack, December 2017, https://www.c-span.org/video/?438777-1/homeland-security-briefing-wannacry-malware-attack, accessed 26/6/2023.

[18] J. Scott, D. Spaniel. The Anatomy of Cyber-Jihad: Cyberspace Is the New Great Equalizer. Institute for Critical Infrastructure Technology (ICIT), Createspace Independent Pub, 2016.

[19] D. Giantas, D. Stergiou. From Terrorism to Cyber-Terrorism: The Case of ISIS, 2018, SSRN 3135927.

[20] Susan W. Brenner. Toward a Criminal Law for Cyberspace: Product Liability and Other Issues, Pittsburgh Journal of Technology Law and Policy, Vol. 5, 2005, DOI: 10.5195/tlp.2005.16.

2

THE GEOPOLITICS OF 5G AND EU DIGITAL SOVEREIGNTY

ANDREW N. LIAROPOULOS

2.1 Introduction

In recent years, the concept of digital sovereignty has dominated the debate about the digital future of the European Union (EU), its strategic autonomy and the geopolitical competition that is taking place in the digital domain between the United States, China, and the EU. The literature that relates sovereignty with the digital domain has produced a number of terms, with the most popular being information sovereignty (mainly advocated by Russia and China), data sovereignty, cloud sovereignty, and technological sovereignty. For the purposes of the present analysis, we chose the term digital sovereignty, since it is a term that largely encompasses the previously mentioned ones and appears frequently in the relevant discourse.

Although it is a term difficult to define, digital sovereignty relates to the governance of data, the protection of critical information infrastructure, and cybersecurity in general, as well as the EU's dependencies in cloud and data infrastructures, semiconductors, and artificial intelligence (AI). Central to the discussion about EU digital sovereignty is also the issue of 5G networks. 5G stands for the fifth-generation technology for mobile telecommunications that will provide faster download speeds, reduced latency and a higher network density, enabling a greater number of users. In contrast to 4G, which consists of networks of towers, 5G will use a broader range of cellular technologies that demands the installation of completely new infrastructure. Thus, the security of 5G networks involves a range of components including radio access networks (RAN), core networks, clouds and

DOI: 10.1201/9781003314721-2

third-party applications. The latter are essential to the digital evolution of the coming generation. The Internet of Things (IoT), the materialization of the metaverse, quantum computing, and in general the Fourth Industrial Revolution will all depend on 5G and in the near future 6G technologies.

The EU has correctly identified the 5G challenge and aims to develop strategies that will eventually reduce its dependency on foreign technologies [1, 2]. The discussion about 5G networks has been framed around two main arguments. The first argument involves security concerns regarding the implementation of an infrastructure, which will soon form the backbone of our digital society. The second argument relates to the first one, but places more emphasis on the geopolitical competition in the digital domain and the fact that the EU is largely dependent on non-EU companies—and in particular Chinese companies like Huawei and ZTE. Despite the promise to ensure digital sovereignty and strengthen its autonomy, the EU has not yet developed a concrete strategy on how to respond to the 5G challenge.

In order to elaborate on how 5G relates to sovereignty and security issues, as well as geopolitical ones, the chapter first explores the discussion on European digital sovereignty. The latter frames the EU both as a digital colony, since the fragmented European digital market has been heavily dominated by Asian and US high-tech companies, and as a regulatory power that manages to set global standards on data regulation and privacy, since many countries have incorporated General Data Protection Regulation (GDPR) provisions in their national legislation. Having identified the narratives on digital sovereignty, the chapter shifts its focus on the security and geopolitical concerns related to the 5G networks. The purpose of this chapter is dual—on the one hand to highlight the issue of 5G networks as an essential element of EU's digital sovereignty, and on the other hand to explore how the EU can place itself in the global race for digital dominance.

2.2 EU Digital Sovereignty: In Search of a Definition and a Strategy

Sovereignty is without a doubt one of the most important terms in international politics, but also one of the most controversial ones.

It relates to concepts like governance, security, independence, exercise of control and autonomy, and it is used within the context of states [3, 4]. It implies autonomy in foreign policy, but also exclusive competence in internal affairs. Thus, a common understanding of sovereignty differentiates between the internal and the external/international sovereignty. The former refers to the supreme power that the state has over its citizens within its borders and therefore the supreme decision-making and enforcement authority over a specific territory and toward a population. The latter refers to the absence of a superior power to states. International sovereignty represents the principle of self-determination in the absence of a supreme international authority [5, 6]. To conclude, sovereignty does not only mean authority within a distinct territorial entity, but it also implies equal membership in the international states system. States, regardless of their power status, are considered sovereign and independent, and they enjoy equal rights under international law.

Placing this state-centric concept within the EU's supranational level is a conceptual challenge, for two reasons. First, the very idea of European sovereignty does not even appear in the EU constitutive treaties [7]. After all, sovereignty is reserved for the member states. Second, it is unclear whether European sovereignty implies the weakening of the national ones, the creation of a shared one or even the construction of a collective sovereignty [8]. To make things even more complex, placing the term digital in front of sovereignty creates a catchphrase that is hard to define, but is nevertheless, widely used by various institutions within the EU. The reason is that the digital domain resembles a non-territorial realm, which challenges the traditional understanding of geographical boundaries and thus state sovereignty. The truth is that the digital domain is, after all, terrestrially based and thus not immune to state control. Thus, the territoriality principle allows states to control cyberspace-related activities occurring within and across their borders, and the effects principle gives them jurisdiction over external activities that cause effects internally. The tricky part is to apply the same analogy to the non-physical elements of the digital domain, since there is no universally accepted understanding of data/information sovereignty [9].

Although hard to define, the concept of European digital sovereignty has emerged due to the security and geopolitical challenges that the EU is facing in the digital domain. A review of the policy papers and regulations published by the EU, as well as the statements that key officials made in recent years, demonstrate EU's struggle to regulate its digital ecosystem, safeguard its citizens' data and privacy, and at the same time compete with China and the United States in the global digital arena [10, 11]. The coronavirus pandemic vividly illustrated the extent to which data, networks and digital technologies constitute the backbone of our societies [12]. Thus, it is only natural that calls within the EU to enhance its level of autonomy in its digital industrial base have increased. The review of the literature reveals that digital sovereignty is about controlling, possessing, and regulating the digital realm. Thus, it is about data and AI, standardization processes and hardware, as well as about services like social media or e-commerce and infrastructures like satellites and undersea data cables. Having conceptualized an understanding of what sovereignty entails in relation to the digital ecosystem, we turn our analysis to the concept of European digital sovereignty.

There are two main narratives on European digital sovereignty [8]. The first one perceives the EU as a weak actor in the digital domain. According to this narrative, the EU struggles to regulate its digital services and to protect its critical infrastructure and values, as well as to shape the global norms regarding cyberspace governance. Concisely, the quest for digital sovereignty is rooted in a perception that the EU has been digitally colonized. It is a fact that in relation to the global digital market, it is Asian and U.S. companies that have dominated, and not European ones [13]. EU dependencies are evident in the cases of cloud and data infrastructures, 5G connectivity and AI. Regarding the latter, the EU is lagging both the United States and China in terms of private investment and adoption of AI technologies by the private sector and by the public sector [14, 15]. As far as communication infrastructure is concerned, the two dominant European companies, Nokia and Ericsson, are unable to compete with their U.S. and Chinese peer competitors for share of the global market. Adding to that, the European market is fragmented with many national players and few giants like Deutsche Telecom, Telefonica, Vodafone and Orange [16]. Likewise, the global cloud storage service market is largely dominated by U.S. companies. According to a survey conducted by Synergy Research Group referring to the second quarter of 2022, Amazon's (AWS) market share amounted to 34%, followed by Microsoft Azure with 21% and Google Cloud with 10% [17].

As a result, most of the data generated in the EU is stored with U.S. cloud providers because there are hardly any European alternatives. By storing data abroad, the EU cannot take full advantage of the available metadata, to identify consumer habits, minimize costs, and modernize supply chains. Thus, Europe's digital economy becomes less competitive [18]. On the other hand, via technological giants like Google, Apple, Facebook, Amazon, and Microsoft, (GAFAM), the United States is collecting a vast amount of data. By exploiting data about online behavior and consumer habits, these companies have a major competitive advantage in relation to other players [19]. Through data capitalism, the United States acts as the gatekeeper of the European digital market [20].

Indicative of the argument that the EU has been digitally colonized are the concerns expressed by the European Parliament in 2019 about the potential security threats of embedded backdoors in 5G equipment provided by two Chinese companies, Huawei and ZTE [18, 21]. It is interesting to point out how the issue of 5G has been securitized in the European discourse in recent years. Most EU member states were rather satisfied with the 3G and 4G networks provided by Huawei. Furthermore, the EU until 2019 framed the 5G networks as a strategic opportunity and not a security challenge. Fears of surveillance and espionage expressed by the intelligence agencies of member states, as well as pressure from the United States on its European partners to exclude Huawei from the future 5G upgrades, led to the gradual securitization of 5G [22, 23]. There was a growing security concern that the Chinese government could influence companies like Huawei to monitor or even shut down critical infrastructure in case of a military or political crisis. According to this argument, China could potentially use its private—yet state-controlled—companies as a new "Trojan Horse". Companies like Huawei and ZTE would be able to control the 5G infrastructure and thereby potentially compromise European critical infrastructure. Even though Huawei was not banned, despite the pressure exercised by the United States, certain member states restrained Huawei's role in their networks. For example, Spain hired Huawei, whereas the Czech Republic decided not to do so. Germany took the middle way, welcoming all companies as long as they adhere to a catalog of safety criteria. For example, suppliers must give a declaration of confidence that no information will reach foreign authorities and that they can refuse to disclose confidential information from or about their customers to third parties [24]. By 2019, it became clear that the choice of 5G operators, infrastructures and their suppliers is not a decision made solely on terms of quality and price, but mainly one made based on security and geopolitical concerns [25]. The 5G market is dominated by Huawei and ZTE (China), Samsung (South Korea), Nokia (Finland) and Ericsson (Sweden). Huawei is considered the cheapest and also the most technically efficient supplier [23]. Adding to that, most of the 5G component supply chain is located outside the EU. 5G technology is dependent on integrated circuits, which are mainly produced in Asia (mostly Taiwan and South Korea) [26].

The coronavirus pandemic and the technological war between the United States and China [27] vividly illustrated how dependent the EU is on imports of raw materials like semiconductors [28]. Since the latter are at the core of the global technological race, it is no surprise that the European Commission proceeded with the Chips Act in the first half of 2022. The Chips Act aims to secure Europe's supply of microchips, encourage innovation and strengthen industrial capacity.

Nevertheless, these dependencies and weaknesses draw only one part of the picture. It is a fact that during recent years, the EU has launched several policies and established institutions to safeguard its infrastructure, boost its digital economy and secure the rights of its citizens. Thus, the second narrative about EU digital sovereignty perceives the EU as a regulatory superpower [10]. From the launch of the Digital Single Market in 2015 to the NIS 2.0 Directive in 2021 and the Chips Act and Data Act in 2022, the EU has vividly demonstrated its willingness to regulate its digital ecosystem. The greatest example of Brussels' regulatory power is the GDPR. This privacy legislation imposed strict conditions on the handling of EU citizens' personal information, even if that data or citizen was physically outside the EU. When it went into effect in May 2018, companies around the world found themselves having to comply with GDPR. As a result, the EU is considered a global standard setter in privacy and data protection, since many countries have incorporated GDPR provisions in their national legislation [20]. Although EU digital sovereignty was rarely mentioned at the time, both the Digital Single Market plan and GDPR were clearly intended to enhance EU digital capabilities and provide citizens with a form of control, over their own personal data [10].

According to recent acts on data and AI, data that is collected and controlled within the EU is managed according to ethical standards that place privacy at the epicenter. The EU's approach toward AI is a human-centric one, meaning that the EU requires compliance with fundamental rights, regardless of whether these are explicitly protected by EU treaties, such as the Treaty on European Union or by the Charter of Fundamental Rights of the European Union. Thus, the AI Act prohibits most facial recognition systems and forces the AI systems to inform citizens if they are exposed to an algorithm that might affect their behavior [29]. Likewise, the Digital Services Act proposes rules intended to reinforce European norms on content, consumer protection, and platform liability. By obliging service providers to comply with transparent terms of service, the Act aims to limit the power of major players, like GAFAM [29]. It should be stressed that EU regulations often have a global impact. Bearing in mind that the EU is one of the world's largest consumer markets, most multinational corporations accept its terms of business as the price of admission. To escape the cost of complying with multiple regulatory regimes around the world, many companies often extend EU rules to their operations globally. That is why so many large non-EU companies follow the GDPR in their operations [30]. Since the introduction of the GDPR, there has been growing pressure in the United States for a federal standardization on data privacy and cybersecurity [16]. It is argued, that the GDPR inspired other acts, like the California Consumer Privacy Act (CCPA) [31] and China's Personal Information Protection Law (PIPL) [32]. Thus, it is fair to argue that the so-called "Brussels Effect" is in play in the digital domain. A recent development highlighting the institutionalization of the Brussels impact is the establishment of the transatlantic Trade and Technology Council (TTC) that aims to shape a common understanding on digital and technological standards [33].

2.3 Digital Geopolitics and the Case of 5G

The preceding analysis of how EU digital sovereignty is conceived is necessary to place the 5G debate in a suitable technological and geopolitical context. The debate on 5G within the EU has economic, social, technological, security and geopolitical dimensions [1, 34]. To begin with, 5G is considered as the essential technology that will enable the digital transformation of society and economy in the coming decade. At the same time, as with any new technology, 5G brings its own fair share of vulnerabilities and risks. The latter are related to the rather unique nature of 5G infrastructure. In sharp contrast to 4G, it is hard with 5G to differentiate the core from the edge of the network, and it is therefore difficult to isolate certain components of the overall network [2]. Due to the plethora of devices and services connected to a 5G software–based system, there are more traffic routing points, more entry points for attackers and thus greater insecurity [35]. In terms of digital geopolitics, the 5G debate has been framed as an issue where China could use Huawei to harm the EU. It is interesting to note that a company under the control of the Chinese government is perceived as a greater threat than a company from another state, like South Korea or the United States [36].

In order to address these complex challenges, the European Commission adopted in March 2019 a recommendation [37] regarding the cybersecurity of 5G networks and in October 2019 adopted the technical report prepared by ENISA, titled "EU Coordinated Risk Assessment of the Cybersecurity of 5G Networks" [38]. This report reflected a consensus on how the EU aims to address the security of 5G networks and identified threats, actors, assets, vulnerabilities and risk scenarios. The report estimated that 5G technology creates a paradigm shift in terms of cybersecurity which the present regulatory framework cannot address efficiently [1]. As a result, the EU in January 2020 adopted another report by the NIS Cooperation Group, titled "Cybersecurity of 5G Networks EU Toolbox of Risk Mitigating Measures" [39]. This document, although not a legally binding one, is a solid statement of the member states and the European Commission to implement the measures recommended by the previous risk assessment [1]. In particular, the document developed a toolbox that provided risk mitigation plans for all the risk areas, earlier identified by the EU coordinated risk assessment document. By applying certain measures, at both national and EU levels, the expected result will be a more secure telecommunication network across Europe [34]. Even though the document does not specifically refer to China, it implies that Chinese companies are high-risk suppliers and stresses that member states are free to choose their telecommunications providers. Bearing in mind that the member states have been divided since 2019 on whether to ban Huawei, it is only natural that this report balances between economic competitiveness and security risks. Although states are free to decide on the operator that will access their telecommunication networks, the European Commission recommends that operators use several suppliers in order to reduce dependence on any particular one—and thus lower the associated risk. Practically, this limits Huawei's market share within the EU [2]. It is obvious that the two European telecommunications giants, Nokia and Ericsson are taking advantage of this development and thus are in a position to increase their share of the European market [2].

The NIS report raises some important issues on how the EU aspires to tackle the 5G challenge. Promoting the diversification of providers and suppliers limits the impact of a potential attack on any specific product but at the same time adds complexity and makes network security more costly. Reaching an agreement on technical standardization between operators, hardware and software manufacturers and states is an enormous task. Thus, if member-states chose to use network and system components from various manufacturers, they should bear in mind that diversity is costly and time-consuming. It demands new governance mechanisms and centralized planning to coordinate a vast number of networks [36]. Another issue to consider is under what circumstances and based on what evidence is a company considered as a high-risk supplier. To be blunt, why should we trust for example Nokia, Ericsson, or a provider from the United States and distrust Huawei and ZTE? In the case of 5G, it seems that the EU is considering whether a state can be sufficiently trusted not to use its companies to harm its interests. Although this is a legitimate security concern, it is more than obvious that this should apply to any state and not only to China. For example, the EU has included both Nokia and Ericsson as partners in the Hera-X project that is responsible for shaping the future 6G infrastructure [40]. If the EU does not objectively clarify under what circumstances a company is characterized as a high-risk one, any decision on such grounds is indiscriminate and challenges the European legal order [36]. After all, it was only a few years ago, when the EU realized—due to the revelations by Edward Snowden—that the United States, a trustworthy ally of the EU, was using its technological giants to conduct global surveillance and collect a vast amount of personal data of EU citizens [41]. Adding to that, there was no hard evidence over the past years that China was using backdoors in the 4G technology that was already deployed in Europe, so it reasonable to question whether China would do so in 5G [42].

It is in this context that it is important to understand how the EU has decided to enact restrictions on high-risk suppliers. Before that, we need to differentiate between the "core" and the "periphery" of the network, which involves the RAN. The core, which resembles the brain or the heart of the network, is where voice and other data is routed across various sub-networks and computer servers to ensure it gets to its desired destination. While in the past much of this involved physical equipment such as routers and switches, much of this has been virtualized in the 5G environment, meaning that software—rather that hardware—is caring out these tasks. The core is distinct from the periphery—the RAN—which includes the base stations and antennas that provide a link between individual mobile devices and the core [43]. In the case of the EU, it seems that the rationale was that by limiting Huawei to the RAN, but banning it from the core, the risk of Chinese involvement would be manageable. Since 2019, there has been a strong consensus among the member states to gradually move away from Chinese 5G technology in the core of the networks. [42]. Nevertheless, bearing in mind that software is increasingly used in all parts of the 5G network, and the tendency is to undertake core operations, it is crucial to focus on the Chinese infiltration in the periphery of the networks, the RAN. Strand Consult, a consulting firm for telecom operators, has published a report that provides data on the share of Chinese and non-Chinese vendors in Europe [44].

Table 2.1 reveals two facts. First, there is a tendency to decrease the percentage of Chinese 5G RAN technology in the European market. Second, it is mainly small EU member states (e.g. Sweden, Denmark, Estonia, Latvia, Lithuania, Slovakia, Czech Republic) that have

Table 2.1   Comparison of 4G (2020) vs. 5G (2022)—Percentage of Installed RAN That Is Chinese

COUNTRY	INSTALLED CHINESE 4G NATIONAL RAN 2020	INSTALLED CHINESE 5G NATIONAL RAN 2022
Austria	67%	61%
Belgium	100%	30%
Bulgaria	67%	65%
Croatia	50%	31%
Czech Republic	92%	0%
Denmark	50%	0%
Estonia	20%	0%
Finland	30%	41%
France	26%	17%
Germany	57%	59%
Greece	67%	25%
Holland	50%	72%
Hungary	75%	53%
Ireland	17%	42%
Italy	41%	51%
Latvia	33%	0%
Lithuania	33%	0%
Luxembourg	67%	0%
Malta	0%	0%
Norway	60%	0%
Poland	58%	38%
Portugal	35%	34%
Cyprus	100%	100%
Romania	61%	76%
Slovakia	25%	0%
Slovenia	25%	48%
Spain	35%	38%
Sweden	75%	0%
Switzerland	43%	43%
UK	41%	41%

taken the issue of non-trusted vendors seriously, and not the big ones. States like Germany, Italy, Spain, and Poland purchase significant amounts of 5G equipment from Chinese vendors. These states make up approximately 50% of the European mobile customer base [44]. The EU is also divided in terms of legislation and restrictions regarding the core and the RAN elements of the 5G networks. Denmark, Estonia, France, Latvia, Lithuania, and Sweden are among the states that have passed legislation and imposed restrictions on both the core and the RAN elements of the 5G networks, whereas Austria, Bulgaria, Germany, Greece, Hungary, Portugal, Slovenia, and Malta have not set any restrictions yet [44].

Last, but not least, the EU's call for diversification of suppliers to prevent over-reliance on high-risk suppliers raises many questions regarding the advantages and disadvantages of open RAN. As mentioned previously, RAN is part of a wireless telecommunications network which uses proprietary equipment to connect individual devices to other parts of the network. If a single company would manufacture all parts of the 5G network, this would offer compatibility and operability, but it would also create monopolies, which eventually lead to technological dependence [45]. Open RAN encapsulates modularity. Modules are units of a larger system that are structurally independent, but also work together [46]. The architecture of open RAN is based on the concept of network slicing and supports the disintegration of hardware and software. This means that the 5G network is developed by using open interfaces and it is broken down in smaller networks [2]. Practically, the operating system may come from company A, microchips from company B and antennas from company C. Such a network architecture is expected to reduce technological dependencies and thus minimize security risks [45]. The liberal rationale behind the open RAN concept is to facilitate competition and therefore avoid the formation of oligopolies. It aims to remove market barriers and therefore amplify technological innovation. Open RAN is not a theoretical exercise but became a reality in 2018 with the creation of the O-RAN Alliance [47]. This technological alliance is a huge international consortium that includes mainly U.S., Chinese, and European partners. Among many others, O-RAN includes AT&T, China Mobile, Deutsche Telecom, Orange, ZTE,

Bell, Meta, Nokia, Ericsson, Samsung, Siemens, Microsoft, Lenovo, IBM, Dell, Cisco, AWS, Vodafone, and China Telecom [47].

It is critical at this point to debunk certain myths regarding the open RAN concept [48]. To begin with, the diversification of suppliers does not necessarily reduce the security risks. On the contrary, by using open-source software, technology is not secure at all. Public access to open-source code is without a doubt a weakness. Thus, we have to strike a balance between the expected benefits regarding the diversification of operators and the boost in technological innovation on the one hand, and the cybersecurity risks of an open network. In the case of O-RAN, it should be noted that 44 Chinese companies have joined the consortium, which automatically enables them to have access to the code and the intellectual property rights. It is at least an oxymoron to consider Huawei as an unreliable operator and at the same time enable dozens of Chinese companies to enter the European 5G ecosystem [2]. The last point to consider is whether open RAN in general and O-RAN in particular serve the U.S. geopolitical interests, since it practically aims to replace untrustworthy foreign (Chinese) manufacturers with U.S. technological giants like Amazon, Google, and Microsoft, which have already established dominant positions in their relevant markets. The rhetoric of openness and the potential of creating a transparent market serves the interest of the United States against China in the arena of digital geopolitics [46].

2.4 Conclusions

There is no doubt that 5G technology is a critical component for the development of the economy and society as a whole. The global reach and implications of 5G technology triggered a technological war between the United States and China, making the EU's vulnerabilities visible. For the latter, the choice of 5G providers has been addressed as part of the digital sovereignty debate and has been characterized as a strategic decision, rather than as a technological one. The EU correctly identified not only the strategic value of 5G for the further digitization of the EU but also the security issues attached to the implementation of such a critical infrastructure. 5G represents a technological and geopolitical battle, where the EU is unable to compete. It has neither the means nor the political will to enter into such a competition with China and the United States.

As part of its search for strategic autonomy, the EU has been gradually building a 5G policy. Bearing in mind that the EU cannot legislate or adopt legally binding acts in the area of 5G, as this is the responsibility of the member states, the European Commission has established a coordination model for the implementation and evaluation of 5G settings, via the EU toolbox on 5G cybersecurity [1]. For the time being, the EU strategy on 5G is based on coordinating national policies and emphasizing supplier diversification. The latter will increase competition and thereby reduce dependency. In the near future, the EU needs to invest more in its technological autonomy and build a consortium of European companies that should not only galvanize its digital sovereignty but also serve as an alternative for other states that share similar concerns and dilemmas. As documented in this chapter, 5G technology has raised national cybersecurity concerns within the member-states, revealed their technological dependencies and placed the demand for larger bandwidths and faster data traffic in a broader geopolitical context.

References

1. Margarita Robles-Carrillo. European Union Policy on 5G: Context, Scope and Limits, *Telecommunication Policy*, 45(8), 1–14, 2021.
2. Julien Nocetti, Europe and the Geopolitics of 5G. Walking a Technological Tightrope. In *Études de l'Ifri*. Ifris, January 2022.
3. Thomas Biersteker and Cynthia Weber, eds. *State Sovereignty as a Social Construct*. Cambridge University Press, 1996.
4. Stephen Krasner. *Sovereignty: Organized Hypocrisy*. Princeton University Press, 1999.
5. Gabriella Slomp. On Sovereignty. In Salmon Trevor and Mark Imber (eds), *Issues in International Relations*, pages 33–45, Routledge, 2008.
6. Tanja Aalberts. Sovereignty. In Felix Berenskoetter (ed.), *Concepts in World Politics*, pages 183–199, Sage, 2016.
7. Theodore Christakis. European Digital Sovereignty: Successfully Navigating between the 'Brussels Effect' and Europe's Quest for Strategic Autonomy, *Multidisciplinary Institute on Artificial Intelligence/Grenoble Alpes Data Institute*, 18 December 2020. Available at: https://ssrn.com/abstract=3748098, last accessed 2023-01-20.

8. Andrew Liaropoulos. The EU in the Era of Digital Geopolitics and the Challenge of Digital Sovereignty. In Van Brett Niekerk, Trishana Ramluckan and Neal Kushwaha (eds), *Modelling Nation-state Information Warfare and Cyber-operations*, pages 35–52, ACPI 2022.

9. Stephen Gourley. Cyber Sovereignty. In Panayotis Yannakogeorgos and Adam Lowther (eds), *Conflict and Cooperation in Cyberspace*, pages 277–290, Taylor & Francis, 2013.

10. Carla Hobbs, ed. Europe's Digital Sovereignty: From Rulemaker to Superpower in the Age of US-China Rivalry, *European Council on Foreign Relations, Policy Brief*, 30 July 2020. Available at: https://ecfr.eu/publication/europe_digital_sovereignty_rulemaker_superpower_age_us_china_rivalry/, last accessed 2023-12-12.

11. Julian Ringhof and José Ignacio Torreblanca. The Geopolitics of Technology: How the EU can become a global player, *European Council on Foreign Relations, Policy Brief*, 17 May 2022. Available at: https://ecfr.eu/publication/the-geopolitics-of-technology-how-the-eu-can-become-a-global-player/, last accessed 2022-12-20.

12. David Ramiro Troitiño. The European Union Facing the 21st Century: The Digital Revolution, *TalTech Journal of European Studies, Sciendo*, 12(1), 60–78, 2022.

13. European Commission. Rethinking Strategic Autonomy in the Digital Age, *EPSC Strategic Note*, 30, 2019. Available at: https://op.europa.eu/en/publication-detail/-/publication/889dd7b7-0cde-11ea-8c1f-01aa75ed71a1/language-en, last accessed 2022-11-11.

14. European Commission. USA-China-EU Plans for AI: Where Do We Stand? *Digital Transformation Monitor*, January 2018. Available at: https://ati.ec.europa.eu/sites/default/files/2020-07/USA-China-EU%20plans%20for%20AI%20-%20where%20do%20we%20stand%20%28v5%29.pdf, last accessed 2022-10-10.

15. Daniel Castro, Michael McLaughlin and Eline Chivot. Who Is Winning the AI Race: China, the EU of the United States? *Center for Data Innovation*, 19 August 2019. Available at: https://datainnovation.org/2019/08/who-is-winning-the-ai-race-china-the-eu-or-the-united-states/, last accessed 2022-11-11.

16. EIT Digital. European Digital Infrastructure and Data Sovereignty. A Policy Perspective, 2020. Available at: www.eitdigital.eu/fileadmin/files/2020/publications/data-sovereignty/EIT-Digital-Data-Sovereignty-Summary-Report.pdf, last accessed 2022-08-07.

17. Felix Richter. Amazon Leads $200-Billion Cloud Market, *Statista*, 2 August 2022. Available at: www.statista.com/chart/18819/worldwide-market-share-of-leading-cloud-infrastructure-service-providers/, last accessed 2022-12-15.

18. Andreas Aktoudianakis. Fostering Europe's Strategic Autonomy. Digital Sovereignty for Growth, Rules and Cooperation, *European Policy Centre*, 18 December 2020. Available at: www.epc.eu/en/publications/Fostering-Europes-Strategic-Autonomy--Digital-sovereignty-for-growth~3a8090, last accessed 2022-11-07.

19. Shoshana Zuboff. *The Age of Surveillance Capitalism*. Profile Books Ltd, 2019.

20. Tambiama Madiega. Digital Sovereignty for Europe. *EPRS—European Parliamentary Research Service*, PE 651.992, July 2020. Available at: www.europarl.europa.eu/RegData/etudes/BRIE/2020/651992/EPRS_BRI(2020)651992_EN.pdf, last accessed 2022-09-09.

21. Andrea Calderaro and Stella Blumfelde. Artificial Intelligence and EU Security: The False Promise of Digital Sovereignty, *European Security*, 31(3), 415–434, 2022.

22. Karsten Friis and Olav Lysne. Huawei, 5G and Security: Technological Limitations and Political Responses, *Development and Change*, 52(5), 1174–1195, 2021.

23. Linda Monsees and Daniel Lambach. Digital Sovereignty, Geopolitical Imaginaries, and the Reproduction of European Identity, *European Security*, 31(3), 377–394, 2022.

24. Phillipp Grüll. Geopolitical Europe Aims to Extend Its Sovereignty from China, *EUACTIV.DE*, 11 September 2020. Available at: www.euractiv.com/section/digital/news/geopolitical-europe-aims-to-extend-its-digital-sovereignty-versus-china/, last accessed 2022-11-07.

25. Mathieu Duchâtel and François Godement. Europe and 5G: The Huawei Case, *Policy Paper, Institut Montaigne*, June 2019. Available at: www.institutmontaigne.org/en/publications/europe-and-5g-huawei-case-part-2, last accessed 2022-11-07.

26. Gerard Pogoral, Antonios Nestoras and Francesco Cappelleti, eds. Decoding EU Digital Strategic Autonomy. Sectors, Issues and Partners, *Techno-Politics Series*, 1, *European Liberal Forum*, 2022. Available at: https://liberalforum.eu/wp-content/uploads/2022/06/Decoding-EU-Digital-Strategic-Autonomy_ELF-Study_Techno-Politics_vol.1-2.pdf, last accessed 2022-11-19.

27. Yan Xuetong. Bipolar Rivalry in the Early Digital Age, *The Chinese Journal of International Politics*, 13(3), 313–341, 2020.

28. Julian Kamasa. Microchips: Small and Demanded, *CSS Analyses in Security Policy*, 295, 2021. Available at https://css.ethz.ch/content/dam/ethz/special-interest/gess/cis/center-for-securities-studies/pdfs/CSSAnalyse295-EN.pdf, last accessed 2023-01-09.

29. Jan Czarnocki. Saving EU Digital Constitutionalism Through the Proportionality Principle and a Transatlantic Digital Accord, *European Review*, 20(2), 150–156, 2021.

30. Anu Bradford. *The Brussels Effect. How the European Union Rules the World*. Oxford University Press, 2020.

31. California Consumer Privacy Act. Available at: https://oag.ca.gov/privacy/ccpa, last accessed 2022-12-19.

32. Julia Zhu. The Personal Information Protection Law: China's Version of the GDPR?, *Columbia Journal of Transnational Law*, 14 February 2022. Available at: www.jtl.columbia.edu/bulletin-blog/the-personal-information-protection-law-chinas-version-of-the-gdpr, last accessed 2022-09-09.

33. Annegret Bendiek and Isabella Stürzer. Advancing European Internal and External Digital Sovereignty, *SWP Comment*, 20, Stiftung Wissenschaft und Politik, 2022. Available at: www.swp-berlin.org/en/publication/advancing-european-internal-and-external-digital-sovereignty, last accessed 2022-11-10.

34. Samuele Dominioni and Fabio Rugge, eds. The Geopolitics of 5G. In *ISPI Dossier*, Italian Institute for International Political Studies, 2020. Available at: www.ispionline.it/sites/default/files/pubblicazioni/dossier_cyber_5g_september_2020.pdf, last accessed 2022-11-10.

35. Keir Giles and Kim Hartmann. Emergence of 5G Networks and Implications for Cyber Conflict. In T. Jančárková, G. Visky and I. Winther (eds), *14th International Conference on Cyber Conflict: Keep Moving*, pages 405–420, NATO CCDCOE, 2022.

36. Tim Rühlig, John Seaman and Daniel Voelsen. 5G and the US-China Tech Rivalry—A Test for Europe's Future in the Digital Age, *SWP Comment*, 29, Stiftung Wissenschaft und Politik, 2019. Available at: www.swp-berlin.org/10.18449/2019C29/, last accessed 2022-12-03.

37. European Commission Recommendation, 2019/534. Cybersecurity of 5G Networks, 26 March 2019. Available at: https://eur-lex.europa.eu/legal-content/EN/TXT/PDF/?uri=OJ:L:2019:088:FULL&from=EN, last accessed 2022-09-10.

38. NIS Cooperation Group. EU Coordinated Risk Assessment of the Cybersecurity of 5G Networks, 9 October 2019. Available at: www.politico.eu/wp-content/uploads/2019/10/Report-EU-risk-assessment-final-October-9.pdf, last accessed 2022-12-15.

39. NIS Cooperation Group. Cybersecurity of 5G Networks EU Toolbox of Risk Mitigating Measures, 29 January 2020. Available at: www.politico.eu/wp-content/uploads/2020/01/POLITICO-Cybersecurity-of-5G-networks-EU-Toolbox-January-29-2020.pdf, last accessed 2022-12-15.

40. HERA-X. Available at: https://hexa-x.eu/, last accessed 2022-12-15.

41. Glenn Greenwald. *No Place to Hide: Edward Snowden, the NSA and the U.S Surveillance State*. Metropolitan Books, 2014.

42. Miguel Otero Inglesias. How Much of Chinese 5G Technology Is Still Used in Europe?, *Real Instituto Elcano*, 30 November 2022. Available at: www.realinstitutoelcano.org/en/commentaries/how-much-of-chinese-5g-technology-is-still-used-in-europe/, last accessed 2023-01-25.

43. Leo Kelion. What Is 5G's Core and Why Protect It? *BBC News*, 28 January 2020. Available at: www.bbc.com/news/technology-51178376, last accessed 2023-01-23.

44. Strand Consult. The Market for 5G in Europe: Share of Chinese and Non-Chinese Vendors in 31 European Countries. Available at: https://strandconsult.dk/the-market-for-5g-ran-in-europe-share-of-chinese-and-non-chinese-vendors-in-31-european-countries/, last accessed 2023-01-20.

45. Antonios Nestoras and Francesco Cappelletti. 5G Geopolitics and European Strategic Autonomy: Security, Standardisation, and the (False?) Promise of Open RAN, *Future Europe*, 1(1), 89–95, 2021.

46. Jean-Christophe Plantin. The Geopolitical Hijacking of Open Networking: The Case of Open RAN, *European Journal of Communication*, 36(4), 404–417, 2021.
47. O-RAN Alliance. Available at: www.o-ran.org, last accessed 2022-12-12.
48. Strand Consult. Debunking 25 Myths of OpenRAN. Available at: https://strandconsult.dk/debunking-25-myths-of-openran/, last accessed 2023-01-20.

3

FROM RULES TO RETRIBUTION

The Problem of Attribution and Regulation in the Age of Cyberwarfare

NATHAN DOWNES AND LEANDROS MAGLARAS

3.1 Introduction

The earliest forms of information warfare are likely lost to the annals of time. Such attacks might include message interception, propaganda, and espionage. The "Caesar cipher", one of the earliest forms of cryptography, was created in ancient Rome to protect messages from being read by third parties [1], a problem which is still relatable today.

By the time of World War II, various methods existed for the "encoding" of messages. These ranged from basic code words to the use of Native American languages [2]. By far the most sophisticated was the German Enigma encryption system, which was eventually broken by Alan Turing [3].

One of the earliest modern cybervulnerabilities to affect government infrastructure was identified by then-U.S. president Ronald Reagan, in 1983 [4, 5]. The vulnerability was not prompted by a rogue state, crime syndicate, or even cyberterrorists, but instead by a film titled *WarGames*. The film details the exploits of a teenage boy who employs contemporary computer hacking techniques [6] to gain access to a U.S. military defence mainframe computer. It impressed upon Reagan to such an extent that he enquired into the possibility of such an attack occurring. In response, he was told "The situation is worse that we think".

DOI: 10.1201/9781003314721-3

Although these vulnerabilities are separated by many years, they all share a common problem: attributing blame for an attack would be difficult, and in some cases impossible. Caesar could not identify who might have cracked his cipher, the Nazis could not prove who might have intercepted a communication and the (Reagan-era) U.S. government would likely have struggled to identify a competent hacker.

The attribution problem persists in the modern age; in addition, we are on the cusp of entering into an era in which malicious technology is becoming weaponised on a national scale. Whereas in the past, information warfare was a tool to be used alongside conventional means (hybrid war [3, p. 26]), modern warfare can now utilise cyberattacks as stand-alone weapons [7]. The dangers of this new age are apparent in that many attacks are indiscriminate in who they target [8]. Such a problem must surely prompt ethical concerns: should we be developing such weapons, and what can be done to regulate them? The goal of this review is to assess the ability to attribute blame for cyberattacks and comment on the likelihood that international cyberwar can be regulated via conventional means.

3.2 Advantages of Technology

Though cyberattacks have proven to be severely damaging, there is still an argument that cyberwarfare is far less harmful to public health and much cheaper than conventional warfare [9–11]. It is considered that cyberwarfare is thinly preferred (over conventional war) by civilian populations [11, 12]. Also, it has the ability to destabilise infrastructure anonymously [13]. Whilst this option has no-doubt appealed to many global governments, it does come with a potential impact on a nation's reputation [14].

3.2.1 Overt Cyberattack

In 2019, the United States blamed Iran for several attacks on foreign oil tankers operating in the Gulf of Oman [15]. Iran shot down a U.S. military drone, which it considered to be operating illegally within Iranian airspace. As an act of retaliation, then-U.S. President Donald Trump authorised the use of military force against Iran.

The U.S. military opted to use a cyberattack against Iran [16] rather than conventional weapons. The attack was sanctioned by the U.S. Department of Defense *Law of War Manual*, which suggested that a cyberattack would be a proportional [14] response [17].

Cyberattacks committed by nation-states have been occurring for some time, albeit in a more clandestine manner [3, 10, 18]. The novelty here is the openness in which the United States carried out the attack, as well as the clarity in which the U.S. "War Manual" offers guidelines on the use of cyberwarfare in place of conventional weapons. The use of a cyberattack undoubtedly saved numerous Iranian lives and was likely a much cheaper option, considering that the U.S. military had already lost one drone to Iranian anti-aircraft systems.

3.2.2 Covert Cyberattack

Most cyberattacks are carried out in a covert manner, with their goals usually being to de-stabilise infrastructure or deny access to services [8, 7, 19]. As an example, we could consider the Stuxnet attack on the Iranian uranium enrichment programme [20, 21]. The original Stuxnet attack was novel, in that its goal was to physically damage/destroy equipment. It could be considered humanity's first well-documented virtual weapon [7]. Whilst it is difficult to attribute blame for this attack, Iran has speculated that United States and Israeli hackers were responsible [17].

Attacks such as Stuxnet pose a real ethical question. Given that Iran has been identified, on the world stage, as a potential rogue state attempting to develop nuclear weaponry [22, 23] and the attack itself is considered illegal by the same U.S. military war manual mentioned in the overt example [17], should such an attack (if carried out by the U.S. military) be considered justified? And if so, who can judge? The advantages of such an attack (for the aggressor) are plain to see, assuming the objective of the attack was to cripple the Iranian nuclear program. A physical attack on a nuclear installation (such as the one we have recently seen during the conflict in the Ukraine [24]) could be environmentally devastating and would likely have been heavily condemned as a breach of international law [19].

3.3 Threats and Vulnerabilities

Alongside the advantages discussed in the previous section, it must also be considered that capabilities possessed by an aggressor could also be developed by their opponent. Such adversaries may pose an "advanced persistent threat" (APT) [13]. To be able to defend against such attacks, an organisation must look to their root causes. The following three case studies will be discussed in this subsection, with focus on the root causes of the attack.

3.3.1 Stuxnet

One of the most infamous cyberattacks ever executed [7], the Stuxnet attack on the Natanz uranium enrichment plant in Iran 2010 [20] was an attack aimed at physically destroying the infrastructure required to enrich uranium. The attack allegedly disabled around 1,000 centrifuges [21]. Though the "dropper" delivering the malware [25] will infect any machine running Microsoft's Windows operating system (OS) and is believed to have infected around 100,000 machines globally, the attack was specifically targeted at a particular vendor's (Siemens) brand of hardware controllers. The plant at Natanz is believed to have been so specific a target that the "warhead" responsible for infecting the controllers in question has not been registered anywhere else in the world [26, p. 13]. Once the malware identified a controller, it interacted with its software only when necessary, making the malicious software hard to detect. The malware is not believed to have been delivered via the internet; the most likely method of delivery was via physical media (USB, etc.) [20]. Once delivered, the attack spread via local networks using vulnerability MS08–067 [27].

Several root causes could be considered. First, physical security and staff screening at the plant was insufficient, allowing the attackers to access machines within the plant. Second, the portion of the attack which allowed the malware to be further distributed (by local networks) exploited a vulnerability (MS08–067) which, at the time, was at least two years old. It is possible that the machines within the plant had not been patched against this vulnerability. Third, the controllers in question are not compatible with anti-virus/malware protection software and are completely unprotected from software attacks [20].

Recommendation: Increase physical security and vetting of employees at the plant. Applying security updates promptly and disabling the use of external peripherals would also have helped. If possible, replacing the hardware controllers would be advised.

3.3.2 WannaCry

A ransomware attack which emerged in 2017 [8], WannaCry is acknowledged as one of the first malware attacks to affect civilian wellbeing on a mass scale [28]. It exploited the Microsoft Windows vulnerability known as "Eternal Blue" [29], which is believed to have been leaked from the U.S. National Security Agency [26, 30]. The vulnerability affected Microsoft's SMB network sharing protocol and was present in most Windows operating systems. The attack operated by encrypting the target machine's hard drive, and a ransom was then demanded (in Bitcoin) for the data to be unencrypted.

Focusing on WannaCry's effects on the National Health Service (NHS) in the UK, it is believed that the malware had been detected in around 80 of the 236 NHS trusts. NHS trusts act in a semi-autonomous manner, and whilst they had been advised to patch their systems against the WannaCry malware, many had not carried out the required updates. In addition to this, trusts had been advised (in 2014) to migrate away from old operating systems (such as Windows XP) by 2015. At the time of the attack in 2017, it is believed that many of the trusts had not carried out the migrations [31].

The root causes are likely to be related to poor communication, bureaucracy, and a lack of information technology (IT) expertise. Whilst trusts had received instruction to update systems, some may have not had access to the resources required. Ultimately, the root cause was a lack of due diligence in maintaining computer software, primarily security and operating system updates.

Recommendation: The NHS should consider creating a centralised IT/cybersecurity department. This department would be responsible for updating and managing hardware/software for all NHS trusts.

3.3.3 BlackEnergy

BlackEnergy was first identified in 2007 as a distributed denial of service (DDoS) botnet (v1); its latest variant (v3) was responsible for the 2015 attack on the Ukrainian power grid [7, p. 4, 19, 26]. The malware was delivered via a Microsoft Excel document distributed through phishing attacks [32], aimed at the public-facing networks of the affected power companies. The malware was then able to infect the supervisory control and data acquisition (SCADA) networks that were responsible for controlling the power grid.

First, the BlackEnergy malware was well known at the time of the attack. The U.S. Department of Homeland Security discovered (in 2014) that the software had been detected within the critical infrastructure of various countries throughout the world [33]. The attack may have been thwarted with better security protocols. Second, the attack was delivered via a phishing scheme. Phishing, a social engineering attack delivered via email, is intended to trick the victim into executing malicious web-links or software [32]. It is easily prevented with proper staff training.

> Recommendation: Improve general cybersecurity practices within the organisation; the vulnerability was well established and could have been diagnosed prior to the attack. Basic training for staff and email screening could greatly reduce the likelihood of phishing attacks being successful.

3.3.4 Similarities

All three cases could have been completely prevented—or at least mitigated—if stricter software update and vulnerability scanning protocols had existed. As all vulnerabilities targeted Microsoft operating systems, running a different OS would have made the systems harder to attack. An increase in cybersecurity training for all staff and the recruitment of more cybersecurity specialists would be recommended.

3.4 Existing Solutions

Several potential solutions exist in the field of regulating cyberwarfare. Many of them follow existing conventional models, such as disarmament, international humanitarian law (IHL), and peacekeeping efforts.

3.4.1 International Humanitarian Law

In recent years, there have been efforts made to establish a globally recognised set of rules to govern cyberwarfare. Just as the Geneva Conventions [34] govern conventional warfare, many are now calling for a similar accord to govern cyberattacks [35]. Although IHL may only govern what it considers to be "armed conflict" [19, 36–38], there are some countries that already interpret cyberattacks to be covered by IHL, such as the United States [37], UK, and Australia [36].

Practitioners of law refer to IHL by its Latin synonym "*jus in bello*" [37]. Schmitt [39] argues that a cyberattack would be considered within scope of IHL if it caused (or had potential to cause) physical harm to people or infrastructure, which might cover an attack such as Stuxnet in Iran; however, many attacks may not fall under this jurisdiction as they target digital resources [36]. Dörmann [40] goes one step further and proposes that computer-based attacks can be considered "acts of violence" under IHL, especially if their targets were considered to be "military objectives". This interpretation would not require physical damage for cyberattacks be considered a violation of IHL. The North Atlantic Treaty Organization (NATO) Cooperative Cyber Defence Centre of Excellence (CCDCOE) promotes research into cyberlaw, in the form of the *Tallinn Manual* [19, 41].

One issue when discussing cyberwarfare and law is the distance in time from authoring to modern day. The Geneva Conventions were penned in 1949, at a time when cyberwar was not even a subject of science fiction [37]. As a result, it may be likely that any real-world legal proceedings against an act of cyberwar could get bogged down in the agreement on an IHL interpretation. Given the speed at which technology advances, a legal case such as this could well become irrelevant before it was concluded.

3.4.2 Cyberdisarmament

Cyberwarfare has become an ever-growing threat; attacks are frequently reported in the public press and are becoming common in theatres of war [42, 43]. Given the growth in willingness to deploy such attacks, it could be argued that it is only a matter of time before cyberdisarmament is proposed [38]. Straub [44] draws an analogy between the nuclear disarmament and reduction programmes of the Cold War [3, 45] and the modern predicament of cyberwarfare. Curtis, however [46], opposes the related concept of "mutually assured destruction"—that either side of a conflict would refrain from using nuclear weaponry through fear of retaliation—on the grounds that cyberattacks could not be used to assure the destruction or disablement of an enemy [14]. Also worth considering is the likelihood that opposing parties would agree to disarmament [38].

The success of a disarmament programme is likely to hinge on several factors. First, can all parties be trusted to disclose their own capabilities, and second, can a country's capability be discerned using military intelligence? Such issues are perhaps not as prevalent when regulating physical weaponry [47], though it is unlikely the same approach can apply to cyberweaponry. How can an organisation be inspected when its digital assets cannot be identified or located?

3.4.3 Cyberpeacekeeping

Both NATO and the United Nations (UN) have defensive cybercapabilities. NATO offers support to its members in the form of access to research, training, strategy, operations, and law [37, 38, 48], and the UN's "digital blue helmets" (DBH) [49] claim similar support. The UN defines peacekeeping as an effort to maintain peace in areas where combat has ceased and measures are being taken to negotiate a permeant end to hostility [9, 50, 51]. UN peacekeeping efforts are guided by three principles [52]:

- Permission of the states involved.
- Impartiality.
- Use of force only in self-defence.

The UN expands further on the concept of "self-defence" and specifies that "robust peacekeeping" may only apply tactical force with "consent from the Security Council and of the host nation and/or the main parties to the conflict" [50]. Considering this, it could be concluded to be difficult to conduct a peacekeeping effort, for instance, if one party refused to acknowledge the attribution of an attack. In contrast, the UN also prescribes the possibility of "peace enforcement". Compared to "robust peacekeeping", [53] peace enforcement does not require the consent of the main parties and may involve the use of military force at the strategic or international level, which is normally prohibited for member states under Article 2(4) of the Charter, unless authorised by the Security Council [53].

Nabeel [54] argues that the DBH currently lacks the expertise or resources to effectively provide either cyberpeacekeeping or cyberpeace enforcement.

3.5 Discussion

When considering the appropriate response to a cyberattack, several factors must be assessed: the attack must be identified, investigated, classified, and—finally—attributed. The context of the attack is also important. This section will discuss the relevance of classification and attribution as they apply to the cases identified earlier in the chapter, and the original research questions will then be addressed.

3.5.1 Classification

Many attempts have been made to classify the nature of cyberattacks [3, 55–57]. Myriam Dunn Cavelty's classification model [55, 58, 59] is mentioned prominently in the literature. The model, in order of severity:

1. *Cyber-activism*
   Including vandalism, hacking, hacktivism.
2. *Cyber-crime*
   The act of committing a criminal act via electronic means.
3. *Cyber-espionage*
   The act of "spying": obtaining secret information illegally via electronic means.
4. *Cyber-terrorism*
   Electronic attacks on national infrastructure.
5. *Cyber-warfare*
   Attacks which occur within the context of a war between states.

As of 2010, it was the opinion of the UK's Government Communications Headquarters (GCHQ) that attacks falling under categories 1 and 2 were manageable, with the main concerns falling into categories 3–5 [58]. Cyberterrorism and cyberwarfare are considered quite loose terms [55], and some assert that cyberterrorism has no clear definition [37, 60].

The manageability of any item under this classification model could be considered questionable; we might consider GCHQ's statement in 2010 to be premature. Acts of cyberactivism and cybercrime might first be determined as isolated incidents, but then later (with more context) be realised as precursors to a larger scale of attacks or even the onset of a hybrid war [3, 19] such as the conflict in Ukraine [61]. As an example, given the lack of state-backed military context and solid attribution, the Stuxnet and WannaCry attacks, as detailed previously, could fall into categories 1, 2, 4, or 5.

3.5.2 *Attribution*

It could be argued that attribution is the virtual "elephant in the room". Much of the literature considers attribution to be one of the main difficulties in appropriating blame and directing retaliation [14, 26, 62]. Anonymity on the internet [63] makes the task even harder. Tran [64, p. 391] proposes that criminal law rarely relies on "absolute certainty" and by arguing that there is "no reasonable doubt" as to the identity of the aggressor is legally sufficient to attribute blame. Rauti [65] discusses the possibility of "attribution through deception", a technique also documented in the MITRE frameworks [66]. Using this technique, cyberdefenders can "lay traps" by exposing bogus vulnerabilities to attackers, in the hope that the attacker's identity can be ascertained whilst the vulnerability is monitored.

Of all the attacks discussed in this chapter, only the overt cyberattack made by the United States against Iran in 2019 can be attributed with certainty. The concept of providing "no reasonable doubt", as Tran suggests [64], could possibly be applied to both the Stuxnet attack against the Natanz plant in Iran (as the United States or an ally) and the BlackEnergy attack against the power grid in Ukraine (as Russia). Tran's approach could be flawed in that it is open to corruption, staged false flag attacks [67], and assumptions based on common enemies [18, 68].

3.5.3 RQ1: How Are Cyberattacks Attributed?

Attempting to attribute blame for a cyberattack is very difficult, and in some cases, it may be impossible. The only guaranteed method is an admission from the aggressor. Tran's suggestion [64] that law can be used to attribute blame feels far too open to abuse. The concept of "attribution through deception" seems reasonable—however, for this to be realistic, industry would need to recruit more cybersecurity specialists, a profession which is already acknowledged to be in short supply [69].

3.5.4 RQ2: How Are Cyberattacks Taxonomised?

The concept of classification, initially, appears to be straightforward. Much thought has already been given to creating a hierarchical taxonomy of the topic [55, 58, 59]. There is danger in applying the theory to practice, especially considering GCHQ's approach [58], in that misclassification could lead to threats being underestimated. The reality of "hybrid" warfare is still currently evolving and is likely to prompt further research into classification as attacks become more severe.

3.5.5 RQ3: Can IHL Regulate Cyberwar?

Many opinions exist on the applicability of international law [39, 40]. The arguments seem reasonable, however there are currently no proven legal cases in which law has been applied to cyberwarfare. International law and accords—such as IHL and the Geneva Conventions—require "buy-in" globally. This feels unlikely, as cyberwarfare is currently highly effective and in an era of high popularity. Progress is being made in this area [35, 41] and it is likely, as attacks become increasingly more devastating, that such agreements may become more appealing.

3.5.6 RQ4: Can Cyberpeacekeeping Be Effective?

Cyberpeacekeeping is a topic much discussed [9, 50, 51], though such efforts have yet to be deployed in the real world, and as large-scale cyberwar has yet to occur [26, p. 13], their pragmatic efficacy is an unknown quantity. Some sources claim that such efforts are very much in their infancy [54]. It is likely that early peacekeeping solutions may be somewhat "blunt" in that the only option available may be to disconnect local networks from the internet [10]. Undoubtedly, as cyberwar becomes a more present threat, resources devoted to developing NATO-style cyberdefence and UN peacekeeping efforts are likely to be become better developed and more sophisticated.

3.6 Conclusion

Though the awareness of cyberwar has existed for several decades, our current reality is still naïve. One cannot help but draw parallels to the early ignorance of nuclear weapons and their long-term effects [70], and as the effects of cyberattacks have already become far-reaching, we must ask the question: once unleashed, can this technology be stopped?—or has the proverbial Pandora's Box already been opened?

To conclude, it is clear from the literature that much research has been conducted into the theory of attributing and regulating cyberwar, though we have yet to see it applied in practice. Many of the efforts reviewed are still in their infancy, and it is likely that we may have to experience the full effects of international cyberwarfare before effective techniques can be developed and agreed upon to combat it on a global scale.

References

[1] A. Eskicioglu and L. Litwin, "Cryptography," *IEEE Potentials*, vol 20, no 1, pp. 36–38, 2001. https://doi.org/10.1109/45.913211

[2] W.C. Meadows, *The Comanche code talkers of World War II*, 2. paperback print ed. Austin: University of Texas Press, 2002.

[3] R. Baloch, "Cyber warfare trends, tactics and strategies: Lessons for Pakistan," *Journal of Development Policy, Research & Practice*, vol 3 & 4, pp. 51–71, 2019. Available at: https://journal.sdpi.org/controlpanels/assets/lib/uploads/1630997693350300.pdf

[4] E. Roche, "Dark territory: The secret history of cyber war. by Fred Kaplan. New York: Simon & Schuster, 2016," *Journal of Strategic Security*, vol 9, no 2, pp. 124–126, 2016. https://doi.org/10.5038/1944-0472.9.2.1532

[5] F.M. Kaplan, *Dark territory*, First Simon & Schuster hardcover edition ed. New York; London; Toronto; Sydney; New Delhi: Simon & Schuster, 2016.

[6] S. Zimmer, *"Demon dialling/war dialling"*. Available at: https://science.jrank. org/; https://science.jrank.org/computer-science/Demon_DialingWar_ Dialing-2.html [Accessed 31 Mar 2022].

[7] M. D. Firoozjaei, N. Mahmoudyar, Y. Baseri and A. A. Ghorbani, "An evaluation framework for industrial control system cyber incidents," *International Journal of Critical Infrastructure Protection*, vol 36, pp. 100487, Mar 2022. https://doi.org/10.1016/j.ijcip.2021.100487

[8] Da-Yu Kao and Shou-Ching Hsiao, "The dynamic analysis of WannaCry ransomware," In *International conference on advanced communications technology*, South Korea, Feb 2018, pp. 159–166. Available at: https:// ieeexplore.ieee.org/document/8323682

[9] M. Papathanasaki, G. Dimitriou, L. Maglaras, I. Vasileiou and H. Janicke, "From cyber terrorism to cyber peacekeeping: Are we there yet?" In *PCI 2020: 24th Pan-Hellenic conference on informatics*, Athens, 2020, pp. 334–339. https://doi.org/10.1145/3437120.3437335

[10] M. Papathanasaki and L. Maglaras, *The current posture of cyberwarfare and cyberterrorism*. Global Foundation for Cyber Studies and Research, 2020. Available at: www.researchgate.net/publication/342437834_The_ Current_Posture_of_Cyberwarfare_and_Cyberterrorism [Accessed 31 Mar 2022].

[11] R. Shandler, M. L. Gross and D. Canetti, "A fragile public preference for cyber strikes: Evidence from survey experiments in the United States, United Kingdom, and Israel", *Contemporary Security Policy*, vol 42, no 2, pp. 135–162, 2021. https://doi.org/10.1080/13523260.2020.1868836

[12] R. Shandler, M. L. Gross, S. Backhaus, and D. Canetti, "Cyber terrorism and public support for retaliation—a multi-country survey experiment," *British Journal of Political Science,* vol 52, no 2, pp. 850–868, 2022. https:// doi.org/10.1017/S0007123420000812

[13] Nasir Khaled, "The evolution of cyber war: The actors and strategies," *Peace and Security Review*, vol 9, no 21, pp. 36–53, 2020. https:// bipss.org.bd/pdf/Review-Volume-9-Number21-First-2020.pdf#page=45

[14] E. Iasiello, "Is cyber deterrence an illusory course of action?" *Journal of Strategic Security*, vol 7, no 1, pp. 54–67, 2014. https://doi. org/10.5038/1944-0472.7.1.5

[15] P. Wintour, "UK joins US in accusing Iran of tanker attacks as crew held", *The Guardian*, 14 June. Available at: www.theguardian.com/ world/2019/jun/14/us-accuses-iran-of-detaining-crew-after-oil-tanker-attack [Accessed 31 Mar 2022].

[16] BBC, "US 'launched cyber-attack on Iran weapons systems'", *BBC*, 23 June. Available at: www.bbc.co.uk/news/world-us-canada-48735097 [Accessed 31 Mar 2022].

[17] J. F. Lancelot, "Cyber-diplomacy: Cyberwarfare and the rules of engagement," *Journal of Cyber Security*, vol 4, no 4, pp. 240–254, 2020. https:// doi.org/10.1080/23742917.2020.1798155

[18] F.W. Kagan and T. Stiansen, *The growing cyberthreat from Iran: The initial report of project pistachio harvest*. The American Enterprise Institute, 2015. Available at: https://policycommons.net/artifacts/1296104/the-growing-cyberthreat-from-iran/1899350/ [Accessed 31 Mar 2022].

[19] D. A. Wallace and S. R. Reeves, "Protecting critical infrastructure in cyber warfare: Is it time for states to reassert themselves?" *U.C. Davis Law Review*, vol 53, no 3, pp. 1607, 2020. Available at: https://heinonline. org/HOL/LandingPage?handle=hein.journals/davlr53&div=33& id=&page=

[20] R. Langner, "Stuxnet: Dissecting a cyberwarfare weapon," *IEEE Security & Privacy*, vol 9, no 3, pp. 49–51, 2011. https://doi.org/10.1109/ MSP.2011.67

[21] D. Albright, P. Brannan and C. Walrond, *Did Stuxnet take out 1000 centrifuges at the Natanz enrichment plant?* Washington, DC: isis-online.org, 2010. Available at: https://isis-online.org/isis-reports/detail/did-stuxnet-take-out-1000-centrifuges-at-the-natanz-enrichment-plant/ [Accessed 31 Mar 2022].

[22] E. Inbar, "The need to block a nuclear Iran," *Middle East Review of International Affairs MERIA*, vol 10, no 1, pp. 85–104, 2006. Available at: https://ciaotest.cc.columbia.edu/olj/meria/meria_mar06/meria_10-1g.pdf

[23] J. Amuzegar, "Nuclear Iran: Perils and prospects," *Middle East Policy*, vol 13, no 2, pp. 90–112, 2006. https://doi.org/10.1111/j.1475-4967.2006.00252.x

[24] T. Sawano, M. Tsubokura, H. Ohto, K. Kamiya and S. Takenoshita, An attack on a nuclear power plant during a war is indiscriminate terrorism. *The Lancet*, 2022. https://doi.org/10.1016/s0140-6736(22)00522-0

[25] Microsoft, "TrojanDropper: Win32/stuxnet.A", *Microsoft*, 7 July. Available at: www.microsoft.com/en-us/wdsi/threats/malware-encyclopedia-description?Name=TrojanDropper%3aWin32%2fStuxnet.A [Accessed 31 Mar 2022].

[26] M. Plachkinova and A. Vo, "A taxonomy of cyberattacks against critical infrastructure," *Journal of Cybersecurity Education, Research, and Practice*, vol 2021, no 2, 2022. Available at: https://digitalcommons.kennesaw.edu/ jcerp/vol2021/iss2/3/

[27] Microsoft, "Microsoft security bulletin MS08-067—critical", *Microsoft*, 23 October. Available at: https://docs.microsoft.com/en-us/security-updates/securitybulletins/2008/ms08-067 [Accessed 31 Mar 2022].

[28] Z. Chang, "Cyberwarfare and international human law," *Creighton International and Comparative Law Journal*, vol 9, no 1, pp. 29–53, 2017. https://dx.doi.org/10.2139/ssrn.2973182

[29] Microsoft, "Microsoft security bulletin MS17-010—critical", *Microsoft*, 9 February. Available at: https://docs.microsoft.com/en-us/security-updates/SecurityBulletins/2017/ms17-010 [Accessed 31 Mar 2022].

[30] A. Koujalagi, S. Patil and P. Akkimaradi, "The WannaCry ransomware, a mega cyber-attack and their consequences on the modern India", *International Journal of Information Technology*, vol 6, no 4, 2018. Available at: www.researchgate.net/publication/324983515_The_ Wannacry_Ransomeware_A_Mega_Cyber_Attack_And_Their_ Consequences_On_The_Modern_India

[31] Auditor General, *National audit office. department of health; investigation: WannaCry cyber-attack and the NHS.* TSO, 2017. Available at: https:// publicinformationonline.com/download/151487 [Accessed 31 Mar 2022].

[32] A. Cherepanov and R. Lipovsky, "BlackEnergy—what we really know about the notorious cyber-attacks", *Virus Bulletin*, 2016. Available at: www.virusbulletin.com/virusbulletin/2017/07/vb2016-paper-blackenergy-what-we-really-know-about-notorious-cyber-attacks/

[33] R. Khan, P. Maynard, K. Mclaughlin, D. Laverty and S. Sezer, *Threat analysis of BlackEnergy malware for synchro phasor based real-time control and monitoring in smart grid*, Belfast: BCS, 2016. https://doi.org/10.14236/ewic/ics2016.7

[34] International Committee of the Red Cross, "The Geneva conventions of 1949 and their additional protocols", *International Committee of the Red Cross*, 1 January. Available at: www.icrc.org/en/document/geneva-conventions-1949-additional-protocols [Accessed 31 Mar 2022].

[35] B. Smith, "Microsoft—the need for a digital Geneva convention", *Microsoft*, 21 February. Available at: https://blogs.microsoft.com/on-the-issues/2017/02/14/need-digital-geneva-convention/ [Accessed 31 Mar 2022].

[36] C. Droege, "Get off my cloud: Cyber warfare, international humanitarian law, and the protection of civilians", *International Review of the Red Cross (2005)*, vol 94, no 886, pp. 533–578, 2012. https://dx.doi.org/10.1017/S1816383113000246

[37] M. Marsili, "The war on cyberterrorism," *Democracy and Security,* vol 15, no 2, pp. 172–199, 2019. https://doi.org/10.1080/17419166.2018.1496826

[38] M. E. Erendor and G. Tamer, "The new face of the war: Cyber warfare," *Cyberpolitik Journal,* vol 2, no 4, pp. 57–74, 2018. Available at: https://dergipark.org.tr/en/pub/cyberj/issue/35147/389922

[39] M. N. Schmitt, "Cyber operations and the jus in bello: Key issues," *Israel Yearbook on Human Rights,* vol 41, pp. 113–136, 2011. Available at: https://ssrn.com/abstract=1801176

[40] K. Dormann, "Applicability of the additional protocols to computer network attacks," In *International expert conference on computer network attacks and the applicability of international humanitarian law,* Stockholm, 19 November 2004. Available at: www.icrc.org/en/doc/resources/documents/misc/68lg92.htm

[41] NATO, "The Tallin manual", *CCDCOE*. Available at: https://ccdcoe.org/research/tallinn-manual/ [Accessed 31 Mar 2022].

[42] D. Sabbagh, "Ukraine accuses Russia of cyber-attack on two banks and its defence ministry", *The Guardian*, 16 February. Available at: www.theguardian.com/world/2022/feb/16/ukraine-accuses-russia-of-cyber-attack-on-two-banks-and-its-defence-ministry [Accessed 31 Mar 2022].

[43] A. Mohee, *Cyber war: The hidden side of the Russian Ukrainian crisis.* NewsRX LLC, 2022. https://doi.org/10.31235/osf.io/2agd3

[44] J. Straub, "Mutual assured destruction in information, influence and cyber warfare: Comparing, contrasting and combining relevant scenarios," *Technology in Society,* vol 59, pp. 101–177, 2019. https://dx.doi.org/10.1016/j.techsoc.2019.101177

[45] A. Schlesinger, "Origins of the cold war," *Foreign Affairs (New York, N.Y.),* vol 46, no 1, pp. 22–52, 1967. https://doi.org/10.2307/20039280

[46] W. Curtis, "The assured vulnerability paradigm: Can it provide a useful basis for deterrence in a world of strategic multi-polarity?" *Defense Analysis*, vol 16, no 3, pp. 239–256, 2000. https://doi.org/10.1080/713604728

[47] OCPW, "Convention on the prohibition of the development, production, stockpiling and use of chemical weapons and on their destruction", *OCPW*, 1 October. Available at: www.opcw.org/chemical-weapons-convention [Accessed 31 Mar 2022].

[48] NATO, "CCDOE about", *CCDCOE*. Available at: https://ccdcoe.org/about-us/ [Accessed 31 Mar 2022].

[49] UN, "Digital blue helmets", *United Nations*. Available at: https://unite.un.org/digitalbluehelmets/ [Accessed 31 Mar 2022].

[50] M. Robinson, K. Jones, H. Janicke and L. Maglaras, "An introduction to cyber peacekeeping," *Journal of Network and Computer Applications*, vol 114, pp. 70–87, 2018. https://doi.org/10.1016/j.jnca.2018.04.010

[51] M. Robinson, K. Jones, H. Janicke and L. Maglaras, "Developing cyber peacekeeping: Observation, monitoring and reporting," *Government Information Quarterly*, vol 36, no 2, pp. 276–293, 2019. https://dx.doi.org/10.1016/j.giq.2018.12.001

[52] United Nations, "What is peacekeeping", *UN*. Available at: https://peacekeeping.un.org/en/what-is-peacekeeping [Accessed 31 Mar 2022].

[53] United Nations, "Principles of peacekeeping", *UN*. Available at: https://peacekeeping.un.org/en/principles-of-peacekeeping [Accessed 31 Mar 2022].

[54] F. Nabeel, "Cyber peacekeeping: Critical evaluation of digital blue helmets program," *NUST Journal of International Peace & Stability*, vol 3, no 2, pp. 17–27, 2020. https://doi.org/10.37540/njips.v3i2.53

[55] Y. Tohirjonovich, S. Komildzhonovna and Y. Dilmurad, "Cyber threats and vulnerabilities," *EPRA International Journal of Research and Development*, vol 5, no 3, pp. 158–162, 2020. Available at: https://epra-journals.com/jpanel/upload/939pm_41.EPRA%20Journals2366.pdf

[56] J. J. Plotnek and J. Slay, "Cyber terrorism: A homogenized taxonomy and definition," *Computers & Security*, vol 102, 2021. https://dx.doi.org/10.1016/j.cose.2020.102145

[57] M. Nasser, R. Ahmad, W. Yassin, A. Hassan, Z. Zainal, N. Salih and K. Hameed, "Cyber-security incidents: A review cases in cyber-physical systems," *International Journal of Advanced Computer Science & Applications*, vol 9, no 1, pp. 499–508, 2018. https://doi.org/10.14569/IJACSA.2018.090169

[58] Debi Ashenden, "Cyber security: Time for engagement and debate," In *European conference on information warfare and security*, p. 11, 1 July 2011. Available at: www.proquest.com/docview/1010346764

[59] A. Collins, *Contemporary security studies*, 3rd ed. Oxford: Oxford University Press, pp. 400–416, 2013.

[60] V. Jangada Correia, "An explorative study into the importance of defining and classifying cyber terrorism in the United Kingdom," *SN Computer Science*, vol 3, no 1, 2021. https://doi.org/10.1007/s42979-021-00962-5

[61] N. Gaind and H. Else, "Global research community condemns Russian invasion of Ukraine," *Nature (London)*, vol 603, no 7900, pp. 209–210, 2022. https://doi.org/10.1038/d41586-022-00601-w

[62]   Pardis Moslemzadeh Tehrani, "Cyber resilience strategy and attribution in the context of international law," In *European conference on cyber warfare and security*, Portugal, 1 July 2019, pp. 501–516. Available at: www.proquest.com/docview/2261006997

[63]   H. L. Armstrong and P. J. Forde, "Internet anonymity practices in computer crime," *Information Management & Computer Security*, vol 11, no 5, pp. 209–215, 2003. https://doi.org/10.1108/09685220310500117

[64]   D. Tran, "The law of attribution: Rules for attributing the source of a cyber-attack," *Yale Journal of Law & Technology*, vol 20, no 1, p. 376, 2018. Available at: https://openyls.law.yale.edu/bitstream/handle/20.500.13051/7830/DelbertTranTheLawofAttrib.pdf?sequence=2

[65]   S. Rauti, "Hybrid Intelligent Systems," In *Towards cyber attribution by deception*, Cham: Springer International Publishing, 2020, pp. 419–428. https://doi.org/10.1007/978-3-030-49336-3_41

[66]   MITRE, "Active defense: Using deception and trickery to defeat cyber adversaries", *MITRE*, January. Available at: www.mitre.org/publications/project-stories/active-defense-using-deception-and-trickery-to-defeat-cyber-adversaries [Accessed 31 Mar 2022].

[67]   F. Skopik and T. Pahi, "Under false flag: Using technical artifacts for cyber attack attribution," *Cybersecurity*, vol 3, no 1, pp. 1–20, 2020. https://doi.org/10.1186/s42400-020-00048-4

[68]   K. Ji-Young, L. Jong In and K. Kyoung Gon, "The all-purpose sword: North Korea's cyber operations and strategies," In *11th international conference on cyber conflict (CyCon)*, Tallin, May 2019, pp. 1–20. https://doi.org/10.23919/CYCON.2019.8756954

[69]   B. J. Blazic, "The cybersecurity labour shortage in Europe: Moving to a new concept for education and training," *Technology in Society*, vol 67, 2021. https://dx.doi.org/10.1016/j.techsoc.2021.101769

[70]   S. L. Simon and A. Bouville, "Health effects of nuclear weapons testing," *The Lancet (British Edition)*, vol 386, no 9992, pp. 407–409, 2015. https://doi.org/10.1016/S0140-6736(15)61037-6

4

CYBERTERRORISM

A New Wave of Terrorism or Not?

ELENI KAPSOKOLI

4.1 Introduction

Terrorism originates from the Latin term terror and the suffix -isme (referring to practice), meaning "practicing or causing terror". The word terror and its practice date back to at least the 1st century CE, but the word terrorism entered our vocabulary from the French Revolution with the "reign of terror" and the "system of terror" in 1793–1794. The "system of terror" was a result of the indiscriminate violence by the French government, while in modern times, terrorism is the killing of a civilian population by non-state actors to achieve political purposes. Terrorism as a tactic has been used by its various proponents, from the Zealots and assassins to Al Qaeda and ISIS.

Terrorism has been used in our everyday life randomly and without a specific context of activities. Terrorism is commonly used to describe violent acts committed by actors against targets such as civilians without discrimination, without limits, only in pursuit of their political goals. The historical evolution of the phenomenon is due to the existence of a variety of modus operandi, political goals, and actors, which are constantly changing, but some elements, such as its nature, remain unchanged over time [1].

The 21st-century digital revolution offers countless possibilities for the collection, spread, and exchange of information in the field of communication, thus enabling actors to overcome geographical and time limitations [2]. Cyberspace provides the services that are the backbone of our society and these days has more than five billion users. In the age of selfies, snaps, likes, shares and hashtags, internet, and social media have transformed our daily lives. It confirms Virilio's

DOI: 10.1201/9781003314721-4

statement that the internet will bring "the end of geography" [3], as there will no longer be any geographical restrictions. The digital revolution and the rapid digitization of society is creating a new security landscape, which has affected almost every human, social, economic, and political aspect as it raises significant challenges.

The challenges emerging from cyberspace concern the development of malicious activities such as cyberattacks, cyberterrorism, cyberespionage, cybercrime, cyberwar, fake news and disinformation. Terrorism has gone through a significant transformation during recent decades, as it has developed an inseparable relationship with cyberspace. Cyberspace serves as a field for enhancing and maintaining terrorism. This is proven by the fact that Islamic terrorism has emerged as one of the most important security challenges. The insecurity caused by Islamic terrorism is due to the size, frequency and scope of its actions, and its ability to adapt [4].

During recent decades, every political actor across the ideological spectrum has exploited digital technology. Thus, terrorist organizations like Al Qaeda and ISIS/Islamic State have digitized their modus operandi. It should come as no surprise that terrorists are able to learn, innovate and adapt to the new technological imperatives of each era. This vicious cycle of their operational innovation and adaptation poses a challenge for counterterrorism. Terrorists have proven to be effective adopters of the emergence of new digital technology and virtual toolboxes as means to create and disseminate material, to radicalize and recruit supporters, to coordinate online and offline activities, and to raise funding. Terrorists use cyberspace to imitate and substitute utilities previously undertaken in the physical world.

As then-U.S. President Barack Obama stated in 2009 during his announcement of the new cybersecurity policy,

> Al Qaeda and other terrorist groups have spoken of their desire to unleash a cyberattack on our country—attacks that are harder to detect and harder to defend against. Indeed, in today's world, acts of terror could come not only from a few extremists in suicide vests but from a few key strokes on the computer—a weapon of mass disruption [5].

In our time, terrorists have both the motivation (religious faith and/or political purposes) for operational action and the means for its effectiveness via cyberspace and information communication technologies (ICTs).

This chapter applies Rapoport's wave theory of terrorism to analyze the transformation of this phenomenon. It also analyzes the empirical evidence at operational level for Al Qaeda and ISIS to trace their evolution. Moreover, it applies the wave theory to examine if cyberterrorism consists of the fifth terrorist wave.

4.2 The Wave Theory of Terrorism

Rapoport's wave theory refers to the existence of four waves that characterize the evolution of modern terrorism [6–8]. The four waves are: the "Anarchist Wave" (1879–1920), the "Anti-Colonial Wave" (1919–1960), the "New Left Wave" (1960–1990), and the "Religious Wave" (1979–2020) [8, 9]. The wave is a cycle of activities in a given period of time, which lasts a few decades at a specific geographical location with specific actors, means, modus operandi, and audiences. In each wave, there are some specific actors who express the dominant energy of the wave [7]. Rapoport highlights the existence of some common characteristics to each wave: 1) the use or the threat of use violence in order to achieve political goals; 2) the international character and impact of their actions; 3) the existence of the wave after a catalytic event; 4) the use of technology as a means at the operational level; 5) the ideological background of the actors; and 6) revolution—the emergence of a new political reality [10].

According to Rapoport, there are some critical variables that affect the beginning of a new terrorist wave, thus the end or the gradual disappearance of the current and its replacement by a new one, or the limitation of its energy, but not its replacement because it may be activated in the future. The critical variables are three: 1) the creation of a new political reality; 2) the adoption of new techniques and means at the operational level; and 3) when the wave's energy is not capable of influencing the creation of new terrorist groups (e.g., to be inspired or imitated by like-minded people). These variables are essential to identify the transformation of terrorism. The consecutive change of the terrorist waves is due to the fact that in each time period, specific actors express greater dynamic at the international level [11].

Rapoport believes that technology is a critical variable at the evolution of terrorism. Each wave uses other means of technology to promote its terrorist actions and to noticeably shrink time and geographical limits. The "Anarchist Wave" used telegraph, daily newspapers, steamship, railroads, gunpowder, and nitroglycerin. The "Anti-Colonial Wave" used faster means of communication such as radio and newspapers. The "New Left Wave" used more sophisticated means such as television, radio, newspapers, mobile phones, digital timers, radar guns, and explosive devices or means of surveillance. The globalization of the ideological background in this wave was through its visibility from movies, songs, magazines or posters. The last one is the "Religious Wave", where there was an increase in the sophistication of improvised explosive devices and the use of the "ultimate smart bomb" (suicide terrorists). In the field of communication and propaganda, we have the rise of the internet and social media [12].

This analysis of the technological variables that influenced previous terrorist waves is significant to trace the evolution and the transformation of this phenomenon at operational level. Nowadays, terrorism acquires a digital character due to the widespread use of ICTs. Terrorists no longer use a printed page, but an encrypted web page. They do not operate in a specific geographical area, but they rather have an expanded field of action. Technology has also served the preserving and promotion of know-how derived from previous terrorist waves which are a source of inspiration for the new terrorists [8]. Undoubtedly, the generation that grew up alongside the technological development is the most dangerous source of terrorists, due to the increased know-how.

4.3 The Synthesis of Cyberspace and Terrorism: Cyberterrorism

Clausewitz stated that "war is the continuation of politics by other means" [13, p. 7]. Similarly, cyberterrorism is the continuation of terrorism by other means. There is a dominant and well-established symbiotic relationship between terrorism and cyberspace [14]. The digital era has offered countless opportunities for those who want to swiftly and easily amplify violent physical actions into the information environment. It is safe to say that without digital technology, many terrorist organizations would never survive and expand. At this point, it could be said without any exaggeration that there is a "digital footprint" in terrorism since every aspect of society is connected to some information means, so it is obvious that cyberspace is a potential field where terrorism can flourish.

There is no commonly accepted definition of cyberterrorism, which leads to conceptual ambiguity. Over the years, policy makers, academics and media outlets have used terms such as "cyber-9/11", "electronic Pearl Harbor", "electronic Chernobyl", "electronic Armageddon" and "electronic pandemic" in order to gain attention and publicity, but also to further securitize the field of cyberspace. There are narrow and broad approaches of cyberterrorism. The narrow approach limits the understanding of what cyberterrorism constitutes and includes exclusively the conduct of malicious cyberactivities [15–17]. The broader approach examines a full spectrum of malicious cyberactivities in order to have a more holistic approach toward cyberterrorism and the true potential that cyberspace offers to terrorist activities [18, 19].

Cyberterrorism reflects the "dark side" of cyberspace. The latter approach enables a full spectrum of terrorist actions to promote their political goals [20]. Terrorists are taking advantage of the potentials of cyberspace, imitating successful tactics from other terrorists, learning from past mistakes and adapting to present and future needs and conditions [21]. It is safe to argue that the extensive use of ICTs enable terrorists by decreasing costs, generating efficiencies, increasing access to new audiences, granting anonymity, enhancing security, decreasing organizing barriers and of course improving, expanding and ensuring the longevity of their actions.

Terrorists use cyberspace for two main reasons. The first is to develop malicious cyberactivities, such as cyberattacks. The possibility of a terrorist organization conducting a cyberattack on a military or financial system is considered as a major security threat [22]. The second reason is to facilitate their actions, which provide a fertile ground for the rise of radical ideas that lead to terrorism [15, 18]. Terrorists can express digitally their religious with the use of this means and the construction of digital religious communities [23].

Figure 4.1   The Digital Jihad model

This chapter adopts the broader approach of cyberterrorism and analyzes the cyberactivities by Al Qaeda and ISIS based on the "Digital Jihad" model (Figure 4.1). The model includes the following uses: radicalization, recruitment, strategic communication/propaganda, operational training, funding and online matching.

4.4 Digital Jihad: Al Qaeda and ISIS

Al Qaeda and ISIS are two anachronistic terrorist organizations that adapted to the new social-political imperatives and to the demands of each era through the use of contemporary means. Their main strategic goals are to restore traditional Islam to modern society, to expand territorially and to spread their ideology [1, 24, 25]. They have launched an extremely sophisticated information campaign targeting a wider audience to gain global support. The oxymoron is that both prohibit modern behaviors (smoking, use of digital technology, fashion outfits, etc.), but they manage to modernize their operational action in a unique way.

Al Qaeda has developed at a time when modernity and social behavior patterns were not dependent on ICTs and cyberspace, and the organization lacked the appropriate equipment and corresponding know-how regarding their use [26, 27]. Al Qaeda turned to cyberspace as a temporary solution to mitigate for the loss of offline actions after 2001. On the contrary, ISIS developed at a time when citizens were dependent on ICTs and social media. Moreover, ISIS tried to control its territory between 2014–2017 through cyberspace as a mean of radicalization, recruitment and propaganda for fighters. The following subsection analyzes the activities of Al Qaeda and ISIS based on the Digital Jihad model.

4.4.1 Radicalization

This process concerns the development and the adoption of radical ideas, which will lead to violent actions to achieve political goals of an individual or a group [28, 29]. Cyberspace provides the ability to construct new "virtual communities" wherein users may be exposed and share more radical and alternative ideas with other like-minded people. Small terrorist organizations can find their voice to attract new members through secure and anonymous communication. Only two things are essential: a smartphone and an internet connection. The users can express their ideas and opinions freely and openly, without the fear of being deplatformed. Cyberspace acts as an amplifier of terrorism since it removes any barriers and acts as a mean of radicalization [30]. The number of people exposed to radical ideas has risen with the growth of the number of internet users and it is expected to increase more.

Quintan Wiktorowicz has written that "Islamic radicalization" includes a "cognitive opening" which is triggered by a crisis—personal, economic, social, political, and religious—during this phase, the person is more vulnerable to radical ideas, values, and beliefs, readjusts these to its daily life and develops a behavioral radicalization [31, 32]. He mentions that there are four phases of radicalization through cyberspace: 1) *pre-radicalization*, the reference to their life before they adopted the Salafist/jihadist ideology; 2) *self-identification*, the exploration of jihadist ideology; 3) *indoctrination*, the intensification of jihadist ideology and complete assimilation into it; and 4) *jihadization*, the acceptance of the ideology and implementing it by waging jihad through terrorist attacks [33].

Radicalized people feel like "scapegoats" or "victims" due to social inequality and injustice, pushing them to adopt radical and extreme ideas which may trigger a "moral shock". Once radicalized, terrorists satisfy their desire of belonging, to regain their lost self-esteem, to give meaning to their life, to get revenge, to increase their prestige and to live an adventure [34–38]. Cyberspace facilitates the formation of a new virtual relationship between the core of the organization and its future members. This relationship is based on promises of friendship, acceptance and a sense of purpose.

Persons who radicalize tend to have criminal records, are usually lonely and socially withdrawn, seek risk and adventure, want revenge for various reasons and are not socially acceptable, and often are relatives or friends of a member. The push factors are the age, prior criminal record, gender, psychopathological characteristics, family background, social circle, relative deprivation (economic, educational), failed integration, personal or collective victimization, social (religious) identity and humiliation. Jihadists have created the concept of "jihadi cool" which refers to the promotion of an ideal image of the life of the radicalized that is equivalent to a star [39, 40]. They created reputations regarding their actions and their political goals based on their general perceptions, to attract more potential terrorists.

The "virtual radicalization" promotes the self-radicalization in a short period of time due to the extensive and effective use of cyberspace [41, 42], with the creation of a complete functional virtual ecosystem [43]. In this complete functional virtual ecosystem, users have access to sources of information that can intensify the radicalization. In cyberspace, there is a common sense of belonging to an "imagined community"—and in the case of Islamic terrorism, an imagined unity of the Ummah with the creation of "virtual Muslim community" where they can share ideas, opinions and best practices [44, 45]. According to Ranstorp, cyberspace is "the virtual base where every dimension of global Jihad could take place" [46, p. 23].

There are some important methods for virtual radicalization: target groups, social mapping and profiling. Those responsible for radicalization place emphasis on the receiver of the message and their behavior because they create specific target groups whereby their approach is adjusted to group's social, economic, religious, and ideological specifications. They also use the method of social mapping and profiling which helps to collect all the necessary information to be used for their approach [47]. Most users forget the daily role of social media and ICTs, and publish all their personal information unfiltered, thus providing all the needed information to malicious actors.

The areas of virtual radicalization are online libraries, jihadi websites and forums which include digital audiovisual material such as videos, magazines, books, manuals, recordings, religious sermons (khutbas) and Arabic songs (Nasheed) [48]. These means create chat rooms for the communication, operational planning, and support of the members that function as "echo chambers"[1] [49]. The online magazines have religious content, use of Arabic symbolic names and publication dates according to the Arabic calendar (hijri), which tend to build a new identity for the potential terrorists. The publications are in different languages (English, French, German, Russian, Hindi, and Arabic) to approach different audiences. Another trend that has emerged mainly in the Western Balkans is the use of online platforms for free religious lectures (sermons) delivered by jihadist preachers (Da'is) to attract followers [50]. They create digital religious classrooms for the believers, to enhance their beliefs. The possibility of effective communication in a digital environment, is reflected in Neumann's description that "online forums are virtual squares, where people meet, bond, and discuss, and where even the most controversial issues can be discussed, without the risk of consequences". The radicalized persons are developing a common digital culture [51, p. 434, 52].

4.4.2 Recruitment

Recruitment is the process whereby individuals voluntarily become part of a grou to share thoughts and goals with other like-minded members. Recruitment is no longer done exclusively by experienced veteran fighters in local training centers, mosques, cultural centers, and other convenient places. This process has been digitized and diversified after the Western military interventions in Afghanistan and Iraq, and the subsequent long-term presence of foreign military forces in these areas [53]. Terrorist groups lost their military training bases and tried to survive through cyberspace, which was the new field of their action.

In particular, recruiters are enabled by the homogeneity of virtual environments, where they can isolate potential fighters from counter narratives into private clusters and ensure that they will be exposed to the desired ideas—their ideas. The recruiter and a potentially radicalized person have developed a "digital relationship" only with a friend request. Important factors in this process are trust and intimacy [51]. This form of recruitments is less risky than in the physical world, due to anonymity and encryption methods. Recruiters have created a "cyber-Caliphate" to unify the Muslims of diaspora through cyber-space so they become "cyberfighters" to conduct offline and online activities.

There are some specific methods of recruitment through cyber-space, which are: digital material (audiovisual material, speeches by leaders, interviews, sermons or actions), chat rooms, online forums, websites, communication platforms, social media and use of animation and videogames to attract younger fighters [54]. For example, ISIS's media company, Nashir News, published a post on LinkedIn with opening positions in the Caliphate for potential fighters. However, an important observation is that recruitment is not only effective through digital means, but also by physical means, as cyberspace is used to identify, gather information, track and select potential fighters.

4.4.3 Operational Training

The process of operational training is promoted by cyberspace because terrorists have access to all kinds of information for their actions without requiring a physical presence [55, 56]. Both terrorist organi-zations have created a "cyber-Caliphate" to enhance all their cyberac-tivities. Potential fighters have access to online material and lectures in the "digital classrooms" [57], containing necessary information and instructions like creation and use of weapons; conduct of espionage and surveillance; collection of information on targets, planning, coor-dination and conduct of offline and online activities; development of hacking activities; and improvement of security and encryption for communications [48]. This kind of digital training converts tradi-tional terrorists into "cyber fighters" [58], because they can develop their knowledge on the use of traditional means and develop their cyberskills to conduct cyberactivities.

Another operational training tactic that was introduced by Al Qaeda, is that of "gamification", which involves the use of videogames, training series and audiovisual material to reduce time-consuming training and minimize the need for economic resources [59]. The videogames offered a type of digital simulation through a "virtual battlefield and training camp" where players could have any kind of operational training, to prepare for the real purpose of their life: to become sahid (martyrs) [60, 61]. The videogames intensify radicalization, and recruitment, because the players are remaining active and zealous for jihadists [62, 63]. Al Qaeda's videogames were the *Quest for Bush*, *Muslim Mali* and *Second Life* [59, 62, 63], and ISIS's were *Call of Jihad*, *Huroof* (*Letters*), *ARMA3 3D FPS* and *Salil al-Sawarim* (*The Clanging of the Swords* 1–4) [64].

Moreover, they used online training materials such as audiovisual material, digital magazines (*Inspire*, *Spoils of War*, *Haqq* and *Rumiyah*), training series (Silsilat), digital technology (global navigation systems, satellite images of the area taken by Google Street View, or three-dimensional panoramic photos) and simulation systems [65, 66]. The training videos are divided into two categories: 1) self-produced videos by fighters or supporters of the organization; and 2) films produced by other supporters (companies of marketing and production) which are available on jihadist websites. The latter category includes videos with instruction for using guns and knives, bomb-making and even instructions for vehicle-ramming attacks [67].

4.4.4 Strategic Communication—Propaganda

Propaganda is a type of manipulation and promotion of specific information and ideas which are based on real or fabricated events to influence the actions, emotions, attitudes and behaviors of the audience. Cyberspace offers freedom of expression in an environment where its users do not filter their ideas and opinions. The anonymity that exists in cyberspace offers room for people to express themselves where under normal circumstances they would not have the opportunity [68–70]. Propaganda through cyberspace and social media offer some unique advantages compared to other traditional media. In fact, the range and scope of online discussions create an almost global digital arena.

Terrorist organizations use propaganda as a means of gaining publicity and resonance for their actions and ideas, to influence and manipulate attitudes and emotions [71]. Bruce Hoffman emphasizes that every terrorist act seeks the maximum publicity, the intimidation, and the subjugation of the audience to achieve their political goals [14]. According to Marshall McLuhan, without communication, terrorism does not exist, which means that its preservation and survival, is through the spread of fear and terror [72, 73]. The more publicity a terrorist action generates by reproducing and spreading terror, the more success and impact will the terrorist's work have to bring the political change that they seek [14]. Brigitte Nacos categorizes the goals of communication in the "political communication triangle" (media, public and government). The three communication goals are the pursuit of media attention, recognition, and publicity, but also gaining respect and legitimacy in certain circles, countries and regions [74].

Lisa Wiechert described terrorists using a four-step strategy in propaganda AIDA (attraction, interest, desire, action). The first step is to generate high media resonance to reach broader audience. The second is to present their fighters to convince potential supporters. The third is to publish content with the experiences of fighters to encourage others to live the same experiences. If the third step is effective, it will recruit fighters and supporters to provide online and offline ideological support, enabling attacks [75].

Another goal of propaganda is to create psychological fear through the use of cyberspace. Timothy Thomas uses the term "cyberfear", which is the result of what a cyberattack could cause or the true cyberskills of terrorists [76]. Cyberspace is a means of power for small groups and presents them as more capable than they might be, so it allows them to create their own narrative about their power and creates a fear in the virtual world.

Al Qaeda's rhetoric aims to achieve three main goals: first, to motivate Muslims to defend their religion against the West; second, to counter political, economic, and social issues with global impact; and third, to reunite Muslims in diaspora for the jihad against the West [77]. Al Qaeda's propaganda is divided in two parts. The first part is based on religious references such as the Quran, hadiths, and religious sermons to promote the image of a terrorist organization which endorses deep religious belief, while in fact it promotes its political goals (religious manipulation) [78]. The propaganda offers a religious justification for the use or threat of use of violence against non-combatant population [79]. The second part of the propaganda concerns the projection of material related to foreign military operations, which have negatively affected the Muslim world and degraded their way of life [78]. However, Al Qaeda also used similes with events of historical importance to the Muslim world to characterize their actions taking place in the present time.

Al Qaeda had audiovisual production companies (Global Islamic Media Front, Global Islamic Media Centre, Global Islamic Media Group) to produce online material in several languages. This online material included newsletters, manuals (*Al Qaeda's Twenty-Year Strategic Plan*, Al Qaeda training manual, *Encyclopaedia of Preparation for Jihad*, *Global Islamic Resistance Call* and *The Administration of Savagery*) and digital magazines (*Inspire*, *Echo of Epic Battles*, *Voice of Jihad*).

On the contrary, ISIS's propaganda is more successful than that of other terrorist organizations, by exploiting Al Qaeda's communication heritage, by utilizing new communication technologies and by the ability of its members to use online communication techniques in practicing cyberjihad. They turned a local terrorist organization into a global brand and operated as a Western-style business since the proclamation of the Caliphate [80], which helped to develop a vast of messages to different media and audiences. ISIS used not only traditional media (radio, video, newspapers) to promote its political goals, but also the full spectrum of ICTs.

ISIS's narratives can be divided into three main themes: political, religious, and social. The political narrative referred to the political aspirations of ISIS. This includes references to Abu Bakr al-Baghdadi as self-proclaimed Caliph, the vision of the Caliphate, the unity of Muslims, the revenge of political and religious adversaries, and the broadcasting of their successful terrorist and military actions. The broadcasting of their success offers visibility and publicity to their actions, and presents them as a powerful organization. This is turn, serves the radicalization of new fighters.

Regarding the religious narrative, it focused on jihad, which is the religious duty of all Muslims[2] [81]. ISIS presented a carefully constructed image of its actions and rhetoric with selective historic Arabic events (Dabiq's fight, Syria's conflict) and Islamic symbols (black banner from the Abbasids and the seal of Muhammed) for the "awakening" of believers to become fighters. It is a type of religious indoctrination. Furthermore, ISIS published their terrorist actions for religious legitimacy. They referred that their actions are as per the Quran and Sunnah to protect Islam. They claimed that ISIS was the main political and religious authority in the Sunni community, and they did not hesitate to declare war against all enemies. They referred to the society with the division into "us" (good jihadists) and "them" (bad enemies). They promoted the message that ISIS's supporters were ready to sacrifice their lives for their cause and to become "suicide attackers" (martyrs). The online religious legitimacy could offer to ISIS a recognition of the Caliphate. Through its content, it presented the use of violence as an integral part of Islam and jihad as the basic means. Its audience are Muslims of the diaspora, presenting their actions as necessary, meaningful and exciting—both inside and outside the Caliphate. But the paradox is that they were trying to radicalize Muslims and non-Muslims, while at the same time framing them as apostates and infidels.

The last narrative, social, includes the promotion of fighter's daily life and operational training. ISIS tried through its propaganda to promote a better life which can be used to influence the younger audiences, who feel socially withdrawn in their home countries. Through this social content, ISIS encouraged potential fighters to join the Caliphate.

ISIS used audiovisual production companies (Al-Hayat Media Center, Al-Furqan Islamic Heritage Foundation for Media Production, Amaq News Agency, and Central Media Department) in different languages (English, Arabic, German, Farsi, Hindi, and French) in order to promote its digital content [82]. Other means of propaganda were the digital radio (Al-Bayan, A'maq Ikhbariyya) [83], newsletters (*Al naba*), sermons—Khutbas [84], songs (nasheed), and videoclips (Salil al-sawarim, province of Aleppo, "Deadly Arrows", "The Killings of Shiites", "My Ummah", "Dawn Has Appeared"), online books and manuals (*Islamic State 2015*, *Anarchist Cookbook*), websites, pages and groups on social media and digital magazines (*Dabiq, al-Naba, Dar al-Islam, Konstantiniyye, Istok, Rumiyah, Voice of Hind*) [80].

The most important tool of ISIS's propaganda were their videos. The videos were based to Hollywood-style imagery (Western culture standards) and graphics, had cinematic motifs and were less than five minutes in duration. The videos were broadcasted in different languages, with the use of Islamic music, and they were shared in real time on social media [85–87]. They can be divided into videos with more emotional and tender images and videos with brutal content and horrific images (such as beheadings, arson, rapes, and mass slaughters). The second category serves two goals. The first is to cause fear and loathing in their enemies, and the second is to attract like-minded supporters [88]. Even if Al Qaeda was the first terrorist group that videotaped the murder of a hostage and published it on social media (e.g., Laurence Michael Foley, Sr. (October 5, 1942–October 28, 2002) was an American diplomat who was assassinated outside his home in Amman, Jordan), ISIS has repeatedly shown horrific images and used a pompous rhetoric with eschatological references [89].

As already mentioned, terrorists use social media and communication platforms extensively to promote their material. They use specific methods to promote their messages. First, they use the tactic "hashtag hijacking" or "textual hijacking", using the hashtag symbol (#) to gain access to other users and their information. Also, by using hashtags, they achieve digital grouping and audience guidance. With this method, hashtags lead users to malicious content posted by fake social media accounts and supporters can have easy digital guidance and access to relevant content [90]. In addition, they use "event crashing", which is the exploitation of a popular event by creating a hashtag to offer digital guidance to the user and to collect necessary information from their accounts. The last one is "persona poaching" or "defamation", which is the creation of fake accounts based on the information from real social media accounts. Users impersonating the real users are trying to approach them [91].

Regarding strategic communication, terrorists use digital technology (personal computers, smartphones, email, chat, forums, online meetings, etc.) to have real-time communication regardless of geographic area [92]. Digital technology has offered a low-cost, efficient, encrypted, and secure vehicle to communicate and network, and ICTs are available to the public and are low-cost—as a result, even terrorist organizations with limited economic sources have the capability of creating and maintaining a digital presence. They use effective encryption methods and hijack foreign accounts to have a secure and stable communication [93, 94].

4.4.5 Funding

The use of cyberspace is low-cost and absorbs fewer resources than conventional terrorism. There is a phenomenon of collecting and transferring funds to support and expand the activities of terrorist organizations. Terrorists use cyberspace to publicize their financial needs with posting requests for funding to their websites and personal accounts, where followers can support their actions and expand their reach [95]. There are several methods of funding. One of the methods is the use of cryptocurrencies like Bitcoin, even though their religion rejects the use of digital currencies. They religiously justified it by saying that the monetary system based on paper money is doomed to decline and is a creation of the West [26]. In addition, terrorists have the necessary cyberskills to conduct cyberattacks on financial systems or personal accounts of citizens to collect financial resources [96]. Moreover, the taxes of faith (zakat) could be deposited by supporters and fighters online, so that they could fulfill their religious obligations according to the Quran [97]. They used e-commerce and online retail platforms to obtain more funds through websites and intermediaries (eBay, Amazon and Etsy). ISIS also conducted illegal sales of cars, houses, antiquities, guns, travel documents or assets—mainly to foreign fighters—over the internet [98, 99]. Some examples of digital funding are financial support through online charities, online bank card fraud, money laundering through online gambling (emoney, ekash, PayPal, etc.) [92], use of peer-to-peer trading services, misuse and theft of digital currencies, and mobile finance.

4.4.6 Online Matching

Online matching is a new trend introduced by ISIS. It is the use of social media and dating platforms for terrorists who search for women who will become their proper companions not only in personal life, but also during jihad [100]. Women traveling to the Caliphate (Syria and Iraq) were given the impression that their life would be ideal (expensive houses, money, security, quality life, possibility of starting a family) [101]. Nevertheless, they soon realized that they could not escape and were forced to stay to ensure the survival of their families [100]. ISIS promoted marriage and childbirth, which contribute

Table 4.1 Digital Jihad model—Al Qaeda and ISIS

DIGITAL JIHAD MODEL—AL QAEDA AND ISIS	
Radicalization	Virtual Muslim community, cyber-Caliphate, social media, chat rooms, social mapping, profiling, target groups, preachers, lectures, songs, books, manuals, online forums, and websites.
Recruitment	Digital classrooms, electronic jihad, audiovisual material (magazines, books, manuals), interviews, declarations of leaders, sermons, online forums, chat rooms, websites, social media, animations, and videogames.
Operational Planning	Cyber-Caliphate, training offline and online actions, cyberskills, live training without physical presence, digital classrooms, high-quality videos, training films—series, manuals, online magazines, videogames, digital technology, simulation programs.
Strategic Communication/ Propaganda	High-quality audiovisual material, sermons, websites, online forums, communication platforms, encryption, and mapping applications, newsletters, social media, digital steganography, hashtag campaigns, persona poaching, event crashing, textual hijacking, violent, or more emotional videos, digital radio, books, magazines, songs.
Funding	Paying taxes of faith, sponsorships, donations, charities with digital campaigns, sales on the dark web, and cyberattacks on financial systems, cryptocurrencies, e-commerce, and online retail platforms.
Online Matching	Social media, communication and dating platforms.

to the growth and expansion of the Caliphate. The women were responsible for the education of their children and the spreading of radical ideology to produce real and proper Muslims, fighters, and future members of ISIS [102]. They used a coded vocabulary while approaching the women to avoid being noticed on social media by counterterrorism agencies. For example, the words "Umm" (mother) and "Zora" (dawn) were used by Twitter's users [103, 104].

Table 4.1 summarizes the empirical evidence of the Digital Jihad model, as applied in the cases of Al Qaeda and ISIS, and demonstrates the various utilities of cyberspace for terrorist actions.

4.5 Conclusions

Islamic terrorism has gone through a transformation, by weaponizing the ICTs. This claim is confirmed by the empirical evidence of Al

Qaeda and ISIS at the operational level based on the Digital Jihad model. This transformation is not in terms of its nature and character, but in terms of how terrorist organizations operate. Cyberspace acts as a facilitator of terrorism and serves to maintain, spread, and inspire its followers. It provides a full spectrum of cyberactivities for terrorists. Rapoport's wave theory is applicable in the cases studies examined, but only some of the criteria are confirmed. Clearly, in terms of the ideological background that characterizes each wave, Al Qaeda and ISIS are placed in the Religious Wave. Regarding the rest of the criteria of each wave, Rapoport believes that technology is a critical variable at the evolution of terrorism. Each wave uses other means of technology to facilitate its terrorist actions, even if it has a specific ideological content. In terms of technology, the fifth terrorist wave involves the widespread use of the internet and social media. The new wave does not have a specific ideological context, but the dynamism of this wave focuses on cyberspace. After all, the activities related to the Digital Jihad model were all conducted via the use of ICTs. The fifth wave is technology-driven and five criteria of the wave theory are met due to cyberspace. Figure 4.2 portrays the characteristics of the fifth wave.

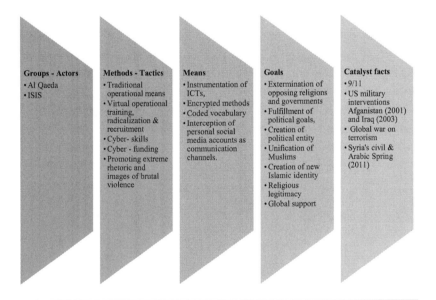

Figure 4.2   Cyberterrorism: the fifth wave of terrorism

In relation to the first criterion, both organizations use violence to achieve their political goals, but in a different way. Al Qaeda conducted bloody terrorist attacks but did not always publish content of its actions, whereas ISIS published content of brutal violent actions to maintain its pompous rhetoric. In relation to the second criterion, the terrorist actions have international character and impact. In this wave, their actions have an international audience due to the extensive use cyberspace. Their actors come from different geographical locations, so we spot the rise of foreign fighters and the conduct of terrorist attacks in various areas. The operational scope is not limited to a single geographical area and terrorist organizations are able to recruit "lone wolves". The terrorists in the diaspora have imitated the tactics and modus operandi introduced by Al Qaeda and ISIS, and adjusted those to their own needs and conditions. The third criterion is the presence of a catalytic event for the emergence of the fifth wave, thus the 9/11 terrorist attacks and the Global War on Terror. ISIS was most affected by the civil war in Syria and the Arab Spring in 2011. The fourth criterion is the extensive use of digital technology at the operational level. The fifth criterion is the creation of a new political reality, which was also expressed in a different way by both actors. Al Qaeda aimed first to unite Muslims in the diaspora and then establish a Caliphate, but eventually it first proceeded with the creation of a cyber-Caliphate. ISIS expanded first territorially into Iraq and Syria and established the Caliphate, and in a latter phase created a cyber-Caliphate to enhance its jihad. Thus, it is safe to conclude that Al Qaeda and ISIS belong to the fifth terrorist wave—that of cyberterrorism—and their know-how, strategy and methods have left behind a legacy for present and future terrorist groups.

Notes

1   Radical ideas are characterized by extreme rhetoric in an echo chamber—a closed system, a digital social environment, with specific group of friends, in which beliefs and ideas are amplified or reinforced from the isolated communication. Users are inevitably caught up in the offensive rhetoric that echoes. The participation at an "echo chamber" provides participants the ability to seek out information that reinforces their existing opinions without encountering opposing opinions. As a result, there is a possibility of social and political polarization and the adoption of extremist ideas. The social media are acting as "echo chambers" for terrorists who are seeking alternative sources of information.

2   After the proclamation of Caliphate, ISIS believed that was the supreme political and religious authority of Muslims as per Allah, and only the Caliph can declare holy war (jihad) against all the opponents in which all Muslims must participate.

References

1. Louise Richardson. *What terrorists want: Understanding the enemy, containing the threat?* Random House Trade Paperbacks, 2006.
2. Morris Mano and Michael Ciletti. *Digital design*, pages 39–40. Pearson, 2018.
3. Paul Virilio. "Un monde surexposé," *Le monde diplomatique*, pages 17, 1997.
4. Brigitte L. Nacos. *Mass-mediated terrorism*, pages 15. Rowman & Littlefield, 2016.
5. White House. *Remarks by the president on securing our nation's cyber infrastructure*, Briefing Room. 29 May 2009.
6. Bruce Hoffman. *The use of internet by Islamic extremists*, pages 1–20. RAND, 2006.
7. David C. Rapoport. The four waves of modern terrorism. In *Attacking terrorism: Elements of a grand strategy*, ed. Audrey Kurth Cronin and James M. Ludes, pages 1–24. Georgetown University Press, 2004.
8. David C. Rapoport. The four waves of rebel terror and September 11, *Anthropoetics* 8, no. 1, 2002.
9. Gerard Chaliand and Arnaud Blin. *The history of terrorism from antiquity to ISIS*. University of California, 2016.
10. Jeffrey D. Simon. Technological and lone operator terrorism: Prospects for a fifth wave of global terrorism. In *Terrorism, identity and legitimacy: The four waves theory and political violence*, eds. Jeffrey E. Rosenfeld, page 45. Routledge, 2010.
11. David C. Rapoport. Fear and trembling: Terrorism in three religious. Traditions, *The American Political Science Review* 78, no. 3, pages 660, 1984.
12. David. C. Rapoport. *Waves of global terrorism*. Columbia University Press, 2022.
13. Carl V. Clausewitz. *On war.* Everyman's Library, 1993.
14. Bruce Hoffman. *Inside terrorism*, pages 40–173. University Press, 2006.
15. Matthew G. Devost, Brian K Houghton and Neal Pollard. Information terrorism: Political violence in the information age, *Terrorism Political Violence* 9, no. 1, pages 78, 1997.
16. Dorothy E. Denning. *Cyberterrorism: Testimony before the special oversight panel on terrorism committee on armed services*, US House of Representatives, Focus on Terrorism, 71, 2000.
17. Dorothy E. Denning. A view of cyberterrorism five years later. In *Internet security: Hacking, counter hacking, and society*, ed. Kenneth Himma, pages 124–126. Jones and Bartlett, 2007.

18. Lee Jarvis, Leela Nouri and Andrew Whiting. Understanding, locating and constructing 'cyberterrorism. In *Cyberterrorism: Understanding, assessment, and response*, eds. Tom Chen, Lee Jarvis and Stuart Macdonald, pages 25–42. Springer, 2014.

19. Sarah Gordon and Richard Ford. Cyberterrorism?, *Computers & Security* 21, no. 7, pages 637, 642–643, 2002.

20. Matthew. J. Morgan. The origins of the new terrorism, *Parameters* 34, no. 1, 40, 2004.

21. Eleni Kapsokoli. The transformation of Islamic terrorism through cyberspace: The case of ISIS. In *Proceedings of the 18th European Conference on Cyber Warfare and Security*, eds. Tiago Cruz and Paulo Simoes, 67. University of Coimbra, 2019.

22. Panagiotis A. Yannakogeorgos. Rethinking the threat of cyberterrorism. In *Cyberterrorism: Understanding, assessment, and response*, eds. Thomas M. Chen, Lee Jarvis and Stuart Macdonald, pages 43–62. Springer, 2014.

23. Cristopher Helland. Religion-online and virtual communities. In *Religion on the Internet: Research prospects and promises*, eds. Jeffrey K. Hadden and Douglas E. Cowan, 205–223. JAI Press, 2000.

24. Alia Brahimi. Ideology and terrorism. In *The Oxford handbook of terrorism*, eds. Erica Chenoweth, Richard English, Andreas Gofas and Stathis N. Kalyvas. Oxford University Press, 2019.

25. Director of National Intelligence. *To the American people*. Dni.gov, 2006.

26. Honiga Or and Yahel Ido. A fifth wave of terrorism? The emergence of terrorist semi-states, *Terrorism and Political Violence* 31, no. 6, pages 2, 2019.

27. Andreas Gofas. The terrorism- democracy nexus and the trade-off between security and civil liberties. In *International Politics in times of change*, ed. Nikolaos Tzifakis, pages 283. Springer, 2012.

28. Thomas Olesen. Social movement theory and radical Islamic activism, *Centre for Studies in Islamism and Radicalization*, pages 7–9, 2009.

29. Thomas Olesen and Farhad Khosrokhavar. Islamism as social movement, *Centre for Studies in Islamism and Radicalization*, pages 1–44, 2009.

30. Rachel Briggs. Radicalisation, the role of the internet. *Institute for Strategic Dialogue*, pages 1–20, 2011.

31. Quintan Wiktorowicz. *Joining the cause: Al Muhajiroun and radical Islam. The roots of Islamic radicalism*, page 7. Yale University, 2004.

32. Quintan Wiktorowicz. *Radical Islam rising: Muslim extremism in the West*. Rowman and Littlefield, 2005.

33. Mina Hamblet. The Islamic State's virtual Caliphate, *Middle East Quarterly* 24, no. 4, pages 1–8, 2017.

34. Jessica Stern. *Terror in the name of God*. Ecco Trade, 2003.

35. Mark Sageman. *Understanding terror networks*. University of Pennsylvania Press, 2004.

36. Clark McCauley and Sophia Moskalenko. Mechanisms of political radicalization: Pathways toward terrorism, *Terrorism and Political Violence* 20, no. 3, pages 415–433, 2008.

37. Arie W. Kruglanski and Shira Fishman. Psychological factors in terrorism and counterterrorism: Individual, group and organizational levels of analysis, *Social issues and policy review* 3, no. 1, pages 10–15, 2009.

38. Holly Mellisa Knapton. The recruitment and radicalization of Western citizens: Does ostracism have a role in homegrown terrorism?, *Journal of European Psychology Students* 5, no. 1, pages 41, 2014.

39. Petter Nesser. *Jihad in Europe—a survey of the motivations for Sunni islamist terrorism in post-millennium Europe.* Norwegian Institute for Defence Research, 2004.

40. Petter Nesser. Military interventions, jihadi networks and terrorist entrepreneurs: How the Islamic State terror wave rose so high in Europe, *CTC Sentinel* 12, no. 3, pages 15–21, 2019.

41. Quintan Wiktorowicz. A genealogy of radical Islam, *Studies in Conflict & Terrorism* 28, no. 2, pages 75–97, 2015.

42. Peter Neumann. *Old and new terrorism*, pages 8–12. Polity, 2009.

43. Brian Levin. The original web of hate: Revolution Muslim and American home-grown extremists, *American Behavioral Scientist* 59, no. 12, pages 1609–1630, 2015.

44. Jonathan Matusitz. Cyberterrorism: Postmodern state of chaos, *Information Security Journal: A Global Perspective* 17, no. 4, pages 185, 2008.

45. Alexander Meleagrou-Hitchens and Nick Kaderbhai. Research perspectives on online radicalisation, a literature reviews 2006–2016, *International Centre for the Study of Radicalisation* 7, 2017.

46. Magnus Ranstorp. The virtual sanctuary of Al Qaeda and terrorism in an age of globalization. In *International relations and security in the digital age*, eds. Johan Eriksson and Giacomello Giampiero, pages 30–39. Routledge, 2007.

47. Foster Provost, Brian Dalessandro, Rod Hook, Xiaohan Zhang and Alan Murray. Audience selection for on-line brand advertising: Privacy-friendly social network targeting, In *Proceedings of the 15th ACM SIGKDD international conference on Knowledge discovery and data mining, Paris, France, June 28–July 1*, 2009.

48. Angela Gendron. The call to jihad: Charismatic preachers and the internet, *Studies in Conflict and Terrorism* 40, no. 1, pages 44–61, 2017.

49. Matteo Cinelli, Gianmarco D.F. Morales, Alessandro Galeazzi, Walter Quattrociocchi and Michele Starnini. The echo chamber effect on social media, *Proceedings of the National Academy of Sciences* 118, no. 9, pages 1–8, 2021.

50. Edina Bećirević, Majda Halilović and Vlado Azinović. Radicalisation and violent extremism in the Western Balkans, *Extremism Research Forum* 28, 2017.

51. Peter Neumann. Options and strategies for countering online radicalization in the United States, *Studies in Conflict and Terrorism* 36, no. 6, pages 434–437, 2013.

52. Ariel Koch. The new crusaders: Contemporary extreme right symbolism and rhetoric, *Perspectives on Terrorism* 11, no. 5, pages 13–24, 2017.

53. Gordon Corera. A web wise terror network. *BBC News*, 6 October 2014.
54. Gabriel Weimann. Using the internet for terrorist recruitment and mobilization. In *Hypermedia seduction for terrorist recruiting*, ed. Ganor Boaz, pages 47–58. IOS Press, 2006.
55. Akil Awan. Radicalization on the internet? The virtual propagation of jihadist media and its effects, *RUSI Journal* 152, no. 3, pages 76–81, 2007.
56. Aaron Y. Zelin. *The state of global jihad online*. New America Foundation, 2013.
57. Aliya Sternstein. New OPM Cyber czar worried about an ISIS hack. *Nextgov*, 14 December 2015.
58. Laith Alkhouri, Alex Kassirer and Nixon Allison. Hacking for ISIS: The emergent cyber threat landscape. *Flashpoint*, 2016. https://iici.io/storage/media/2016/6/1014833787/files/474992437698232546.pdf.
59. Brian Jenkins. *Stray dogs and virtual armies radicalization and recruitment to jihadist terrorism in the United States Since 9/11. RAND*, 2011.
60. Jay Caspian Kang. ISIS's call of duty. *New Yorker*, 18 September 2014.
61. Terrence McCoy. The Islamic State's 'call of duty' allure. *Washington Post*, 28 October 2014.
62. Thomas Holt, Adam Bossler and Kathryn Seigfried-Spellar. *Cybercrime and digital forensics: An introduction*. Routledge, 2018.
63. Martin Rudner. Electronic jihad: The internet as Al-Qaeda's catalyst for global terror, *Studies in Conflict and Terrorism* 40, no. 1, pages 10–23, 2017.
64. Paul Tassi. ISIS uses 'GTA 5' in new teen recruitment video. *Forbes*, 20 September 2014.
65. Lia Brynjar. Al Qaeda Online: Understanding jihadi internet infrastructure. *Jane's Intelligence Review*, 1–16, 2006.
66. Stenersen Anne. The Internet: A virtual training camp?, *Terrorism Political Violence* 20, no. 2, pages 215–233, 2008.
67. Thomas Joscelyn. AQAP claims responsibility for cargo planes plot, *FFD's Long War Journal*, 6 November 2010.
68. Robert E. Schmidle. Positioning theory and terrorist networks, *Journal for the Theory of Social Behavior* 40, no. 1, pages 65–78, 2009.
69. Robyn Torok. Make a bomb in your mums' kitchen: Cyber recruiting and socialization of white moors and home-grown jihadists, *Edith Cowan University Research Online*, 2010.
70. Su Yin Yeap and Jenna Park. Countering internet radicalisation: A holistic approach, *RSIS Commentaries*, no. 078, pages 1–3, 2010.
71. Garth Jowett and Victoria O'Donell. *Propaganda and Persuasion*. Sage, 2012.
72. Marshall McLuhan and Bruce R. Powers. *The Global Village: Transformations in World Life and Media in the 21st Century*. Oxford University Press, 1989.
73. Manuel Torres Soriano. Terrorism and the mass media after al Qaeda: A change of course, *Athena Intelligence Journal* 3, no. 1, pages 1–20, 2008.
74. Brigitte L. Nacos. *Terrorism and counterterrorism*. Penguin Academics, 2010.
75. Lisa Wiechert. *The marketing of terrorism: Analyzing the use of social media*. Studylab, 2017.

76. Timothy Thomas. Al Qaeda and the internet: The danger of cyber planning, *Parameters* 23, no. 1, pages 112–123, 2003.
77. Michael Scheuer. *Osama Bin Laden*. Oxford University Press, 2012.
78. Marcin Styszynski. Al-Qaeda's structure according to propaganda techniques, *Acta Asiatica Varsoviensia* 24, pages 125–136, 2011.
79. Llyod H. Goodall. *Counter narrative*. Left West Coast Press, 2010.
80. Charlie Winter. *The virtual Caliphate, understanding Islamic State's propaganda strategy*, pages 6–18. Quilliam Foundation, 2015.
81. Matteo Colombo and Luigi Curini. *Discussing the Islamic state on Twitter.* Palgrave Macmillan, 2022.
82. Gari Siboni, Daniel Cohen and Tal Koren. The Islamic state's strategy in cyberspace, *Military and Strategic Affairs* 7, no. 1, pages 127–144, 2015.
83. Asma Ajroudi. It sounds like BBC: ISIS seeks legitimacy via 'caliphate' radio service. *Al-Arabiya News*, 20 May 2020.
84. Linda Jones. *The power of oratory in the medieval Muslim world*, pages 195–232. Cambridge University Press, 2012.
85. Erin M. Saltman and Charlie Winter. *Islamic state: The changing face of modern jihadism*. Quilliam Foundation, 2014.
86. Graeme Wood. *The way of the strangers*. Random House, 2019.
87. Adam Lankford. A psychological re-examination of mental health problems among the 9/11 terrorists, *Studies in Conflict & Terrorism* 41, no. 11, pages 875–898, 2018.
88. Chun Yeung. *A critical analysis on ISIS media strategies*, pages 1–18. University of Salford, 2015.
89. William McCants. *The ISIS apocalypse: The history, strategy, and doomsday vision of the Islamic state*, pages 43–45. St. Martin's Press, 2015.
90. Yannick Veilleux-Lepage. Retweeting the Caliphate: The role of soft sympathizers in the Islamic State's social media strategy, *Turkish Journal of Security Studies* 18, no. 1, pages 53–69, 2014.
91. Katerina Grigorova. Hijacking heads & hashtags, *Global ejournal, ISIS Media* 10, no. 56, 24 August 2017.
92. E. Dilipraj. *Cyber Enigma: Unravelling the terror in the cyber world*. Routledge, 2019.
93. International Telecommunication Union (ITU). *ICT Facts and Figures— The world in 2015*, report, 2015.
94. Michele Zanini and Edwards Sean. The networking of terror in the information age. In *Networks and netwars: The future of terror, crime, and militancy*, eds. John Arquilla and David Ronfeldt. RAND, 2001.
95. Yariv Tsfati and Gabriel Weimann. www.terrorism.com: Terror on the internet, *Studies in Conflict & Terrorism* 25, no. 5, 2002.
96. Raphaeli Nimrod. Financing of terrorism: Sources, methods, and channels, *Terrorism and Political Violence* 15, no. 4, pages 59–82, 2010.
97. Eckart Woertz. How long ISIS will last economically, *Notes internacionals CIDOB*, no. 98, pages 1–5, 1 October 2014.
98. Jessica Stern. ISIL and the goal of organizational survival. In *Beyond convergence*, eds. Hilary Matfess and Michael Miklaucic, pages 195–214. World without Order, 2016.

99. Jessica Stern and J. Berger. *ISIS: The state of terror.* Ecco Trade, 2016.

100. Louisa Loveluck. In Syrian camp for women and children who left ISIS caliphate, a struggle even to register names. *Washington Post*, 28 June 2020.

101. Ashley A. Binetti. A new frontier: Human trafficking and ISIS's recruitment of women from the west, *Georgetown Institute for Women, Peace and Security*, 3–6, 2015.

102. Gina Vale. Women in Islamic state: From caliphate to camps. *ICCT Policy Brief*, October 2019.

103. Christina Shori Liang. Cyber Jihad: Understanding and countering Islamic State propaganda, *GCSP Policy Paper* 2, pages 1–12, 2015.

104. Jytte Klausen. Tweeting the Jihad: Social media networks of western foreign fighters in Syria and Iraq, *Studies in Conflict and Terrorism* 38, no. 1, pages 1–22, 2015.

5

MACHINE LEARNING–BASED TCP CONGESTION CONTROL STRATEGIES FOR CYBERTERRORISM ACTIVE DEFENSE ON SMART GRIDS

KONSTANTINOS DEMERTZIS,
DIMITRIOS TAKETZIS, CHARALABOS
SKIANIS, PANAYOTIS KIKIRAS,
AND LAZAROS ILIADIS

5.1 Introduction

Driven by international climate policy and recent circumstances whereby Europe—following Russia's invasion of Ukraine—is facing a worsening energy crisis, smart energy networks [1] are again at the center of modern research and technology, with a view to optimal management of energy balances [2]. In addition, the management in question should consider the increase in fuel costs, government directives for the pushing and use of electric vehicles, and the increasing share of new forms of load consumption such as heat pumps and electric HVAC (heating, ventilation, and air conditioning) systems, etc. The unpredictable use of these distributed energy resources introduces additional severe challenges for grid operators, who are called upon more than ever to optimally to handle peak demand and power (supply/demand) imbalances.

Demand response until recently, when electricity could not be easily stored, was handled by utilities by matching and adjusting the generation rate, acquiring generating units, or importing power from other utilities, usually in neighboring states. Thanks to recent developments in information and communication technologies (ICT), the

DOI: 10.1201/9781003314721-5

development of large-scale data analysis techniques, and especially intelligent technologies [3], historical data are used for pattern learning, with the aim of real-time demand forecasting and response, electric load forecasting, estimation status, the detection of energy theft, and other actions which until now were impossible to carry out—and while the digital technologies in question undoubtedly improve the efficiency of networks and the operations of energy providers, their adoption is accompanied by significant challenges, the most important of which are the constant threats to cybersecurity [4].

The protection of intelligent energy networks incorporating the most modern digital energy ICT technologies and advanced algorithmic standardization for intelligent energy control are ideal targets for large-scale methodical cyberattacks such as advanced persistent threats (APT). Cybercriminals in APT attacks have absolute expertise in advanced tools; they do not consider time and are mostly related to cyberterrorism. APT attacks, which usually manifest as distributed denial of service (DDoS) attacks [5], target widespread services commonly used in intelligent networks such as the transmission control protocol (TCP), which is mainly implemented in Layers 3 and 4 of open systems interconnection (OSI) [6], to ensure fairness and prevent the network from crashing in cases of network congestion [7]. Specifically, agents respond to signals from the central management authority of the smart energy grid to limit load when the grid is congested. The most dangerous consequence of the violation of congestion control (CC) [8] is DDoS attacks caused by flows that make the service unable to accept other connections by generating illegitimate connection requests for amplification and targeting the parties that have a management role in smart grids (SGs) so that they cannot serve other potential customers and the network collapses [9].

Given that the amount of information in an intelligent network is vast and specific attacks are now challenging to discover through manual analysis and human expertise, we present in this chapter machine learning (ML)-based TCP CC strategies for active defense on SGs. In particular, the methods of using ML methods [10] are presented in network programming, the adjustment of its parameters and the optimal distribution of its resources, as well as how to ensure an estimated model of acceptable accuracy in cases of DDoS attacks, such as load change patterns and network resource performance optimization [11].

5.2 Literature Review

In 2020, Gunduz and Das [12] provided a comprehensive survey backed by a thorough examination of prior research. They examined current studies of the grid from a security standpoint and introduced the intelligent grid's history before discussing its advantages, features, and critical components. They studied the challenges and possible remedies of the sensor SG, concentrated on cyberattack types, and presented a comprehensive assessment of the SG's cybersecurity status. They focused on the debate and investigation of security flaws, attack responses, and security needs. They wanted to provide a comprehensive knowledge of cybersecurity weaknesses and remedies, and a roadmap for future research prospects.

Ding et al. [13] in 2022 gave a comprehensive review of the effect of incumbent cyberattacks on the whole intelligent grid ecosystem in their study. They examined the different dangers to the SG that have two fundamental domains: the system's inherent vulnerability and external cyberattacks. Likewise, they assessed the risks of all SG components (technology, software, and data transfer), data processing, services, applications, operating environment, development, and sophisticated SGs. A structured SG design and worldwide SG cyberattacks and their effects from a 12-year timeframe are described. They then examined the topic taxonomy of intrusions on SGs to highlight attack techniques, repercussions, and related research. In addition, prospective cybersecurity solutions for SGs are discussed within the framework of blockchain and artificial intelligence (AI) approaches. Finally, technological suggestions for the future based on the study were presented to protect SGs against cyberattacks.

Xu et al. [14] explored networking difficulties by exploiting developing deep learning to propose an experience-driven strategy that allows a network or protocol to discover the optimal way to regulate itself based on its expertise (e.g., running statistics data), similar to how a person learns a skill. They presented design, implementation, and assessment of deep reinforcement learning (DRL) for CC. This DRL-based management framework fulfills their experience-driven design approach for multi-path TCP CC. DRL-CC employs a single agent (rather than numerous separate agents) to execute congestion management dynamically and cooperatively for all active streams on an end host to maximize overall utility. Utilizing a modular recurrent neural network (RNN), LSTM (long-term/short-term), inside a DRL structure for learning a model for all ongoing flows and coping with their dynamics is innovative to their design.

Rivas and Abrão [15] published a comprehensive evaluation of SG flaws from the most influential research databases and cutting-edge research articles. Aiming to create a comprehensive typology of the applicable requirements, they viewed fault recognition and tracking as a critical element to SG durability and included categorizing various fault scenarios in detail within a comprehensive framework involving system-level applications. In addition, the survey provides researchers, academics, and professionals with a complete perspective on the relationships between SGs monitoring and fault detection and/or location methodologies. Finally, it offered a foundation for the further investigation and growth of knowledge and understanding of SGs monitoring fault detection and/or location methodologies.

In their review, Gumpu et al. [16] described several methodologies and techniques of congestion management. In addition, they presented a complete study of CC techniques. On modified multibus systems, CC strategies were evaluated and tested. Future research could concentrate on determining the optimal transmission switching strategy for CM, based on the trade-off between turning off the transmission line and turning on a capacitor at the receiving end of the line, as well as identifying alternative techniques to reduce the computational burden.

Going one step further, this chapter proposes— for the first time in the literature —a ML-based CC for active defense on SGs.

5.2.1 *Machine Learning–Based TCP CC Strategies*

ML is one of the most critical and widespread fields of AI that includes those computational methods of studying and building algorithms that can learn from suitable data sets and—based on this experience—improve the performance of a system or make accurate future predictions. The concept of experience refers to the hidden knowledge contained in past data, which may be in the form of sets appropriately classified by humans or derived from interaction with the environment [17].

More specifically, the goal of an ML algorithm is to estimate a function $f: R^N \rightarrow T$, where the domain R is the set of real numbers, while the domain T can be either $T = R^M$ in regression problems or a set of labels in classification problems. Given a set of pairs $(x_1, f(x_1)), \ldots, (x_n, f(x_n))$, the goal of a typical ML algorithm is to compute an optimal approximation of $\widehat{f}: R^N \rightarrow T$ of the function $f: R^N \rightarrow T$ such that for $x_0 \in R^N$, with $x_0 \neq x_i$, $i \in \{1, \ldots, n\}$, the estimated $\widehat{f}(x_0)$ is as "close" as possible, in some sense, to the true $f(x_0)$. The process of calculating the function $\widehat{f}: R^N \rightarrow T$ from the set of pairs $(x_1, f(x_1)), \ldots, (x_n, f(x_n))$ is called learning or training, while the process of calculating the value (x_0) for $x_0 \neq x_i$, $i \in \{1, \ldots, n\}$, is called generalization. A primary goal of any learning process is an acceptable ability to generalize [18].

ML in networking is a specialized but at the same time an effective tool in dealing with the most critical challenges in its field of application [17, 19]. Classification and prediction are essential in network problems such as intrusion detection and performance prediction. Based on evaluation criteria, different protocols can be addressed to differentiate the services provided to the user and apply the appropriate security policies accordingly. In addition, ML is the preeminent decision support system which can contribute to planning the network, adjusting its parameters, and optimally allocating its resources according to current needs. Accordingly, with its inherent high flexibility, adaptability, and computational capabilities, ML can provide an estimated model of acceptable accuracy for network problem cases arising from interaction with complex system environments when they are significantly sophisticated enough to accurately create analytical models to represent complex system behaviors such as content delivery network (CDN) load change patterns and optimization based on their performance characteristics [20].

There are several classes of learning which are entirely dependent on the nature of the problem to be solved and show substantial differences in the type of data available, the method by which the training data is obtained and the test data for evaluating the system. The primary learning categories found in the literature and used for CC are presented in what follows [3, 16]:

5.2.2 Supervised Learning

This is the most general category of learning, in which a set of well-defined observation data—with samples categorized into classes—is taken as a training set, based on which predictions are made about the new data. Given a set N of training data of the form $\{(x_1, y_1), \ldots, (x_N, y_N)\}$, where x_1 is a feature vector and y_1 is its corresponding class, a supervised learning algorithm seeks a function $g: X \rightarrow Y$, where X is the input space and Y is the output space. The function g is an instance of the possible functions G in the hypothesis set. Sometimes it is convenient to implement g using a score function, e.g., $f: X \times Y \rightarrow R$ such that g returns the highest scoring y value calculated as follows, considering that F characterizes the set of possible scoring functions that can be used [21].

$$g(x) = \underset{y}{\operatorname{argmax}} \, f(x, y) \tag{5.1}$$

Although G and F can be any function, many learning algorithms are probabilistic models, which forces g to take the form of a conditional probabilistic model of the form $g(x) = P(y \mid x)$, or its equivalent case in which f takes the form of a joint probability model of the form $f(x, y) = P(x, y)$.

A loss function of the form $L : Y \times Y \rightarrow R^{\geq 0}$ is used to measure the performance of the supervised learning model, i.e., whether it has correctly classified the control set data. Specifically for a training example (x_1, y_1), the prediction error $\hat{y}$ is $L(y_1, \hat{y})$ and is defined by calculating the empirical risk, which essentially constitutes the average of the ranking error of the points of the training set and can be measured by the following equation [22].

$$R_{emp}(g) = \frac{1}{N} \sum_{i} L\left(y_1, g(x_i)\right) \tag{5.2}$$

Supervised learning methods for congestion detection in end-to-end networks are used in networking [23].

5.2.2.1 Congestion Detection in End-to-End Networks
Congestion signal prediction consists of loss classification and delays prediction.

5.2.2.1.1 Loss Classification
Congestion loss (wireless loss, contention loss, and reordering loss) is a critical point of network valuation, and the

loss classification technique can be an indirect signal to detect congestion. Still, it only gives feedback to network nodes when it has already occurred. Basic CC algorithms based on loss classification cannot distinguish the cause of packet loss, and intelligent automatic loss recognition is therefore necessary to understand more general CC [8, 24].

Supervised learning techniques show advantages in classifying loss types in different network scenarios and specifically in the following cases [23, 25].

1. Maximizing throughput. To maximize performance, bandwidth usage is assumed to be high. High throughput contrasts with low round-trip time (RTT) or flow completion time (FCT), as high throughput means the environment tolerates high queue lengths, which can cause long delays.
2. Minimizing RTT or FCT. Minimizing RTT or FCT is a basic requirement that must be met to have serious expectations from a network. For each task, the completion time reflects the delay, which is assumed to be as small as possible.
3. Minimizing packet loss rate (PLR). PLR minimization is a key and enduring goal of CC algorithms. A low PLR means a stable low-latency network environment that satisfies sophisticated services.
4. Fairness. The distribution of resources must be done dynamically and as fairly as possible between users, considering the different priority requirements of the applications—services they serve.
5. Responsiveness. Updating the congestion window (CoWi) adjustment frequency policy can affect the responsiveness of the algorithms. High responsiveness is expected, which also implies high resource consumption. Therefore, responsiveness must be balanced based on different usage scenarios and general requirements.

A general description of the loss classification mechanism with supervised learning is presented in Figure 5.1 [23].

However, there are some issues associated with supervised CC learning algorithms [26]. Specifically, the Classification Error or Misclassification Rate is a severe issue. For example, in wireless networks, the predefined parameters determine the errors when

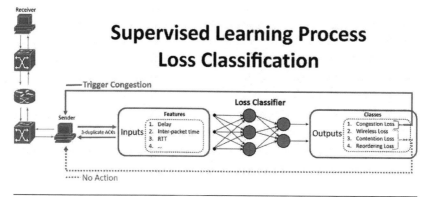

Figure 5.1   Loss classification mechanism with supervised learning

classifying congestion loss and wireless loss. If congestion loss is easier to classify than wireless loss, the classifier performs poorly in wireless networks, as the network is supposed to react when a loss is detected. However, due to the misclassification, the network considers congestion loss as wireless loss and does not quickly control the sending speed. Therefore, congestion cannot be reduced [26].

Conversely, if the wireless loss is more easily classified as congestion loss, the algorithm is inefficient in wireless scenarios because there are significant wireless losses. As a result, the wireless network may overreact to lost signals. Therefore, the parameters used each time as input to the algorithms must be carefully considered to balance the performance in different network scenarios. For example, in a wireless networking scenario, if we accept as output (classes) wireless loss and congestion loss, some inputs (features) that lead the intelligent algorithms to correct predictions are the standard deviation, minimum and maximum of the one-way delay, and inter-packet time. Of course, as said, everything should be checked before use, and the applications—services that are served each time—should be taken into account.

Also, the balance between computational complexity and classification accuracy is another critical issue that should be considered. Some algorithms achieve greater accuracy but consume much more network resources. Therefore, considering the possibilities available in computational resources, trade-offs should be taken to create a robust environment where the classification accuracy will be balanced against the computational cost, which is also inextricably linked to the time to complete the classification process. For example, in the preceding scenario, categorization of wireless loss and congestion loss in a wireless network, suitable algorithms that will balance the classification accuracy without requiring high consumption of resources are decision trees, including all other tree algorithms (XGBoost, Random Forest, C4.5, CART, etc.)—as they are algorithmic approaches that create highly accurate predictive models without requiring too much experience and complex hyperparameters, they are relatively easy to interpret, and most importantly, they offer stability and generalization, which is the main requirement in ML [26].

5.2.2.1.2 Delays Prediction   As a signal of congestion, transmission delay reflects the amount of uninterrupted data, which indicates the overall load on the network. Some classic delay-based CC algorithms can measure it accurately; however, in dynamic networking environments, these traditional CC algorithms are not flexible enough. In contrast, supervised learning techniques have high learning potential and are effective in predicting future delays, thus offering possibilities for quick reactions to avoid congestion [16].

For delay prediction in managing queue length for network-assisted networks, the basic idea of the approach is that the network states form a continuous time series, whereby the future state can be predicted from past states. A general description of the delay prediction mechanism with supervised learning is shown in Figure 5.2 [23].

For the exact approach of the problem, which is reduced to a time series analysis-prediction problem, the goal is to find the mathematical relationship that can model the historical data of the network and the way they are shaped about time. The general modeling method

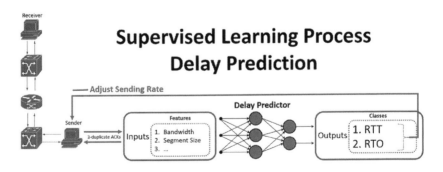

Figure 5.2   Delay prediction mechanism with supervised learning

uses non-parametric techniques offering significant advantages over conventional methods. They offer a possibility to overcome the statistical problems associated with normality and linearity assumptions necessary in traditional or linear regression methods.

The assumption of the underlying technique suggests that the predictors have a cumulative structure, which allows for their easy interpretation and modeling while at the same time not requiring a detailed search for the transformation of each variable. More specifically, the estimate of the dependent variable Y, in this case for a single independent variable, can be given by the following equation [23–25]:

$$Y = s(X) + error \tag{5.3}$$

where s(X) is an unspecified smoothing function, while *error* is the error which usually has zero mean and constant variance. For example, the smoothing function can be determined from the running mean or the running median or the local least squares method, the kernel method, the LOESS method, or the spline method. The term running means the serial calculation of statistics applied to overlapping intervals of values of the independent variable, such as, for example, the running mean. In modeling through generalized additive models (GAMs), the classical linear assumption is extended to include any probability distribution (Poisson, gamma, Gaussian, binomial and inverse Gaussian) of error from the exponential group.

Also, this particular methodology can adjust as components, many linear and non-linear functions of time, where in their simplest form, three basic elements are used: trend, seasonality, and events—which are combined in the following equation [22, 27]:

$$y(t) = g(t) + s(t) + ev(t) + e(t) \tag{5.4}$$

where:
1. $g(t)$ = trend models *non-periodic* changes (i.e., growth over time)
2. $s(t)$ = seasonality presents *periodic* changes (i.e., weekly, monthly, yearly)
3. $ev(t)$ = ties in effects of events (on potentially irregular schedules ≥ 1 day[s])
4. $e(t)$ = covers idiosyncratic changes not accommodated by the model

More generally, the whole equation can be written as follows:

$$y(t) = piecewise\_trend(t) + seasonality(t)$$
$$+ events\_effects(t) + noise(t) \tag{5.5}$$

In a more thorough analysis, the variables under consideration can be structured as follows:

1. Trend. The process includes two possible trend models for g(t), namely a saturating growth model and a piecewise linear model as follows [3, 18, 22]:

   a. Saturating growth model. If the data suggests the promise of saturation:

   $$g(t) = \frac{C}{1 + exp(-k(t - m))} \tag{5.6}$$

   where C is the carrying capacity, k is the growth rate, and m is an offset parameter

   It is possible to incorporate trend changes into the model by explicitly specifying the change points where the growth rate is allowed to change. Assuming that there are S change points during periods S_j, $j = 1, \ldots, S$, the methodology defines a vector of rate change settings δ_j at a time S_j with $\delta \in R^S$, so at each time t, the rate k can be expressed as $k + \sum_{j:t>S_j} \delta_j$. If in this relationship the vector $a(t) \in \{0, 1\}^S$ is defined so that:

   $$a_j(t) = \begin{cases} 1, & if \ t \geq S_j \\ 0, & otherwse \end{cases} \tag{5.7}$$

   then the rate at time t is $k + a(t)^T \delta$. When the rate k is adjusted, the shift parameter m must also be adjusted to connect the endpoints of the segments. The correct setting at the change point j is easily calculated as:

   $$y_j = \left(S_j - m - \sum_{i<j} y_t \right) \left(1 - \frac{k + \sum_{i<j} \delta_t}{k + \sum_{i \leq j} \delta_t} \right) \tag{5.8}$$

The final function is completed as follows:

$$g(t) = \frac{C(t)}{1 + exp\left(-\left(k + a(t)^\mathrm{T}\delta\right)\left(t - \left(m + a(t)^\mathrm{T} y\right)\right)\right)} \tag{5.9}$$

b. Linear trend with changepoints. This is a piecewise linear model with a constant growth rate, which is calculated as follows:

$$g(t) = \left(k + a(t)^\mathrm{T}\delta\right)t + \left(m + a(t)^\mathrm{T} y\right) \tag{5.10}$$

where k is the growth rate, δ has the rate adjustments, m is the offset parameter, and to make the function continuous, y_j is set to $-S_j\delta_j$.

c. Automatic changepoint selection. To identify change-points, it is recommended to identify a large number of changepoints as follows:

$$\delta_j \sim Laplace(0, \tau) \tag{5.11}$$

where τ directly controls the flexibility of the model in altering its rate. It should be emphasized that a sparse prior adjustment δ does not affect the primary growth rate k, so that τ evolves to 0 and the adjustment reduces normal (no piecewise) logistic or linear growth:

d. Trend forecast uncertainty. When the model deviates beyond history to make a prediction, the trend $g(t)$ will have a constant rate. The uncertainty in the forecast trend is estimated by extending the forward generation model where there are S change points over a history of T points, each of which has rate change $\delta_j \sim Laplace$ (0, τ). Simulating future rate changes (which mimic those of the past) is achieved by replacing τ with a variance inferred from the data, which is achieved by maximum likelihood estimation of the rate scale parameter as follows:

$$\lambda = \frac{1}{S}\sum_{j=1}^{S}|\delta_j| \tag{5.12}$$

The future sample change points are randomized in such a way that the mean frequency of the change points matches the corresponding historical points as follows:

$$\forall_j > T, \begin{cases} \delta_j = 0 \; w.p.\dfrac{T-S}{T} \\ \delta_j \sim Laplace(0,\lambda) \; w.p.\dfrac{S}{T} \end{cases} \quad (5.13)$$

2. Seasonality. The seasonal variable $s(t)$ provides adaptability to the model by allowing periodic changes based on daily, weekly, and annual seasonality. Modern time series analysis methodologies rely on the Fourier series to provide a malleable model of periodic simulations, whereby approximately arbitrary smooth seasonal snapshots are convolved with a standard Fourier series:

$$s(t) = \sum_{n=1}^{N} \left(a_n \cos\left(\frac{2\pi nt}{P}\right) + b_n \sin\left(\frac{2\pi nt}{P}\right) \right) \quad (5.14)$$

3. Events. The $ev(t)$ component reflects predictable events of the year, including those on irregular schedules, which introduce serious biases into the model. Assuming that the outcomes of the events are independent, seasonality is accounted for by the model by creating a regression matrix:

$$Z(t) = \left[1(t \in D_1), \dots, 1(t \in D_L) \right]$$
$$h(t) = Z(t)k \quad (5.15)$$

Thus, supervised learning CC algorithms can be smarter and significantly faster than traditional algorithms. In particular, the methodology—e.g., in real-time video applications over wireless networks—can predict the impending delay, thus giving possibilities to the managers of the applications in question to adjust the sending rate. Also, in cases of interactive video applications, by predicting the RTT—which also allows the prediction of other vital parameters such as the re-transmission timeout (RTO)—they will enable the balancing of the sending rate and RTT, resulting in a very satisfactory result which gives added value possibilities to similar services [19, 26].

It is also important to say that delay prediction is also a critical process for delay-sensitive networks that require networks with increased responsiveness. It should also be noted that a significant parameter directly related to delay prediction is the assurance of low computational complexity and parallel high prediction accuracy, which is also achieved here by choosing appropriate parameters and corresponding algorithmic approaches.

5.2.2.2 Queue Length Management in Network-Assisted Networks   Queue length management (QLM) is a key priority of CC algorithms, as the detection in question creates serious conditions for meaningful interaction with the network environment. The operation of the classical algorithms in question, based on detection, is a passive treatment of a severe network problem, which is a brake for applications that require quality of service (QoS). On the contrary, a process of predicting the future length of the queue based on supervised learning techniques, a general representation of which is presented in Figure 5.3, is the most appropriate way to deal with the problem in question proactively [23].

Their logic focuses on the proven hypothesis of long-term dependence between past movement patterns and the future behavior of a queue. For this reason, the used supervised learning algorithms use the time series analysis methodologies of the previous movement as input without taking into account different parameters of the network. Also, an important development in the investigation of the dependencies between the relevant parameters of a queue and the

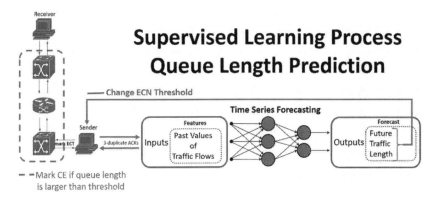

Figure 5.3   Queue length prediction

ways that even their recurrent characteristics can be combined can be found in the methods of recurrent models such as RNNs, LSTM networks, etc. [7].

In general, the technologies and the purpose that are usually used for supervised learning for queue length prediction are [24]:

1. Networks supporting ATM (asynchronous transfer mode):
   a. Predict future traffic based on past flows.
   b. Use the estimated average queue length to calculate the losses and then control the packet sending rate.

2. Networks supporting AQM (active queue management):
   a. Estimate future packet traffic based on past flow characteristics and then determine an optimal relationship between flow packets.
   b. Use adaptive techniques to estimate the instantaneous length of the queue and determine the modes for the benefit of the served applications/services.

3. Networks supporting NDN (named data networking):
   a. Calculate the average queue length based on the prediction of pending entries of the interest table.

5.2.3 Unsupervised Learning

In contrast to the previous category, unsupervised learning is the ability to detect patterns in an input stream, i.e., training data is taken for which the classes are not known, and the system produces predictions based on some distribution or some quantitative measures of evaluation and characterization of the similarity of the data in corresponding groups. In general, unsupervised learning techniques [28, 29] are used when the data class is unknown and the set of samples must be grouped according to some common feature to minimize the gap within the group and maximize the distances between groups. Compared to supervised learning algorithms, unsupervised learning CC algorithms are not widely used, as their contribution is usually focused on cases where the interest is focused on the accumulation of loss and delay features. The way to use the unsupervised learning methodology in CC is detailed below.

5.2.3.1 Congestion Detection in End-to-End CC Algorithms Congestion detection consists of loss clustering and delays prediction.

5.2.3.1.1 Loss Clustering In networking, unsupervised learning techniques are used for clustering and specifically for cluster loss so that different resource allocations are made in other groups to achieve CC. Clustering is the process of classifying samples into clusters based on some distinct similarity measure. Elements that belong to a cluster show greater or relatively greater similarity. The training of a model with the clustering method is called to calculate and finally classify into clusters, data $x_1, \ldots, x_n$ without giving the target values $f(x_1), \ldots, f(x_n)$. The general description of the methodology is shown in Figure 5.4 [23].

More specifically, the general technique is based on the idea that a data set $D = \{x_1, x_2, \ldots, x_n\}$, where $x_i = (x_{i1}, x_{i2}, \ldots, x_{ir})$ is a feature from the set $X \in R^r$ and r is the number of features (dimensions) in the data. After the set of clusters K is defined, each point $x^{(i)}$ of the data set is assigned to some cluster C_k so that the funtion $Score\ (C, D))$ is maximized or minimized as appropriate [8]. The following function gives the calculation method [22, 30–32]:

$$Score(C,D) = \sum_{k=1}^{K} d\left(x, c_k\right) \tag{5.16}$$

where $c_k = \dfrac{1}{n_k} \sum_{x \in c_k} x$ and $\mathrm{d}\left(x, y\right) = \left\| x - y \right\|^2$

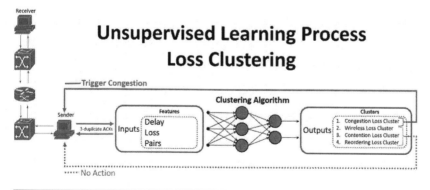

Figure 5.4   Loss clustering

the probability of misclassification is:

$$P_B \leq P_C \leq P_B + \frac{1}{\sqrt{ke}} \qquad (5.17)$$

where P_B is the optimal Bayesian error which expresses the probability that the value of the dependent variable C is c based on the values $x = (x_1, x_2, \ldots, x_n)$ of the features $X = (X_1, X_2, \ldots, X_n)$ and is given by the relation:

$$P(c \mid x) = P(c) \cdot \prod_i^n P(x_i \mid c) \qquad (5.18)$$

The main applications of using the algorithms in question are mainly focused on the following [24]:

1. Wired/wireless networks use pairs of delay-loss values to aggregate data into multiple groups and assigns a predefined optimal sending rate to each group.
2. Optical burst switching networks cluster loss into contention loss and congestion loss to optimally adapt the environment to applications with special requirements.

Unsupervised learning applications work on packet delay variations, which reflect available bandwidth and more specific types of loss. Therefore, loss-delay pairs can describe the loss in networks with relative precision, so the considered pairs can be grouped into similar clusters. Also, when a packet is lost, it will be marked with the RTT value, so with this indication, the losses can be grouped into wireless losses and congestion losses. Congestion losses have a higher mean RTT value, while wireless losses have a lower mean and higher variation for RTT.

In conclusion, it should be said that unsupervised learning techniques are instrumental in helping achieve training in complex environments where there is no prior knowledge of the state of the networks. Still, by themselves, they cannot satisfy the requirements of complex network architectures.

5.2.3.1.2 Delay Prediction   Only a limited number of CC algorithms are based on unsupervised learning techniques. This is because they are not considered suitable for delay prediction due to their high processing requirements, equating to a considerable computing resource

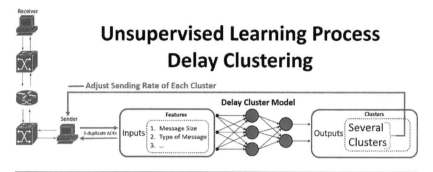

Figure 5.5   Delay clustering

consumption. A typical depiction of how unsupervised learning algorithms work is presented in Figure 5.5 [19, 23, 33].

A very relevant mechanism of the considered architecture is applied in vehicular ad hoc networks, whereby the data is gathered in different clusters based on message size, message validity, message types, the distance between vehicles, roadside units (RSUs), and the direction of the message sender. Then the clusters receive a dispatch-service rate according to their priority, always aiming for the lowest possible delay so that based on delay measurement, CC can be achieved.

5.2.4 Reinforcement Learning

It is a class of training based on the trial-and-error method, inspired by the corresponding analogues of learning with reward and punishment found as learning models of living beings. The purpose of the learning system, which actively interacts with the environment, is to maximize a function of the numerical reinforcement signal (reward), for example, the expected value of the reinforcement signal in the next step. The system is not guided by an external supervisor as to what action to take, but must discover which actions will bring the most rewards. The consideration of a reinforcement learning model is related to problems whereby the learning agent is unaware of its mode of action. It thus has to discover an action policy to maximize the expected gain, which is defined by the rewards it receives during its interaction with the learning environment. At the time t (t = 0,1,2, . . .), the learning agent—or agent, as it is called—receives a state S_t and based on the information provided by the location and time it is located, gets an action a_t. Then the agent receives a reinforcement signal or reward r_{t+1}. In the infinite time domain case, the expected profit is defined as follows [34, 35].

$$R_t = \sum_{k=0}^{\infty} \mu^k r_{t+k+1} \tag{5.19}$$

where μ, $0 < \mu \le 1$, is the rate that determines the value of the rewards

Although reinforcement learning algorithms can be applied to specific networks to improve CC efficiency, reinforcement learning has gained the most attention among different learning-based CC algorithms. It is implemented in a variety of modern applications. Significantly different from supervised learning techniques, reinforcement learning algorithms continuously monitor the state of the environment and react to it to optimize a utility function. This makes these algorithms suitable for variable and unstable network environments, such as data centers and cloud computing, requiring efficient CC algorithms to deal with complex network topologies [3, 18].

In these dynamic environments, reliability is paramount, given the variance that can occur in the supported systems. Reinforcement learning algorithms adapt to errors in time-based on learning and feedback from the dynamic environment, making them the ultimate and most specialized tool in dealing with CC. A typical example of such a dynamic environment is the wireless architectures of mobile devices, which connect to wireless networks often in an ad hoc manner. Therefore, flexible network topologies and diverse flows constitute a significant challenge. Traditional ML approaches based on trained models are insufficient for the environments in question, as they are not dynamic enough to deal with successive changes.

In general, CC algorithms based on reinforcement learning are used to update the CoWi based on different scenarios in end-to-end networks, and to manage the queue length in network-assisted environments.

5.2.4.1 Window Updating in End-to-End Networks Compared to supervised learning and unsupervised learning techniques, reinforcement learning algorithms respond to changes in the environment. Instead of predicting congestion loss and delay, CC algorithms learn CC rules based on different information directly extracted from the

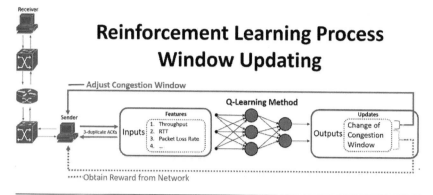

Figure 5.6   Window updating

environment. Also, given that these algorithms can integrate network conditions based on interaction and determine corresponding actions, they are suitable for real-time CC control systems. This feature is unique to the capabilities of other ML techniques [9, 10].

The mechanism of CC algorithms based on reinforcement learning to update CoWi based on different scenarios is shown in Figure 5.6 [23, 31].

In general, the purpose usually used reinforcement learning techniques for window updating in end-to-end networks use the technologies described in the following subsections [2, 3, 36].

5.2.4.1.1 ATM Networks   ATMs are the best networks to support multimedia applications, as they offer different QoS features, such as different cell loss rates and delays, for various multimedia streaming services. However, the very different time-varying traffic patterns significantly increase the uncertainty of the network traffic. In addition, the small cell transmission time and low buffer sizes require more adaptive and highly responsive CC algorithms. Reinforcement learning techniques minimize PLR and maintain high quality in related services such as video/voice. They focus their operation on performance based on corresponding characteristics such as cell loss rate and voice quality. The algorithm measures action against performance at each step, so different traffic patterns are associated with related activities.

5.2.4.1.2 SDN   An SDNs (software-defined network) provides a new architecture whereby the forwarding and control layers are optimally separated, with the control layer managing the entire network centrally. The functions in question require efficient and especially adaptive CC algorithms to implement high-availability and long-term performance SDN networks. Reinforcement learning addresses the challenges, as the dynamics of the techniques in question create adaptive counterparts that operate based on interaction with the environment, achieving extremely high link utilization to achieve efficient CC.

5.2.4.1.3 NDN The main feature of NDN (named data networking) is connectionless operation, providing content services and network caching, with typical applications in changing mobile communications and high-demand real-time communications. As easily understood, CC algorithms are required to deal differently with dynamic content and automatically adapt to the active feedback mode to be efficient. Reinforcement learning technologies and, in particular, DRL architectures—taking into account the diversity of different content through a set of self-adaptive settings, specialized memory retrieval mechanisms for relevant content searches, addressing techniques and advanced ways of assigning attention weights to memory vectors—facilitate learning specialized techniques for extracting useful intermediate representations, significantly reduces CC time, and produces improved stability, high performance, and remarkable content categorization accuracy.

5.2.4.1.4 Satellite Communications Satellite communication networks are dynamic and have time-varying flows. High bandwidth and high elasticity are their key features. One of the most common satellite communications services is real-time video streaming. However, the frequent satellite handover process is a severe problem, leading to routing failures, packet blocking, channel quality impacts, and generally multiple unspecified failures. To deal with these problems, reinforcement learning technologies are used in the multi-path TCP design, where by measuring the re-transmission rate of each sub-flow, the RTT and ACK (acknowledgment) number, the algorithm significantly degrades the handover probability, upgrading thus the quality and performance of the services offered, especially in low earth orbit satellite communications.

5.2.4.1.5 Internet of Things   Internet of Things (IoT), as a product of a rapidly evolving wireless technology, includes features such as local computing, high usage variability, and potential on-demand computing requirements. Reinforcement learning, with its powerful learning capabilities, satisfies the different and varied demands of IoT networks, as its self-adaptive capabilities perfectly match the real-time processors and memory demands supported by IoT.

5.2.4.1.6 Wired Networks with Under-Buffered Bottleneck Links   Although wired networks are not typical usage scenarios for reinforcement learning technology in the CC domain, the networks in question are much more stable than wireless networks. Nevertheless, in situations when there are very high requirements for CC, the specific algorithms—including multiple parameters such as input acknowledgment inter-arrival time, packet inter-sending time, the ratio of the current RTT, minimum RTT, the slow start threshold, and CoWi size for download adaptation information—achieved significantly higher stability between throughput and delay, which is directly related to much more efficient offered services, particularly demanding in QoS adaptations [24, 35].

5.2.4.1.7 Ad Hoc Wireless Networks   Ad hoc wireless networks (AWN) are the prime application field for CC algorithms based on reinforcement learning, as they are a collection of mobile wireless nodes without any fixed infrastructure. The participating devices usually have limited resources, limited processing capacity, and unpredictable mobility related to the ever-changing dynamic environment. In most of the use cases of these algorithms, the only possibility is to quickly learn the state of the network from reduced information and a finite number of actions. These functions are achieved by entering data such as the inter-arrival times of ACKs and duplicate packets and outputting the window size while taking into account the throughput and RTT when viewing the state spaces and the corresponding action spaces, which are differentiated by dynamic action probability distribution, which is related to the individual characteristics of CC methods.

5.2.4.1.8 Queue Length Management in Network-Assisted Networks   For the QLM of CC algorithms based on reinforcement learning,

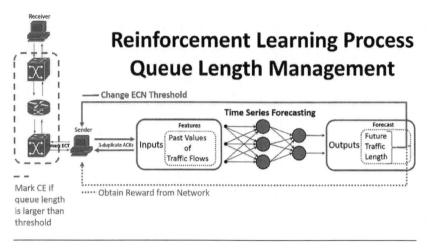

Figure 5.7   Queue length management

modeling techniques are used based on the current situation and with the primary purpose of maintaining the queue length within a defined target limit framework while calculating the probability of fluctuation. A representative architecture is shown in Figure 5.7 [23, 37].

5.2.4.1.9 Networks Supporting Active Queue Management (AQM)   The purpose that reinforcement learning techniques are usually used for QLM in network-assisted networks per technology is that by intelligently adjusting parameters that balance the network operation, such as stabilizing the router queue length by parameterizing traffic loading per usage scenario, RTTs and bottleneck link capacities, an optimal queue length can be maintained around an ideal target queue length, which can also be understood as a dynamic threshold, to calculate and thus predict the dropping probability in the future, thus achieving a remarkable CC [3, 18, 27].

5.2.4.1.10 Disruption-Tolerant Networks   In the cases of these networks, congestion state information is widely used to support congestion notifications and further ensure CC. Compared to the window updating technology in end-to-end networks, QLM in network-assisted networks for CC algorithms is much more demanding in computing resources because to ensure quality controls and timely and valid prediction of future states, multiple nodes must be used for CC, such as routers, active equipment, etc. In addition, the current

QLM and calculations based on reinforcement learning techniques is covered only by limited state parameters such as the past queue length and the buffer size, which creates more parameter optimization requirements to improve the performance of CC algorithms.

In conclusion, it appears that CC algorithms based on reinforcement learning can satisfy different network scenarios with high adaptability and robust flexibility. However, there are some limitations. For example, convergence is complicated to ensure for continuous tasks of long-time intervals, especially in complex situations of constantly changing environments. Moreover, the abstractness imposed by the condition of limited resources is challenging. The algorithms in question require significant computational resources for their processing, such as storage resources, memory resources, processing resources, etc., as their computational complexity is relatively high.

5.3 Conclusion

Distributed denial of service (DDoS) attacks, specifically DDoS protocol assaults, are one of the most destructive types of address resolution protocol (ARP) attacks. These are attacks often predicated on the functioning of the transmission control protocol (TCP) to maintain fairness and avoid collapse by applying congestion management. Due to the increasing complexity of threats, the ever-changing environment, and the importance of critical infrastructures, advanced persistent threat assaults may directly or indirectly result in significant financial losses and even the death of innocent people.

In this chapter, we described machine learning (ML)-based TCP congestion management solutions for active cyberterrorism protection on smart grids, given that the relevant threats against this protocol have been identified by manual study and human knowledge. It is an analytical demonstration of how to use ML methods in network planning, adjusting its parameters, and ideally allocating its resources, as well as how to ensure a model of acceptable accuracy, such as load change patterns and performance enhancement of network resources, in the event of DDoS attacks.

Future extensions concern the optimization of the algorithms to reduce their complexity and allow the reduction of the computational resources needed for their operation.

References

[1] A. Mohammed and G. George, "Vulnerabilities and Strategies of Cybersecurity in Smart Grid—Evaluation and Review," in 2022 3rd International Conference on Smart Grid and Renewable Energy (SGRE), March 2022, pp. 1–6. doi: 10.1109/SGRE53517.2022.9774038.

[2] G. Kaur, V. Saxena, and J. P. Gupta, "Detection of TCP targeted high bandwidth attacks using self-similarity," J. King Saud Univ. Comput. Inf. Sci., vol. 32, no. 1, pp. 35–49, Jan. 2020, doi: 10.1016/j.jksuci.2017.05.004.

[3] L. Alzubaidi, J. Zhang, A. J. Humaidi, A. Al-Dujaili, Y. Duan, O. Al-Shamma, J. Santamaría, M. A. Fadhel, M. Al-Amidie, and L. Farhan, "Review of deep learning: Concepts, CNN architectures, challenges, applications, future directions," J. Big Data, vol. 8, no. 1, p. 53, Mar. 2021, doi: 10.1186/s40537-021-00444-8.

[4] K. Demertzis, L. S. Iliadis, and V.-D. Anezakis, "An innovative soft computing system for smart energy grids cybersecurity," Adv. Build. Energy Res., vol. 12, no. 1, pp. 3–24, Jan. 2018, doi: 10.1080/17512549.2017.1325401.

[5] K. Tsiknas, D. Taketzis, K. Demertzis, and C. Skianis, "Cyber threats to industrial IoT: A survey on attacks and countermeasures," IoT, vol. 2, no. 1, Art. no. 1, Mar. 2021, doi: 10.3390/iot2010009.

[6] K. Demertzis, K. Tsiknas, D. Taketzis, D. N. Skoutas, C. Skianis, L. Iliadis, K. E. Zoiros, "Communication Network Standards for Smart Grid Infrastructures," Network, vol. 1, no. 2, Art. no. 2, Sep. 2021, doi: 10.3390/network1020009.

[7] S. Jero, E. Hoque, D. Choffnes, A. Mislove, and C. Nita-Rotaru, "Automated attack discovery in TCP congestion control using a model-guided approach," in Proceedings of the Applied Networking Research Workshop, New York, NY, Apr. 2018, p. 95. doi: 10.1145/3232755.3232769.

[8] J. P. Astudillo León, T. Begin, A. Busson, and L. J. de la Cruz Llopis, "Towards a distributed congestion control mechanism for smart grid neighborhood area networks," in Proceedings of the 16th ACM International Symposium on Performance Evaluation of Wireless Ad Hoc, Sensor, & Ubiquitous Networks, New York, NY, Aug. 2019, pp. 29–36. doi: 10.1145/3345860.3361520.

[9] U. Saxena, J. Sodhi, and Y. Singh, "An analysis of DDoS attacks in a smart home networks," in 2020 10th International Conference on Cloud Computing, Data Science & Engineering (Confluence), Jan. 2020, pp. 272–276. doi: 10.1109/Confluence47617.2020.9058087.

[10] K. Dermetzis and L. Iliadis, "AI threat detection and response on smart networks," in Computational Collective Intelligence: 13th International Conference, ICCCI 2021, Rhodes, Greece, September 2–October 1, 2021, Proceedings. Springer-Verlag, Berlin, Heidelberg, 2021, pp. 685–695. doi: 10.1007/978-3-030-88081-1_51.

[11] E. Özer and M. İskefiyeli, "Detection of DDoS attack via deep packet analysis in real time systems," in 2017 International Conference on Computer Science and Engineering (UBMK), Jul. 2017, pp. 1137–1140. doi: 10.1109/UBMK.2017.8093526.

[12] M. Z. Gunduz and R. Das, "Cyber-security on smart grid: Threats and potential solutions," Comput. Netw., vol. 169, p. 107094, Mar. 2020, doi: 10.1016/j.comnet.2019.107094.

[13] J. Ding, A. Qammar, Z. Zhang, A. Karim, and H. Ning, "Cyber threats to smart grids: Review, taxonomy, potential solutions, and future directions," Energies, vol. 15, no. 18, p. 6799, Sep. 2022, doi: 10.3390/en15186799.

[14] Z. Xu, J. Tang, C. Yin, Y. Wang, and G. Xue, "Experience-driven congestion control: When multi-path TCP meets deep reinforcement learning," IEEE J. Sel. Areas Commun., vol. 37, no. 6, pp. 1325–1336, Jun. 2019, doi: 10.1109/JSAC.2019.2904358.

[15] A. E. Labrador Rivas and T. Abrão, "Faults in smart grid systems: Monitoring, detection and classification," Electr. Power Syst. Res., vol. 189, p. 106602, Dec. 2020, doi: 10.1016/j.epsr.2020.106602.

[16] S. Gumpu, B. Pamulaparthy, and A. Sharma, "Review of congestion management methods from conventional to smart grid scenario," Int. J. Emerg. Electr. Power Syst., vol. 20, no. 3, Jul. 2019, doi: 10.1515/ijeeps-2018-0265.

[17] M. Komisarek, M. Pawlicki, R. Kozik, and M. Choraś, "Machine learning based approach to anomaly and cyberattack detection in streamed network traffic data," J. Wirel. Mob. Netw. Ubiquitous Comput. Dependable Appl., vol. 12, no. 1, pp. 3–19, Mar. 2021, doi: 10.22667/JOWUA.2021.03.31.003.

[18] F. Emmert-Streib, Z. Yang, H. Feng, S. Tripathi, and M. Dehmer, "An introductory review of deep learning for prediction models with big data," Front. Artif. Intell., vol. 3, p. 4, 2020, doi: 10.3389/frai.2020.00004.

[19] M. Soysal and E. G. Schmidt, "Machine learning algorithms for accurate flow-based network traffic classification: Evaluation and comparison," Perform. Eval., vol. 67, no. 6, pp. 451–467, Jun. 2010, doi: 10.1016/j.peva.2010.01.001.

[20] K. J. Danjuma, "Performance evaluation of machine learning algorithms in post-operative life expectancy in the lung cancer patients," https://arxiv.org/ftp/arxiv/papers/1504/1504.04646.pdf.

[21] S. B. Kotsiantis, D. Kanellopoulos, and P. E. Pintelas, "Data preprocessing for supervised leaning," Int. J. Comput. Inf. Eng., vol. 1, no. 12, pp. 4104–4109, Dec. 2007.

[22] T. W. Anderson, An Introduction to Multivariate Statistical Analysis. Wiley, 2003, ISBN: 978-0-471-36091-9.

[23] H. Jiang et al., "When machine learning meets congestion control: A survey and comparison," Comput. Netw., vol. 192, p. 108033, Jun. 2021, doi: 10.1016/j.comnet.2021.108033.

[24] M. Wang, Y. Cui, X. Wang, S. Xiao, and J. Jiang, "Machine learning for networking: Workflow, advances and opportunities," IEEE Netw., vol. 32, no. 2, pp. 92–99, Mar. 2018, doi: 10.1109/MNET.2017.1700200.

[25] P. Akubathini, S. Chouksey, and H. S. Satheesh, "Evaluation of Machine Learning approaches for resource constrained IIoT devices," in 2021 13th International Conference on Information Technology and Electrical Engineering (ICITEE), Jul. 2021, pp. 74–79. doi: 10.1109/ICITEE53064.2021.9611880.

[26] Y. Kong, H. Zang, and X. Ma, "Improving TCP congestion control with machine intelligence," in Proceedings of the 2018 Workshop on Network Meets AI & ML, New York, NY, Dec. 2018, pp. 60–66. doi: 10.1145/3229543.3229550.

[27] A. Gasparin, S. Lukovic, and C. Alippi, "Deep learning for time series forecasting: The electric load case," ArXiv190709207 Cs Stat, Jul. 2019, Accessed: Mar. 27, 2022. [Online]. Available: http://arxiv.org/abs/1907.09207

[28] E. I. Papageorgiou, C. Stylios, and P. P. Groumpos, "Unsupervised learning techniques for fine-tuning fuzzy cognitive map causal links," Int. J. Hum. Comput. Stud., vol. 64, no. 8, pp. 727–743, Aug. 2006, doi: 10.1016/j.ijhcs.2006.02.009.

[29] L. Tulczyjew, M. Kawulok, and J. Nalepa, "Unsupervised feature learning using recurrent neural nets for segmenting hyperspectral images," IEEE Geosci. Remote Sens. Lett., vol. 18, no. 12, pp. 2142–2146, Sep. 2021, doi: 10.1109/LGRS.2020.3013205.

[30] J. O. Berger, "Bayesian analysis," in Statistical Decision Theory and Bayesian Analysis, J. O. Berger, ed. Springer, 1985, pp. 118–307. doi: 10.1007/978-1-4757-4286-2_4.

[31] K. Md. R. Alam, N. Siddique, and H. Adeli, "A dynamic ensemble learning algorithm for neural networks," Neural Comput. Appl., vol. 32, no. 12, pp. 8675–8690, Jun. 2020, doi: 10.1007/s00521-019-04359-7.

[32] M. Kumar and R. Mathur, "Unsupervised outlier detection technique for intrusion detection in cloud computing," in International Conference for Convergence for Technology, Apr. 2014, pp. 1–4. doi: 10.1109/I2CT.2014.7092027.

[33] Y. Gao and L. Jia, "Stability in measure for uncertain delay differential equations based on new Lipschitz conditions," J. Intell. Fuzzy Syst., vol. 41, no. 2, pp. 2997–3009, Jan. 2021, doi: 10.3233/JIFS-210089.

[34] W. Li, F. Zhou, K. R. Chowdhury, and W. Meleis, "QTCP: Adaptive congestion control with reinforcement learning," IEEE Trans. Netw. Sci. Eng., vol. 6, no. 3, pp. 445–458, Jul. 2019, doi: 10.1109/TNSE.2018.2835758.

[35] A. Ndikumana, S. Ullah, D. H. Kim, and C. S. Hong, "DeepAuC: Joint deep learning and auction for congestion-aware caching in Named Data Networking," PLoS ONE, vol. 14, no. 8, p. e0220813, Aug. 2019, doi: 10.1371/journal.pone.0220813.

[36] T. Zhang and S. Mao, "Machine learning for end-to-end congestion control," IEEE Commun. Mag., vol. 58, no. 6, pp. 52–57, Jun. 2020, doi: 10.1109/MCOM.001.1900509.

[37] H. Worthington, R. S. McCrea, R. King, and R. A. Griffiths, "Estimation of population size when capture probability depends on individual states," J. Agric. Biol. Environ. Stat., vol. 24, no. 1, pp. 154–172, Mar. 2019, doi: 10.1007/s13253-018-00347-x.

6

SPEED 2 COMES TRUE

Cyberattacks against Ships

GEORGIOS KAVALLIERATOS
AND SOKRATIS KATSIKAS

6.1 Introduction

The shipping industry, influenced by the Fourth Industrial Revolution, has increased the automation and connectivity of both shore-side and ship-side systems, and leverages technologies such as the Internet of Things (IoT), artificial intelligence (AI), and Big Data analytics. This trend has been named "Shipping 4.0", a term that was first coined in 2016 [1] to describe the new developments in the digitalization of shipping that reflect the very similar developments in the manufacturing industry that commonly go under the name "Industry 4.0". Digitalization in the shipping industry has two facets: the digitalization of the enterprise operations of shipping companies and the digitalization of the shipping infrastructure, i.e., the vessels themselves. In this chapter, we focus on the latter, and in particular on the onboard cyber–physical systems (CPSs).

Despite the indisputable benefits of leveraging emerging technologies towards achieving the goals of shipping 4.0, these very same technologies increase the cyberattack surface and make the ship infrastructure prone to cyberattacks. Such concerns have already been raised in both the scientific literature and among stakeholders in the maritime domain [2–5]. The more interconnected the ship infrastructure is, the more vulnerable are the onboard cyber–physical systems. Therefore, adversaries can launch cyberattacks that may cause physical, financial, or reputation damage to humans, companies, or the environment.

Even though the possibility of launching a cyberattack against a ship was at the core of the plot of the 1997 movie *Speed 2: Cruise*

DOI: 10.1201/9781003314721-6

Control [6], in which an onboard hacker took control of the ship's communication and engine control systems, the first cyberattack in the real world that was reported in the media occurred in 2010 and the first fully documented such attack was demonstrated in a laboratory environment in 2013 [7]. Since then, the frequency, diversity, and sophistication of cyberattacks against ships have been increasing.

Over 80% of the volume of international trade in goods is carried by sea [8]. Because of the importance of the maritime sector for the world's economy, and the increasing digitalization of the sector, maritime cybersecurity has been studied extensively in the past decade. The European Network and Information Security Agency (ENISA) published a report that analyzes the main cybersecurity issues that arise in the maritime sector, focusing on shore-side and port information and communications technology (ICT) systems and policy and regulation aspects [9]. Cybersecurity threats and vulnerabilities in the maritime sector have been also analyzed in the scientific literature [10, 11]. The cybersecurity of onboard CPSs, including for autonomous or remotely controlled ships, has been systematically studied [12–18]. A survey of cybersecurity threats faced in the maritime sector and in onboard systems has been presented [19]. Park et al. [20] analyzed incidents caused by cyberattacks in the maritime sector. Farah et al. [21] provide a classification of possible cyberattacks in the maritime sector, based on the target of the attack, vulnerabilities exploited, and cybersecurity objectives. Meland et al. [22] proposed a taxonomy for cybersecurity incidents in the maritime sector and used it to analyze 46 such real-world incidents. Of these, 13 involved and affected onboard CPSs. In response to the rising need for guidance regarding cybersecurity in the maritime sector, several organizations have made available guidelines [4]. Proposed strategies and countermeasures for mitigating cyberattacks against onboard CPSs have been proposed [15, 17]. Recent developments and research directions in maritime cybersecurity have been identified [23].

This chapter presents an analysis of cyberattacks against CPSs onboard ships that have either occurred in the wild or whose feasibility has been demonstrated in a laboratory environment. The sources used are from the scientific literature, technical reports by the shipping industry, and media reports. However, not all of the reported incidents could be analyzed in detail, due to lack of detailed information. The chapter aims to provide a comprehensive understanding of the landscape of cyberattacks on onboard CPSs, to raise cybersecurity awareness in the shipping industry, and to identify potential solutions to mitigate such attacks. This work also proposes a taxonomy of the current state of play of cyberattacks against onboard CPSs. The proposed taxonomy is based on the guidelines in [24]; each cyberattack is characterized by the attributes *actor*, *motive*, *category*, *target*, *impact*, *means*, and *vulnerabilities*.

Concretely, this chapter provides the following.

- A comprehensive review and discussion of the major cyberattacks against onboard CPSs that have occurred in the real world. This enables a comprehensive understanding of the attackers' tactics, techniques, goals, and procedures.
- A taxonomy to analyze the cyberattacks on onboard CPSs, based on the type of the attack, adversary actions, target CPS onboard, impact of the attack, and vulnerability(ies) exploited.
- Mitigation techniques and strategies that could have prevented the incident, had they been followed before the attack.

The remainder of this chapter is structured as follows. Section 6.2 presents a brief overview of the CPSs onboard a modern ship, focusing on those that have been identified as the most vulnerable ones [14]; these systems have also been the targets of most of the real-world cyberattacks, which are reviewed in Section 6.3. Section 6.4 presents our proposed taxonomy for analyzing the reviewed cyberattacks and discusses the findings of the analysis. Section 6.5 proposes possible mitigation measures and, finally, Section 6.6 summarizes our conclusions.

6.2 Onboard Cyber–Physical Systems

A generic architecture for the onboard CPSs was proposed in [25, 26]. Three groups of such systems are identified, namely the *engine automation systems (EAS)*, *bridge automation systems (BAS)*, and *ICT infrastructure*.

The EAS include all the systems that generate and manage the ship's power and propulsion systems. These are:

- The *autonomous engine monitoring and control (AEMC)* that monitors the mechanical parts of the ship and includes the *autonomous control of the engine room (AC-ER)* that monitors and controls the propulsion system, the power generation system, the fuel system, rudder systems, and the evaporation system; *emergency handling (EmH)* that includes the alarm systems; and the *engine data logger (EDL)* that records all information about the operation of the ship's engines.

- The *engine efficiency system (EES)* that monitors and controls the ship's engine efficient operation, and includes preventive tools for maintenance.
- The *maintenance interaction system (MIS)* that provides for technical, managerial, and administrative maintenance in the engine room. It also includes an instance of the EmH.

The BAS includes all the sub-systems on the bridge, most notably those for navigation and control of the ship. These are the following.

- The *integrated navigation system (INS)* that provides for navigating the ship, i.e., for determining aspects such as position, speed, and direction during travel. The INS includes the *voyage data recorder (VDR)* that gathers and stores all the information about the ship's condition, its position, its movements, and recordings from engine and radio systems; the *automatic identification system (AIS)*, a communication system using four worldwide channels in the VHF (very high frequency) maritime mobile band, for the exchange of navigation data; the *electronic chart display and information system (ECDIS)*, a geographic information system used for nautical navigation that complies with International Maritime Organization (IMO) regulations as an alternative to paper nautical charts; the *advanced sensor system (ASS)* that provides information about the ship's position; and a number of navigational aids, such as the *autopilot, radar, sonar, echo sounder, gyro compass, and collision avoidance (CA) system*. The global positioning system (GPS) offers satellite-based positioning, speed, and time information. A GPS receiver is installed on vessels for navigational purposes. A detailed presentation of all possible components of an INS and a reference architecture for the INS has been proposed [26].
- In autonomous or remotely controlled vessels, the *autonomous ship controller (ASC)* complements the shore control center

in assessing the data provided by the sensors to control the ship's operations. Such vessels are out of the scope of the present chapter, as no cyberattacks have been demonstrated or occurred against these.

The *ICT infrastructure* includes all the networking and computing equipment used in the vessel; systems such as the *access control (AC) system*, responsible for controlling access to the ship, be it physical or remote; and the *passenger service system (PSS)* that serves the ship's customers/passengers with the goal of implementing efficient identity management and AC in the ship's infrastructure and services. Such systems are also out of the scope of this chapter.

6.3 Cyberattacks in the Real World

As already mentioned, in this chapter, we consider cyberattacks that have either occurred in the wild or whose feasibility has been demonstrated in a laboratory environment. The attacks span the period 2010–2022. Some of the attacks have been thoroughly analyzed in the scientific literature. For others, limited information is available, mostly through posts in relevant websites. As the latter do not lend themselves well to further analysis, they are listed in a separate subsection.

6.3.1 *Fully Analyzed Attacks*

Most of the fully analyzed attacks were demonstrated in a laboratory environment. The systems mostly involved are navigational aids such as the AIS, the GPS, and the ECDIS.

M. Balduzzi et al. demonstrated two cyberattacks that targeted the AIS and its communication protocols [7]. The goal of the cyberattacks were to alter transmitted data by leveraging vulnerabilities of the AIS communication protocol to send fake collision alerts and spoof the identify of other ships in the vicinity, and to impersonate marine authorities. In a subsequent publication, M. Balduzzi et al. demonstrated several cyberattacks targeting the AIS [27]. The goal of the attacks were to spoof the identity of another vessel in the vicinity and cause a ship collision. An AIS spoofing attack that occurred in the wild was analyzed by Lloyd's List Intelligence [28]. According to the report, this was a state-sponsored attack and its goal was to alter the route of a UK-flagged tanker. Another spoofing cyberattack was launched by North Korean ships to avoid detection from authorities [29]. The malicious ships broadcasted wrong AIS signals by spoofing the Maritime Mobile Service Identity (MMSI) number of another ship in the vicinity. A. Androjna et al. [30] analyzed an AIS spoofing attack which aimed to spoof a vessel identity so as to be recognized as a Dutch-flagged naval unit. This was achieved by sending thousands of AIS messages that were artificially generated and had different identification codes, positions, routes, and speeds. The goal of the attack was to alter navigational information and, by so doing, to impact the safety of vessels in the area. S. Khandker et al. [31] demonstrated cyberattacks on the AIS that leveraged remote radio frequencies and used transmission-enabled software-defined radio. The demonstrated cyberattacks were: 1) spoofing the identity of other ships in the vicinity; 2) producing fake "man overboard" alerts; 3) jamming AIS communication channels; 4) tampering AIS messages to change the MMSI number; and 5) a denial of service (DoS) attack to overflow AIS receivers with fake signals. The goal of the cyberattacks was to analyze AIS vulnerabilities and investigate the security posture of the system. The U.S. Department of Transportation's Maritime Administration issued a warning about an Iran-sponsored GPS spoofing attack against ships sailing in the Arabian Gulf, Strait of Hormuz, and Gulf of Oman regions [32]. The goal of the attack was to spoof the identity of commercial vessels in the vicinity by leveraging AIS vulnerabilities. W.C. Leite Jr. et al. [33] demonstrated a cyberattack that targeted navigational systems, namely the radar and the AIS. The goal of the attack was to spoof the identity of other ships in the vicinity and alter the vessel's position by utilizing an installed malware.

Naval Dome demonstrated a cyberattack on ECDIS [34]. The goal of the attack was to alter the ship's position during its voyage. The attack was performed by leveraging the chart update process. O.S. Hareide at al. [35] demonstrated a cyberattack against ECDIS. The cyberattack installed a malware onboard that acted as a man-in-the-middle and changed the ship's position on the navigational charts by injecting faulty values of the speed and position of the ship. M.S. Lund et al. demonstrated a proof of concept cyberattack against the INS with particular focus on the ECDIS [36]. The attack vector included a malware that aimed to alter GPS coordinates.

M. Psiaki et al. [37, 38] demonstrated and analyzed a GPS spoofing attack against a superyacht's GPS. The goal of the attack was to affect the voyage of the yacht by broadcasting wrong GPS signals through spoofing the identity of a navigational satellite.

A.V. Harish et al. [39] demonstrated and analyzed a cyberattack against the VDR. The attack was launched by leveraging a pre-programmed USB drive that enabled remote access to the targeted system.

B. Croteau et al. demonstrated a cyberattack that caused damage to the rudder of a ship [40]. The attack was launched against a model ship testbed, with the goal to analyze the impact of a cyberattack to the onboard machinery systems. The cyberattack aimed at the ship's rudder, freezing the rudder to a fixed location by tampering the data sent to actuators.

6.3.2 *Attacks about Which Limited Information Is Available*

In 2010, a drilling rig en route from South Korea to Latin America had to be shut down because of malware that infected even the computers controlling its blowout preventer, a critical piece of safety equipment. That infection could have caused the preventer and other systems to be unresponsive if the rig were drilling, possibly leading to a well blowout, explosion, oil spill, and loss of life. The same malware had infected and adversely affected the operation of several other rigs at the same time [41]. Little is known about another attack against an offshore platform which took place in October 2012. The attack had targeted communication networks installed on an Iranian offshore platform in the Persian Gulf [42, 43]. In 2013, the drilling operation on a rig in the Gulf of Mexico was disrupted because of a malware infection that affected communication between the dynamic positioning system and the thrusters. The infection was caused when members of the crew inadvertently connected malware-infected PCs and USB drives to the rig's network [22].

In April 2016, South Korea announced that around 280 vessels were under a GPS jamming attack that forced the affected vessels to return to port, and claimed that the attack was organized by North Korea [44, 45].

In February 2017, hackers reportedly took control of the navigation systems of a German-owned 8,250 TEU (20-foot equivalent unit) container vessel en route from Cyprus to Djibouti for 10 hours. The result was that the ship was not possible to maneuver. While details are limited, it is possible that the 10-hour attack was carried out by "pirates" who gained full control of the vessel's navigation system, intending to steer it to an area where they could board and take over. The crew attempted to regain control of the navigation system but had to bring ICT experts on board, who eventually managed to get them running again after hours of work [46, 47].

On 22 June 2017, a ship off the Russian shore notified the U.S. Coast Guard Navigation Center about a problem with GPS, one that had also affected 20 more ships in the area. According to the report, the ship's GPS showed the wrong position. The ship's GPS gave a position inland, even though the vessel was drifting more than 25 nautical miles from the given coordinates. Investigations revealed that this was a GPS spoofing cyberattack that has been attributed to Russia [48, 49]. A similar incident involves a ship exposed to GPS spoofing in the Black Sea. The ship was at sea, but the geolocation system onboard claimed that it was on land. During the course of three days, this happened four times, each lasting up to 30 minutes [22].

In 2018, multiple incidents involving GPS interference took place across the island of Cyprus. No reason for two of these was identified, and they appeared as "Unknown Interference" in the USCG NAVCEN 2020 records [50]. The Norwegian Shipowner's Mutual War Risks Insurance report focuses on the probability of GPS interference occurring around the island of Cyprus caused by Turkey [47, 51].

In February 2019, a large ship bound for New York City radioed the U.S. Coast Guard warning that the vessel was "experiencing a significant cyberincident impacting their shipboard network." The Coast Guard led an incident response team to investigate the issue and found that malware had infected the ship's systems and significantly degraded functionality. Fortunately, essential systems for the control of the vessel were unimpeded [52].

On several occasions throughout 2018 and 2019, the GPS signals in Troms and Finnmark (northern Norway) were switched off. The disturbances have affected civil aviation and ship traffic to some extent, but fortunately have not had serious consequences. As the activity was high at, among other things, the NATO exercise Trident Juncture, according to the Norwegian Intelligence Service, there is reason to believe that some of the cases were intentional interference from the Russian side, while other cases may have been unintended effects in Norway as a result of Russian exercise activity [53].

In the same year, 2019, the administration server of a tanker near the port of Naantali in Finland was infected by ransomware, and the backup disk was wiped. Remote desktop protocol (RDP), a USB device, or an email attachment were identified as probable attack vectors. The same vessel was infected again four months later near the same port [22].

Also in 2019, two ships of the same ownership were infected by the ransomware Hermes 2.1. The infection was caused by a macro-enabled Word document attached to an email, and multiple workstations on the administrative networks were affected [22].

In 2020, the server and multiple PC clients onboard a vessel anchored near Tynemouth, UK, were infected with the Ryuk ransomware. A full reinstall was necessary to restore the systems [22].

Also in 2020, three ships sailing under the U.S. flag had their administrative systems infected by the ransomware Sodinokibi. This virus also threatened to leak information ("ransomtheft"), in addition to encrypting data [22].

6.4 A Taxonomy of Attacks

The goal of a taxonomy of cyberattacks on onboard systems is to provide a comprehensive overview of the current situation in the cybersecurity of marine vessels and to allow the identification of likely targets, their mostly exploitable vulnerabilities, and associated threats and adversaries, with an eye toward prioritizing systems in need of enhanced cybersecurity protection and toward identifying measures that can mitigate the accordant risks. The taxonomy proposed herein is based on the following attributes of a cyberattack.

- **Actor:** An individual or a group of people who take(s) part in setting up or executing any phase of the attack.
- **Motive:** The motive of the adversary. It can be experimental or malicious.
- **Category:** This attribute follows the categories of the STRIDE threat modeling method, namely spoofing, tampering, repudiation, information disclosure (privacy breach or data leak), DoS, elevation of privilege. Each one of these categories maps one-to-one onto the breaching of the following security attributes: authenticity, integrity, non-repudiability, confidentiality, availability, and authorization.
- **Target:** The targeted systems.
- **Impact:** The impact that the attack had. This can be operational or informational, or both [54]. The former aims to impact the ship's operations and functions, while the latter aims to impact information and data exchange.
- **Means:** The means and tools used for carrying out the attack. Such means can be physical attack, information exchange, script, or user command [55].
- **Vulnerabilities:** Vulnerabilities that the attack exploited. These are categorized as follows: zero-day vulnerability (V1), known vulnerabilities (V2), insecure protocols (V3), insecure configuration (V4), and social engineering (V5) [40].

Table 6.1 provides the result of the categorization of the cyberattacks discussed in Section 6.3.1 according to the preceding taxonomy. The cyberattacks discussed in Section 6.3.2 have not been categorized, as most of the taxonomy attributes are unknown.

We notice that the number of cyberattacks against ships has increased manyfold during a recent three-year span (2019–2022); this is not surprising, considering the ongoing digitalization process. The motives of the cyberattacks that occurred between 2013 and 2018 have been experimental, and hence benign. On the contrary, four

Table 6.1 Categorization of Cyberattacks against Ships

SOURCE	YEAR	ACTOR	MOTIVE	CATEGORY	TARGET	IMPACT	MEANS	VULNERABILITIES
[7]	2013	Research lab	Experimental	Tampering/spoofing	Data network	OI, II	Information exchange	V3, V4
[27]	2014	Research lab	Experimental	Spoofing	Data	OI	Information exchange	V3
[37, 38]	2016	Research lab	Experimental	Spoofing	Data network	OI	Information exchange	V3
[34]	2017	Research lab	Experimental	Tampering	Data user OS	II	Information exchange, user command	V4, V5
[35]	2018	Research lab	Experimental	Tampering	Data network	II	Information exchange script	V2, V5
[36]	2018	Research lab	Experimental	Spoofing/tampering	Data user OS	OI, II	Physical attack, user command	V4, V5
[28]	2019	Nation-state	Malicious	Spoofing	Data	OI	Information exchange	V3, V4
[32]	2019	Nation-state	Malicious	Spoofing	Data	OI	Information exchange	V3, V4
[29]	2019	Nation-state	Malicious	Spoofing	Data	OI	Information exchange	V3, V4
[40]	2019	Research lab	Experimental	Tampering	Data	OI, II	Physical attack, user command, information exchange	V2, V4, V5
[56]	2020	Nation-state	Malicious	Tampering/elevation of privileges	Data network	OI, II	Information exchange	V2, V4
[33]	2021	Research lab	Experimental	Spoofing/tampering	Data OS	OI, II	Information exchange	V3, V4
[30]	2021	Research lab	Experimental	Spoofing	Data	OI	Information exchange	V3
[39]	2022	Research lab	Experimental	Tampering/information disclosure	Data user	OI, II	Information exchange script	V3, V4
[31]	2022	Research lab	Experimental	Spoofing/tampering, denial of service	Data network	OI, II	Information exchange, user command	V2, V3, V4

out of nine incidents that occurred in 2019–2022 were malicious actions, aiming at inflicting damage to the ship and consequently to the reputation of the shipping company that owned it. Most of the analyzed cyberattacks are of the *spoofing* and *tampering* categories, and targeted navigational systems with the aim to alter the route of the vessel. However, in recent years, cyberattacks have become more sophisticated and include attacks in the *information disclosure, elevation of privileges*, and DoS categories. Although the targets of the cyberattacks have mostly been the transmitted data and the network in bridge systems, some cyberattacks exploited the lack of security awareness of the crew onboard. Most of the presented cyberattacks have had both operational and informational impact. Most of the attacks leveraged *information exchange*, while only two were more sophisticated and deployed a malicious script. Additionally, four attacks leveraged a faulty *user command*; this may have been the result of lack of security awareness among the crew. The discussed cyberattacks exploited vulnerabilities such as *insecure protocols* and *insecure configurations*. Four out of 15 attacks exploited social engineering techniques, and four cyberattacks leveraged well-known vulnerabilities of the onboard systems.

6.5 Mitigation Controls

A number of sources [57–59] propose sets of security controls to mitigate cyberattacks at large. However, such sources focus on information systems and do not capture aspects of cyber–physical systems; therefore, their applicability to the onboard systems is limited. The National Institute of Standards and Technology (NIST) *Guide to Industrial Control Systems (ICS) Security* [60] provides the ICS overlay, which is a partial tailoring of the controls and control baselines that add supplementary guidance specific to ICS [58, 59]. By leveraging identified security controls [16, 61] for onboard systems and the approach for their selection, Table 6.2 presents potential mitigation techniques for the analyzed attacks. The coding used to identify controls is that used in [58, 59]. We notice that all considered cyberattacks can be mitigated by these controls.

Table 6.2 Mitigation Controls

CYBERATTACK	DEVICE IDENTIFICATION AND AUTHENTICATION (IA-3)	PORT AND I/O DEVICE ACCESS (SC-41)	SOFTWARE, FIRMWARE, AND INFORMATION INTEGRITY (SI-7)	CRYPTOGRAPHIC KEY ESTABLISHMENT AND MANAGEMENT (SC-12 [1])	CRYPTOGRAPHIC PROTECTION (SC-13)	INTERNAL SYSTEM CONNECTIONS (CA-9)	INFORMATION SYSTEM BACKUP (CP-9) (1), (2), (3), (5))	POWER EQUIPMENT AND CABLING (PE-9)	DENIAL OF SERVICE PROTECTION (SC-5)	INTERNAL SYSTEM CONNECTIONS (CA-9)	MONITORING PHYSICAL ACCESS (PE-6)
[7]	✓		✓								
[27]	✓	✓									
[37, 38]	✓										
[34]		✓	✓								
[35]		✓	✓								
[36]	✓	✓	✓								
[28]	✓										
[32]	✓										
[29]	✓										
[40]		✓	✓	✓							
[56]		✓	✓							✓	✓
[33]	✓	✓	✓								
[30]	✓	✓	✓	✓	✓						
[39]		✓	✓			✓	✓	✓	✓		
[31]	✓	✓	✓								

6.6 Conclusions

The cyberthreat landscape against marine vessels has been expanding in the past few years, fueled by the ongoing process of digitalization of the shipping industry. In this chapter, we reviewed and analyzed cyberattacks against marine vessels that have occurred in the real world in the past 12 years. Further, we proposed a taxonomy of such attacks that provides insight into the workings of such attacks and allows for both drawing useful conclusions and for identifying baseline security controls that may be useful in mitigating them. As it is expected that the cyberthreat landscape in the maritime domain will continue to evolve for some time, systematic monitoring and analysis of relevant attacks appears to be in order, to coordinate action among both companies and nations.

References

[1] SINTEF. Shipping 4.0 presented at Singapore maritime week.

[2] Victor Bolbot, Gerasimos Theotokatos, Evangelos Boulougouris, and Dracos Vassalos. Safety related cyber-attacks identification and assessment for autonomous inland ships. In *Proceedings of the International Seminar on Safety and Security of Autonomous Vessels (ISSAV), Aalto University, Espoo, Finland*, 17–20 September 2019.

[3] GL DNV. Dnvgl-rp-0496-cyber security resilience management in 2016.

[4] BIMCO, CLIA, ICS, INTERCARGO, INTERMANAGER, INTERTANKO,IUMI,OCIMFandWORLDSHIPPINGCOUNCIL. *The Guidelines on Cyber Security Onboard Ships; Technical Report*, Bagsværd, Denmark: BIMCO, 2018.

[5] Masitoh Indriani. International Maritime Organization (IMO) guidelines on maritime cyber risk management: Isu dan Tantangan Bagi Indonesia. *Jurnal Majelis*, (10):1–16, 2019.

[6] Wikipedia. Speed 2: Cruise control. https://en.wikipedia.org/wiki/Speed2:CruiseControl.

[7] Marco Balduzzi, Kyle Wihoit, and Alessandro Pasta. Hey captain, where's your ship? Attacking vessel tracking systems for fun and profit. In *Proceedings of the 11th annual Hack in the Box (HITB) Security Conference in Asia, Kuala Lumpur, Malaysia*, 14–17th October 2013. https://conference.hitb.org/hitbsecconf2013kul/m aterials/D1T1%20-%20Marco%20Balduzzi,%20 Kyle%20Wilhoit%20Alessandro%20Pasta%20-%20Attackin g%20Vessel% 20Tracking%20Systems%20for%20Fun%20and%20Profit.pdf.

[8] United Nations Conference on Trade and Development. Review of maritime transport 2020. https://unctad.org/webflyer/review-maritime-transport-2020.

[9]   Dan Cimpean, Johan Meire, Vincent Bouckaert, Stijn Vande Casteele, Aurore Pelle, and Luc Hellebooge. *Analysis of Cyber security Aspects in the Maritime Sector*, Athens: ENISA, 2011.

[10] Kevin D Jones, Kimberly Tam, and Maria Papadaki. Threats and impacts in maritime cyber security. Master's Thesis, University of Plymouth, Plymouth, 2016.

[11] Frank Akpan, Gueltoum Bendiab, Stavros Shiaeles, Stavros Karam-Peridis, and Michalis Michaloliakos. Cybersecurity challenges in the maritime sector. *Network*, 2(1):123–138, 2022.

[12] Sokratis Katsikas and Georgios Kavallieratos. Cybersecurity of the unmanned ship. In *Cybersecurity Issues in Emerging Technologies*, pages 21–42. CRC Press, 2021.

[13] Sokratis K. Katsikas. Cyber security of the autonomous ship. In *Proceedings of the 3rd ACM Workshop on Cyber-Physical System Security*, CPSS'17, page 55–56, New York, NY: Association for Computing Machinery, 2017.

[14] Georgios Kavallieratos, Vasiliki Diamantopoulou, and Sokratis K. Katsikas. Shipping 4.0: Security requirements for the cyber-enabled ship. *IEEE Transactions on Industrial Informatics*, 16(10):6617–6625, 2020.

[15] Georgios Kavallieratos and Sokratis Katsikas. Attack path analysis for cyber physical systems. In Sokratis Katsikas, Frederic Cuppens, Nora Cuppens, Costas Lambrinoudakis, Christos Kalloniatis, John Mylopoulos, Annie Anton, Stefanos Gritzalis, Weizhi Meng, and Steven Furnell, editors, *Computer Security*, pages 19–33, Cham: Springer International Publishing, 2020.

[16] Georgios Kavallieratos and Sokratis Katsikas. Managing cyber security risks of the cyber-enabled ship. *Journal of Marine Science and Engineering*, 8(10):768, 2020.

[17] Georgios Kavallieratos, Georgios Spathoulas, and Sokratis Katsikas. Cyber risk propagation and optimal selection of cybersecurity controls for complex cyberphysical systems. *Sensors*, 21(5), 2021.

[18] Georgios Kavallieratos, Sokratis Katsikas, and Vasileios Gkioulos. Cyber-attacks against the autonomous ship. In Sokratis K. Katsikas, Frederic Cuppens, Nora Cuppens, Costas Lambrinoudakis, Annie Anton, Stefanos Gritzalis, John Mylopoulos, and Christos Kalloniatis, editors, *Computer Security*, pages 20–36, Cham: Springer International Publishing, 2019.

[19] Imran Ashraf, Yongwan Park, Soojung Hur, Sung Won Kim, Roobaea Alroobaea, Yousaf Bin Zikria, and Summera Nosheen. A survey on cyber security threats in IOT-enabled maritime industry. *IEEE Transactions on Intelligent Transportation Systems*, 24(2):2677–2690, https://doi.org/10.1109/TITS.2022.3164678, 2023.

[20] C Park, W Shi, W Zhang, C Kontovas, and CH Chang. Cybersecurity in the maritime industry: A literature review. In *20th Commemorative Annual General Assembly, AGA 2019-Proceedings of the International Association of Maritime Universities Conference*, IAMUC 2019, pages 79–86, 2019.

[21] Mohamed Amine Ben Farah, Elochukwu Ukwandu, Hanan Hindy, David Brosset, Miroslav Bures, Ivan Andonovic, and Xavier Bellekens. Cyber security in the maritime industry: a systematic survey of recent advances and future trends. *Information*, 13(1):22, 2022.

[22] P.H. Meland, K. Bernsmed, E. Wille, Ø.J. Rødseth, and D.A. Nesheim. A retrospective analysis of maritime cyber security incidents. *TransNav, the International Journal on Marine Navigation and Safety of Sea Transportation*, 15(3):519–530, 2021.

[23] Victor Bolbot, Ketki Kulkarni, P¨aivi Brunou, Osiris Valdez Banda, and Mashrura Musharraf. Developments and research directions in maritime cybersecurity: A systematic literature review and bibliometric analysis. *International Journal of Critical Infrastructure Protection*, 100571, 2022.

[24] Igor Nai-Fovino, Ricardo Neisse, Jose Hernandez-Ramos, Nineta Polemi, Gian-Luigi Ruzzante, Malgorzata Figwer, and Alessandro Lazari. A proposal for a European cybersecurity taxonomy (Tech. Rep. No. EUR 29868 EN). Luxembourg: Publications Office of the European Union. https://doi.org/10.2760/106002, 2019.

[25] Georgios Kavallieratos, Sokratis Katsikas, and Vasileios Gkioulos. Modelling shipping 4.0: A reference architecture for the cyber-enabled ship. In Ngoc Thanh Nguyen, Kietikul Jearanaitanakij, Ali Selamat, Bogdan Trawinski, and Suphamit Chittayasothorn, editors, *Intelligent Information and Database Systems*, pages 202–217, Cham: Springer International Publishing, 2020.

[26] Aybars Oruc, Vasileios Gkioulos, and Sokratis K. Katsikas. Towards a cyber-physical range for the integrated navigation system. *Journal of Marine Science and Engineering*, 10(107), 2022.

[27] Marco Balduzzi, Alessandro Pasta, and Kyle Wilhoit. A security evaluation of ais automated identification system. In *Proceedings of the 30th Annual Computer Security Applications Conference*, pages 436–445, 2014.

[28] Michelle Wiese Bockmann. Seized UK tanker likely 'spoofed' by Iran. https://lloydslist.maritimeintelligence.informa.com/LL1128820/ Seized- UK-tanker-likely-spoofed-by-Iran.

[29] Colin Zwirko. North Korean vessels exploiting tracking system flaws to evade sanctions: report. www.nknews.org/2019/06/north-korean-vessels-exploiting-tracking-system-flaws-to-evade-sanctions- report/.

[30] Andrej Androjna, Marko Perkovič, Ivica Pavic, and Jakša Mišković. Ais data vulnerability indicated by a spoofing case-study. *Applied Sciences*, 11(11):5015, 2021.

[31] Syed Khandker, Hannu Turtiainen, Andrei Costin, and Timo Hämäläinen. Cybersecurity attacks on software logic and error handling within ais implementations: A systematic testing of resilience. *IEEE Access*, 10:29493–29505, 2022.

[32] Sam Chambers. US warns merchant shipping of Iranian GPS spoofing threat. https://splash247.com/us-warns-merchant-shipping-of-iranian-gps-spoofing-threat/.

[33] Walmor Cristino Leite Junior, Claudio Coreixas de Moraes, Carlos EP de Albuquerque, Raphael Carlos Santos Machado, and Alan Oliveira de Sá. A triggering mechanism for cyber-attacks in naval sensors and systems. *Sensors*, 21(9):3195, 2021.

[34] American Journal of Transportation. Cyber penetration tests underscore maritime industry's nightmare security scenario. www.ajot.com/news/cyber-penetration-tests-underscore-maritime-industrys-nightmare-security-sc.

[35] Odd Sveinung Hareide, Øyvind Jøsok, Mass Soldal Lund, Runar Ostnes, and Kirsi Helkala. Enhancing navigator competence by demonstrating maritime cyber security. *The Journal of Navigation*, 71(5):1025–1039, 2018.

[36] Mass Soldal Lund, Odd Sveinung Hareide, and Øyvind Jøsok. An attack on an integrated navigation system. *Necesse*, 3:149–163, 2018.

[37] Mark L Psiaki, Todd E Humphreys, and Brian Stauffer. Attackers can spoof navigation signals without our knowledge. Here's how to fight back gps lies. *IEEE Spectrum*, 53(8):26–53, 2016.

[38] B Brewin. University of Texas team hijacks 80 million yacht with cheap GPS spoofing gear. Accessed: Oct. 10, 2021. [Online]. Available: https://www.nextgov.com/cio-briefing/2013/07/universitytexas-team-hija%cks-80-million-yacht-cheap-gps-spoofing-gear/67625, 2013.

[39] Avanthika Vineetha Harish, Kimberly Tam, and Kevin Jones. Investigating the security and accessibility of voyage data recorder data using a USB attack. 2022.

[40] Brien Croteau, Ryan Robucci, Chintan Patel, Nilanjan Banerjee, Kiriakos Kiriakidis, Tracie Severson, and Erick Rodriguez-Seda. Alternative actuation paths for ship applications in the presence of cyber-attacks. In *2019 Resilience Week (RWS)*, volume 1, pages 91–97. IEEE, 2019.

[41] Sam Chambers. Malware on the off-shore rig: Danger lurks where the chips fail. www.houstonchronicle.com/business/energy/article/Malware-on-the-offshore-rig-Danger-lurks-where-4470723.php.

[42] Hansdeep Singh. Cyber security in maritime industry the exposures, risks, preventions and legal scenario. Master's thesis, University of Oslo, Oslo, 2019.

[43] The Maritime Executive. Iran's offshore platforms become target of recent cyber attacks. www.maritime-executive.com/article/iran-s-offshore-platforms-become-target-of-recent-cyber-attacks.

[44] Luke Graham. Shipping industry vulnerable to cyber attacks and GPS jamming. www.cnbc.com/2017/02/01/shipping-industry-vulnerable-to-cyber-attacks-and-gps-jamming.html.

[45] Jonathan Saul. Cyber threats prompt return of radio for ship navigation. www.reuters.com/article/us-shipping-gps-cyber/cyber-threats-prompt-return-of-radio-for-ship-navigation-idUSKBN1AN0HT.

[46] Tanya Blake. Hackers took 'full control' of container ship's navigation systems for 10 hours. https://rntfnd.org/2017/11/25/hackers-took-full-control-of-container-ships-navigation-systems-for-10-hours-ihs-fairplay/.

[47] Aybars Oruc. Claims of state-sponsored cyberattack in the maritime industry. In *Proceedings, 15th International Naval Engineering Conference and Exhibition*. INEC, 2020.

[48] David Hambling. Ships fooled in GPS spoofing attack suggest Russian cyberweapon. www.newscientist.com/article/2143499-ships-fooled-in-gps-spoofing-attack-suggest-russian-cyberweapon/.

[49] Dana Goward. Mass GPS Spoofing Attack in Black Sea? www.maritime-executive.com/editorials/mass-gps-spoofing- attack-in-black-sea.

[50] Aybars Oruc, *Claims of State-Sponsored Cyberattack in the Maritime Industry*. Institute of Marine Engineering, Science and Technology, 2020.

[51] Tu"rkiye GPS Jammer ile Yunan Araştırma Gemilerini Engelliyor Mu? www.denizcilikbilgileri.com/turkiye-gps-jammer-ile-yunan-arastirma-gemilerini-engelliyor-mu/.

[52] Robert Lemos. Coast guard warns shipping firms of maritime cyberattacks. www.darkreading.com/vulnerabilities-threats/coast- guard-warns-shipping-firms-of-maritime-cyberattacks.

[53] Nasjonal sikkerhetsmyndighet (NSM). Risiko 2020. Technical report, Nasjonal sikkerhetsmyndighet (NSM), 2020.

[54] Chris Simmons, Charles Ellis, Sajjan Shiva, Dipankar Dasgupta, and Qishi Wu. Avoidit: A cyber attack taxonomy. Technical Report CS 09-003, University of Memphis, 2009.

[55] John D Howard and Thomas A Longstaff. A common language for computer security incidents. Technical report, Sandia National Lab. (SNL-NM), Albuquerque, NM (United States); Sandia, 1998.

[56] Tanya Blake. Hackers took 'full control' of container ship's navigation systems for 10 hours. www.asket.co.uk/post/2017/11/26/hackers-took-full-control-of-container-ships-navigation-systems-for-10-hours-aske-toperati.

[57] Federal Office for Information Security. It-grundschutz-catalogues:13th version. 2013.

[58] Joint Task Force. Security and privacy controls for federal infor- mation systems and organizations. *NIST Special Publication*, 800-53, Revision 5, 2020.

[59] Joint Task Force. Control baselines for information systems and organiza- tions. *NIST Special Publication*, 800-53B, 2020.

[60] Keith Stouffer, Victoria Pillitteri, Abrams Marshall, and Adam Hahn. Guide to industrial control systems (ics) security. *NIST Special Publication*, 800(82):247, 2015.

[61] Georgios Spathoulas, Georgios Kavallieratos, Sokratis Katsikas, and Alessio Baiocco. Attack path analysis and cost-efficient selection of cyber-security controls for complex cyberphysical systems. In *European Symposium on Research in Computer Security*, pages 74–90. Springer, 2021.

7

Cyberwarfare in Ukraine

Incidents, Tools and Methods

THEODOROS KOMNINOS AND DIMITRIOS SERPANOS

7.1 Introduction

The current war in Ukraine, which started in February 2022, is a hybrid conflict. Although most of the news in the media—traditional and social—have been focusing on aspects of the physical war, there have been several reports of cyberwarfare incidents. Cyberoperations have targeted critical infrastructure with goals ranging from destruction and disruption of services to data theft. Disinformation and misinformation campaigns have also developed. Clearly, cyberwarfare is a significant part of the ongoing war. Analogous safety and cybersecurity incidents in the geographic area of the war have been occurring for a long time, demonstrating the geopolitical problems and indicating that the cyberwar started long ago, before the physical one.

This cyber part of the current conflict affects multi-location parties in addition to the actual opponents, such as NATO countries and allies. The effects of cyberwarfare were emphatically proved by the announcements of CISA (Cybersecurity & Infrastructure Security Agency) for Common Vulnerabilities and Exposures (CVE) [1]. There has been a 35% increase in CVEs for Q1 and 30% for Q2 of 2022. Additionally, the indicators of compromise (IoC) that the Open Threat Intelligence Community of AlienVault has released as of September 9, 2022 indicate that there were about 322 attacks targeting Ukraine and 246 against Russia [2].

DOI: 10.1201/9781003314721-7

7.2 Actors Involved in Cyberwar and Tools Used

In cyberwar, one expects that the main actors are countries and nations. They are the main participating entities and have significant cyber-resources, typically. However, the current war has revealed other involved actors, as well. Hacking groups (Electrum/Sandworm, APT28/29, Red October, Conti, Anonymous, and others), hacktivists, cybercriminals and individuals, and sympathizers of each side, have been involved in reported incidents.

Some well-known hacking groups (advanced persistent threat [APT] groups) have a predefined arsenal of tools used, including the following.

- APT28 uses Koadic, Mimikatz, Net, Responder, Tor, USBStealer, Zebrocy.
- APT29 uses Mimikatz, Net, Cobalt Strike, PsExec, CosmicDuke, FatDuke, GeminiDuke, PowerDuke, SeaDuke.
- SUNBURST Sandworm team engages Mimikatz, Net, PsExec, BlackEnergy, Industroyer, NotPetya, KillDesk.
- Wizard Spider team deploys Mimikatz, Net, Cobalt Strike, PsExec, Empire, Bazar, Conti, Dyre, Emotet, GrimAgent, Ryuk, TrickBot.
- Dragonfly 2.0 team is attacking usually with Net, PsExec, Reg, CrackMapExec, Impacket.

The listed APT groups employ a range of malware and software tools in their cyberattacks, including both commercial and open-source software as well as specially created programs with malicious intent. In MITRE ATT&CK site [3] there are 680 different software, malware, backdoors, and other tools that are used by attacking groups. Following is a short description of some of them.

Mimikatz is an open-source program that allows users to read and store authentication credentials such as Kerberos tickets. The toolset is compatible with the most recent version of Microsoft Windows operating system (OS) and comes with a variety of network attacks to assist identification of vulnerabilities. Mimikatz is frequently used by attackers to steal passwords and elevate privileges because endpoint security software and anti-virus programs frequently fail to identify or remove the attack.

Pen testers, on the other hand, employ Mimikatz to find and take advantage of vulnerabilities in your networks so you can patch them. Attackers commonly use Mimikatz to steal credentials and escalate privileges because in most cases, endpoint protection software and antivirus systems will not detect or delete the attack. Conversely, pen testers use Mimikatz to detect and exploit vulnerabilities in your networks so you can fix them.

Net is part of Windows OS and it is used for the control of users, groups, services, and network connections. It is used by adversaries for acquiring network and system information navigating SMB/Windows administrator shares laterally via net use commands, and communicating with services.

Cobalt Strike is an adversary simulation tool created to simulate targeted attacks and advanced threat actors' post-exploitation behaviors. In addition to its own capabilities, Cobalt Strike leverages the capabilities of other well-known tools such as Metasploit and Mimikatz.

Koadic is a Windows post-exploitation framework and penetration testing tool that is publicly available on GitHub. Koadic has several options for staging payloads and creating implants, and performs most of its operations using Windows Script Host.

PsExec is a free Microsoft tool that can be used to execute a program on another computer. It is used by information technology (IT) administrators and attackers.

Empire is an open-source, cross-platform remote administration and post-exploitation framework that is publicly available on GitHub. While the tool itself is primarily written in Python, the post-exploitation agents are written in pure PowerShell for Windows and Python for Linux/Mac OS. Empire was one of five tools singled out by a joint report on public hacking tools being widely used by adversaries.

Responder is an open-source tool used for LLMNR, NBT-NS and MDNS poisoning, with built-in HTTP/SMB/MSSQL/ FTP/LDAP rogue authentication server supporting NTLMv1, NTLMv2, LMv2, extended security NTLMSSP, and basic HTTP authentication.

Impacket is an open-source collection of modules written in Python for programmatically constructing and manipulating network protocols. It contains several tools for remote service execution, Kerberos manipulation, Windows credential dumping, packet sniffing, and relay attacks.

BlackEnergy is a malware toolkit that has been used by both criminals and APT actors. It dates back to at least 2007 and was originally designed to create botnets for use in conducting distributed denial of service (DDoS) attacks, but its use has evolved to support various plug-ins. It is well known for being used during the confrontation between Georgia and Russia in 2008, as well as in targeting Ukrainian institutions. Variants include BlackEnergy 2 and BlackEnergy 3.

Industroyer is a sophisticated malware framework that was used in the attacks on the Ukrainian power system in December 2016. It is intended to interfere with industrial control systems (ICSs) and specifically electrical substation components. This is the first publicly documented malware that was created with the intent of affecting and targeting electric grid operations.

NotPetya virus was employed by Sandworm Team in a global assault that began on June 27, 2017. Although NotPetya looks to be a type of ransomware, the attackers never meant to make the encrypted data recoverable. Instead, their major goal was to delete data and disk structures on infected devices. As a result, NotPetya might be better described as a type of wiper malware. NotPetya uses the SMBv1 exploits EternalBlue and EternalRomance to spread across a computer network utilizing worm-like characteristics.

USBStealer is malware that has been used by APT28 since at least 2005 to extract information from air-gapped networks. It does not have the capability to communicate over the internet and has been used in conjunction with ADVSTORESHELL.

Bazar is a downloader and backdoor that has been used since at least April 2020, with infections primarily against professional services, healthcare, manufacturing, IT, logistics, and travel companies across the United States and Europe. According to reports, Bazar is connected to TrickBot campaigns and can be used to spread further software, such as ransomware, as well as to steal personal information.

Conti is the first ransomware-as-a-service (RaaS), identified in December 2019. TrickBot has been used to deploy Conti against significant businesses and governmental organizations. Actors employing the Conti ransomware family, like those using other ransomware families, steal private files and information from infected networks and threaten to make this material public unless a ransom is paid.

Emotet is a modular malware variant which is primarily used as a downloader for other malware variants such as TrickBot and IcedID. Emotet first appeared in June 2014 and has been primarily used to target the banking sector.

Ryuk is a ransomware designed to target enterprise environments that has been used in attacks since at least 2018. Ryuk shares code similarities with Hermes ransomware.

TrickBot is a Trojan spyware program written in C++ that first emerged in September 2016 as a possible successor to Dyre. As part of "big game hunting" ransomware efforts, Wizard Spider created and first employed TrickBot to target financial websites in North America, Australia, and all of Europe. Since then, it has been utilized against all industries globally.

Zebrocy is a Trojan that has been used by APT28 since at least November 2015. The malware comes in several programming language variants, including C++, Delphi, AutoIt, C#, VB.NET, and Golang.

CosmicDuke is malware that was used by APT29 from 2010–2015.

FatDuke is a backdoor used by APT29 since at least 2016.

GeminiDuke is malware that was used by APT29 from 2009–2012.

PowerDuke is a backdoor that was used by APT29 in 2016. It has primarily been delivered through Microsoft Word or Excel attachments containing malicious macros.

SeaDuke is malware that was used by APT29 from 2014–2015. It was used primarily as a secondary backdoor for victims that were already compromised with CozyCar.

GrimAgent is a backdoor that has been used before the deployment of Ryuk ransomware since at least 2020; it is likely used by FIN6 and Wizard Spider.

CrackMapExec (CME) is a post-exploitation tool developed in Python and designed for penetration testing against networks. CrackMapExec collects active directory information to conduct lateral movement through targeted networks.

All available infrastructures—including the internet, cloud, and web services—are being weaponized by the actors, who use their expertise and resources accordingly. TikTok, for example, is exploited by sympathizers to distribute pro-war [4] or anti-war [5] videos, depending on their side. Software providers distribute targeted malware in an effort to sabotage and disrupt services of the enemy of their preferred side. It becomes clear that, in general, all digital infrastructures and services can be weaponized, from networks and power grids to supply chains and social media.

Besides the organized and usually state-backed groups, there are pro-Ukrainian and pro-Russian volunteers who support attacking their opponents in this cyberwar. Such a case is the open call made on Twitter by Mykhailo Fedorov, Ukraine's vice prime minister and minister for digital transformation, "for digital talents and tasks for everyone" [4]. There is a group in the chat app Telegram called "IT Army of Ukraine" for which about 300,000 people have signed up and are assigned tasks designed—among other things—to disrupt Russian internet services.

There are also stories about citizens of Ukraine with expertise in IT that help the military with their knowledge. One such story [5] is that of Nikita Knysh who formed a volunteer team of developers called Hackyourmom and began retaliation. It is rumored that he and Fedorov, the tech entrepreneur and head of Ukraine's digital ministry, are the men behind the Elon Musk's Starlink deployment in Ukraine. Understanding that Musk wanted to demonstrate Starlink's capabilities, Fedorov tweeted him publicly pleading for assistance. Musk responded by sending several hundred Starlink terminals to Poland, from where the Ukrainian digital ministry installed them in hospitals, governmental buildings, train stations, and other crucial infrastructure [6]. Although Starlink have a range of 90 meters from the satellite antenna, when they are are spread in an area, they form a distributed mesh network—making it difficult to jam or destroy the link.

Using Starlink, they hacked thousands of security and traffic cameras in the occupied parts of Ukraine and in Belarus, filtering out military moves using machine learning algorithms and informing the Ukrainian armed forces about troop locations and movements. They used a mix of online collaboration and rapid development done on GitHub and Signal to solve problems and develop solutions. Currently, pro-Ukraine hackers, opportunistic criminal organizations, and—as some security researchers fear—government-backed entities from Western countries are pursuing Russia in cyberspace.

Malware, known or emerging, has been extensively used up to now for targeting all types of systems, from web servers to cyber–physical systems in the field. As infrastructures are increasingly weaponized, sophisticated attacks combine botnets, DDoS, hijacking, jamming, misinformation, etc. The goals of these increasingly sophisticated attacks include not only intelligence acquisition for field operations but diplomatic espionage as well. Importantly, the scope and effect of these attacks becomes global at an unprecedented rate, making the need for mitigation a worldwide concern.

On the other hand, Russia is still enlisting its own cyberforces. A new organization known as "Cyber Spetsnaz" has been discovered as a result of recruiting efforts made by a group known as the "Killnet Collective." The first sub-unit, "Zarya," was identified in April 2022. Phoenix, Vera, FasoninnGung, Miri, Jacky, DDoS Gung, and Sakura Jima are a few other well-known sub-units. Another new sub-unit named "Sparta" was discovered on June 2. The power of these units is unknown. The group's declared goal is to attack the North Atlantic Treaty Organization (NATO). Their cyberattacks have thus far mostly targeted short-term disruptions and poorly designed WEB servers, rather than NATO installations or organizations.

When the conflict in Ukraine first broke out, the group Conti declared its support for the Russian invasion, only to face opposition from many of its own members, who are also Ukrainians. The group's internal conversations—as well as other technical information, including scripts, configurations, and ransomware source code—were soon leaked by a user with the twitter name "contileaks." Ironically, a group going by the name of Network Battalion 65 (NB65) began attacking Russian businesses with ransomware code derived from Conti.

The increasing sophistication of cyberattacks in the Ukrainian conflict reveals a worldwide need to take measures to avoid the weaknesses, vulnerabilities, and exploitations in computing systems and networks, as well as to analyze and evaluate methods and tools for cyberwarfare operations. This need places a high priority considering the increasing digitization of services worldwide, which is based on increasing connectivity, wider availability of technology, emerging service access, smart governance, and integration of digital critical infrastructures in the emerging smart cities. Importantly, in this emerging digital environment, conflicts are increasing at several fronts—such as cultural, economic, trade, and industrial—independently of the existence of physical military conflict.

7.3 Incident Timeline, Technologies, and Tools Used

Cyberattacks in the region started well before the current war. Operation Gamaredon in 2013 against the Ukrainian government and its military and law enforcement officials was an attempt to steal information. Since 2008, the Snake (or Uroboros) cyberespionage campaign has compromised government and diplomatic networks, mostly in Europe, employing spear-phishing emails and watering hole attacks. In 2017, the Snake group was linked to a backdoor installed at Germany's Federal Foreign Office network for data stealing and in 2019 to attacks against military, defense contractors, and government agencies worldwide.

The first known cyberattack on a power grid took place on December 23, 2015, when the Ukrainian power grid was successfully attacked, leading to power disruptions for a large number of citizens and for several hours. The attack exploited the BlackEnergy Trojan malware infecting ICSs, mainly SCADA, of three Ukrainian power operators (providers to the Kyiv, Ivano-Frankivsk, and Chernivtsi regions). More specifically, the attack inserted the BlackEnergy and KillDisk malware on systems after spear-phishing emails. With the attack, ICSs were hijacked and controlled remotely, systems were disabled (uninterruptable power supplies [UPS], modems) and files were erased; during these activities, a denial of service (DoS) attack on call centers disconnected consumers from credible updates. The results of the attack had an impact on 50 substations and led to power interruptions for almost 230,000 consumers lasting 1–6 hours, 135 megawatts (MW) of load impact, and damages to hundreds of servers, workstations, and field devices; the damage required several months for full repairs.

The BlackEnergy Trojan used an unknown SSH backdoor to deliver a new version of KillDisk that—in addition to destroying some 4,000 different file types and rendering machines unbootable—accepts a command line argument to set a specific time delay when the destructive payload should activate. It also deletes Windows event logs: application, security, setup, system. Security analysts revealed that the BlackEnergy config file has a unique text string variable named build_id that is used to identify different infection campaigns and targets. One of the most intriguing characteristics of the damaging BlackEnergy variant employed in the attacks is that the virus tries to halt and eliminate a service called "sec service." This service, which is a part of Eltima's "Serial to Ethernet Connector" driver, enables network connections to remote serial ports. This depicts that the hackers had adequate knowledge of SCADA systems used and particularly developed the virus to target them. RTU (remote terminal unit or remote telemetry unit) communications that were used in these SCADA architectures were utilize by Sandworm group to communicate remotely with control systems and track device failure [7].

A year later, on December 17, 2016, a second attack occurred against ICSs, exploiting the Industroyer malware, which disrupted power services in Kyiv for approximately an hour. The use of four payload components by Industroyer—which are intended to take direct control of switches and circuit breakers at an electrical distribution substation—distinguishes it from other malware that targets infrastructure. The main components found in Industroyer are: a main backdoor; a secondary backdoor, camouflaged as the Notepad application in Windows designed to connect back to control servers if the main backdoor is revealed and disabled; a wiping module, dedicated to erase critical files and registry keys to make system unbootable; and a command and control module that receives commands and reports back to attackers. Industroyer malware is highly customizable and designed to target the following communication protocols: IEC 60870–5–101, IEC 60870–5–104, IEC 61850, and OLE for Process Control Data Access (OPC DA) [8]. The damage had an outage with average duration of 1.25 hours and 200 MW of load impact.

In an apparent retaliation effort in May 2016, two Ukrainian operations—namely "Groundbait" and "May 9"—targeted several sites, including Russian sites of anti-Ukrainian propaganda, sites of the separatist group "Donetsk People's Republic," and resources of Russian private military companies.

In October 2016, the Surkov Leaks revealed 2,337 emails from the period between September 2013 and December 2014, with hundreds of attachments, which include Russian plans for seizing Crimea and promoting separatist unrest in the region of Donbas in eastern Ukraine.

The NotPetya ransomware was used in June 2017 for a massive supply chain attack which compromised successfully Ukrainian critical infrastructure and commercial systems. NotPetya spread worldwide quickly, infecting systems worldwide and leading to billions of dollars in damages. NotPetya was characterized as "the most destructive and costly cyberattack in history" by the White House [9].

As time progressed and the war was approaching, cyberattacks increased. A selective list of incidents is provided in what follows, demonstrating the plurality of events, targets, and methods used. As the conflict is still ongoing, related information is clearly limited and requires further confirmation. The event list that we provide is definitely incomplete, and several aspects require deeper analysis. However, the list includes events that have been publicized by credible sources or documented in reports, such as by the UK-based Centre for Strategic Cyberspace + International Studies (CSCIS) [10].

During a three-day period of January 2022, from January 14–16, Ukrainian government websites were attacked, hijacked, and filled with threatening messages. Data were erased at several Ukrainian agencies on January 18 by an attack that exploited an SQL elevation-of-privilege vulnerability which inserted "wiper" malware in Ukrainian servers several days before the attack. In the meantime, Microsoft's Threat Intelligence Center (MSTIC) disclosed detection of "destructive cyberattacks directed against Ukraine's digital infrastructure" in an online article that was released on January 15 [11].

On February 15 and February 23, 2022, DDoS attacks occurred against various Ukrainian targets, including government, military, telecommunications, and financial. During the February 23 attacks, a new malware, named HermeticWiper, was uncovered; it had been inserted with various methods, including spreading by a worm.

On February 24, an attack on Viasat's KA-SAT network disrupted its broadband services in the Ukraine and elsewhere in Europe. At that time, the Russian National Computer Incident Response and Coordination Center was issuing warnings to owners of critical infrastructure for increased threats on Russian IT systems. Outages of Russian government websites were reported at the time.

Ukraine announced on February 26 that it established an "IT Army" in order to wage cyberwarfare against Russia, listing 31 websites of Russian business and state organizations as the first targets.

On March 2, the Russian government announced lists of internet protocol (IP) addresses and domains that were involved in attacks against Russian targets, including at least 17,500 IP addresses and 175 domains. The same day, Microsoft was warning about continuing HermeticWiper attacks in Ukraine.

A Russian Space Institute's website was successfully attacked on March 3, leaking stolen information.

On March 5, the known group Anonymous claimed that it had launched successful attacks against the website of the Russian intelligence agency Federal Security Service (FSB), and on March 7 against Russian streaming services (Wink and Ivi) and live TV channels (Russia 24, Channel One, and Moscow 24) broadcasting war videos from Ukraine.

On March 8, the hacktivist group International Legion Information Technology Battalion 300 (ILIT300), claimed a "phone bombing" attack exploiting software developed by Ukrainian hacktivists. The attack targeted Russian citizens in order to alert them and motivate them to express objections to the ongoing war.

On March 9, Cisco's Talos Group announced an attack by cybercriminals against Ukrainian sympathizers. The attackers advertised offensive cybertools (malware, DDoS software) against Russian entities, but the downloaded software infected user systems, stealing personal information.

On March 10, a file wiper malware named RURansom was revealed, which targets Russian systems.

On March 18, RIAEvangelist, developer and maintainer of the popular open-source software node-ipc, was criticized for customizing the software to disrupt users in Russia and Belarus. Specifically, in a first version of the customization, code was added to the tool in order to erase data on computers that used node-ipc (an inter-process communication open-source server environment), and in a second version, it added peace messages on desktops.

Ukrtelecom, Ukraine's largest terrestrial broadband provider was attacked on March 28, resulting to nationwide connectivity disruptions for several hours.

On April 8, a regional Ukrainian energy operator suffered a cyber-attack which employed the Industroyer2 malware and targeted high-voltage electrical substations. While Industroyer2 and its predecessor are similar, the new version has more specific capabilities. The new variant solely implements the IEC 60870–5–104 (IEC-104) communications protocol, as opposed to the original version, which used additional modules to support four distinct OT protocols. IEC-104 is mostly used in Europe and the Middle East for power system monitoring and control through TCP. The new malware type gives the attacker the ability to implant specific configurations that change the malware's response to particular intelligent electronic devices (IEDs) such as protection relays, merging units, etc., in the targeted environment. More technical information about the new variant can be found in Mandiant's threat intelligence report [12].

In addition to the directly involved countries, Russia and Ukraine, additional countries became targets for related political purposes. On March 7, phishing attacks that originated from Belarus targeted the Polish military. On April 12, as Ukrainian President Volodymyr Zelenskyy delivered a speech at Finland's Parliament, Finnish government websites suffered a DoS attack.

Reports depict a May 2022 Gamaredon campaign spreading documents that have a relation with humanitarian assistance for refuges, targeting Latvia. [13]

The SolarWinds cyberespionage actors (APT29) introduced two malware families in 2022 and sought to evade detection by retooling and abusing Atlassian's Trello service. They have also launched new phishing campaigns against European, U.S., and Asian diplomats.

During this campaign, APT29 delivered spear-phishing emails posing as embassy administration updates in order to penetrate a target environment. The authentic—but hacked—email addresses in these phishing emails came from different diplomatic organizations. The malicious HTML dropper (ROOTSAW) that was used in these phishing emails uses HTML smuggling to deliver an IMG or ISO file to a victim computer. Two more files, a malicious dynamic link library (DLL) and a Windows shortcut (LNK) file, are included in the picture file.

The "Target" command will run normally if the user clicks the LNK file. By tricking the victim into opening the LNK file, the malicious DLL is unintentionally launched. Files contained within image files, such as mounted ISO files, would not have the Zone.Identifier alternate data stream (ADS) flag that indicates that the files were an internet download (also known as the "mark of the web"). This stops a warning message from appearing on the Windows operating system when files are opened from ISO or IMG image files, resulting in delivery and execution of the BEATDROP, a downloader written in C that makes use of Trello for command and control on system, BOOMMIC (or VaporRage) shellcode downloader that communicates over HTTPS, ROOTSAW (EnvyScout) for encoding/decoding ISO/IMG file and BEACON which is a backdoor part of Cobalt Strike. More technical reading can be found in Mandiant report [14].

Attacks and ransomware incidents have been reported on governmental services by countries that impose sanctions on Russia targeting ICSs (PIPEDREAM malware, by CHERNOVITE threat group [15]) and systems in wind power companies (Nordex experienced ransomware attacks by Conti and Deutsche Windtechnik in Germany by Black Basta [16]), liquid natural gas (LNG) facilities, gas pipeline organizations (Colonial Pipeline, TGS Latin America, by ALPAV/BlackCat ransomware group [17]), energy market companies, etc.

Pro-Russian ransomware actors and hacktivists have continued disruptive activity that includes declaring "war" on whole countries.

The following DDoS attacks against European countries have been blamed on the pro-Russian hacker collective Killnet.

On May 7, 2022, the German Minstry of Defence, the Bundestag (federal parliament), and the federal police suffered a DDoS cyberattack [18].

On May 10 and 14, Killnet launched a DDoS attack against the Eurovision Song Contest, delaying the voting procedure for 13 minutes [19].

On May 11 and 12, Killnet attacked the websites of Italy's senate, military, and National Institute of Health [20]. The same group targeted Lithuanian state institutions and businesses on June 29, 2022. A Norwegian public administration portal, the corporate page of a Norwegian online banking identification service, and the Norwegian Labor Inspection Authority were among the affected sites with a DDoS attack of Killnet group on June 30 [21]. The same group on August 17 targeted more than 200 state and private Estonian institutions including the Estonian Tax and Customs Board, which became unavailable for 10 minutes [22]. The DDoS attack was the most extensive cyberattack since 2007, but Estonia has now the fourth strongest cyberdefense infrastructure in the world, behind the United States, UK, and Saudi Arabia, according to the Global Cybersecurity Index [23].

Pro-Ukrainian hackers continue to cause destruction on Russian computer networks.

The Russian video platform RuTube was disrupted, Russian radio stations were hacked to broadcast Ukrainian music, and DDoS assaults or data breaches against targets like Russian media websites, Russian law firms, Russian Railway employees, and Belarussian ministries were credited to them.

On June 17, the St. Petersburg International Economic Forum suffered a DoS cyberattack against its accreditation system, forcing Russian President Vladimir Putin to delay a scheduled address by one hour [24].

On August 20, it is rumored that Ukrainian hackers hacked the television in Russian-occupied Crimea, broadcasting instead an address by Zelenskyy [25].

On August 30, hackers attacked the online broadcasting of the radio station Radio Crimea and "State Anthem of Ukraine" was broadcasted [26].

On September 2, hackers directed Yandex Taxi cabs in Moscow to go to the same location by breaching the company's app, generating a three-hours traffic jam [27].

Lately, it is said that they revealed a remote Russian base near Melitopol using fake profiles of attractive women on Facebook and Russian social media, tricking soldiers to send back photos, which then they located by photos' geolocation properties [28]. They also used their expertise to hack smart TVs, television satellites, and broadcasters and social media accounts, then sending photos of victims and anti-war messages to Russian citizens on Victory Day [29].

7.4 Mitigation Response

The more targeted industries by now are the financial services; utilities; power producers and distributors; retail and supply chains; television, news, internet, and social media sites; federal, state, and local governments; and education. In order to deal with possible attacks on computer systems in countries involved in the Russia–Ukraine cyberwarfare, taking the following proactive measures is recommended.

- Review and update incident response plans, business continuity plans, playbooks, escalation lists, and contact information.
- Patch systems and application software, as threat actors usually take advantage of software vulnerabilities.
- Audit event logs for domain controllers.
- Stay alerted for Cobalt Strike and webshells, as they are used for lateral movement and persistence.
- Isolate backups from internet and network connections (offline backup storage) and test backups frequently.
- Be ready for incident handling by testing readiness of incident response (IR) groups and continuity of business continuity plans.
- Implement network segmentation between users and servers and IT networks from those of OT networks.
- Audit event logs of service and administrator accounts with no interactive login rights.

- Enforce strong password rules.
- Install anomaly detection systems.
- Disable *all* non-essential ports and protocols.
- Ensure that all access to the organization's network (including remote, privileged, and administrative) uses multi-factor authentication.
- Have a second look at ingress traffic from rival countries (both sides).
- Refer to CISA, Talos, and AlienVault Known Exploited Vulnerabilities catalog for alerts and IoCs.
- Update IoCs in firewalls, intrusion prevention systems (IPS) and intrusion detection systems (IDS).
- Hunt indications from known APTs (sophisticated long-term malicious attacks that are spying on the target infrastructure for months or years before a break in the network appears) and tactics, techniques, and procedures (TTPs) adversaries use to attack.
- Educate/train network users on security awareness—especially about phishing, best practices for password setting, and updating of software.

7.5 Discussion and Conclusions

The world is picking sides in a global cyberwar alongside numerous cybercriminal gangs and dispersed hacktivist groups. The most powerful groups in cyberspace have unleashed their capacities along ideological, ethical, and geopolitical lines in response to the Ukraine–Russia conflict. There has never been a larger risk of a major catastrophe as a result of the rise in offensive cyberactivity, particularly the possibility of cyber–physical strikes on vital infrastructure. Future cybersecurity risks, due to the Ukraine war, are increasing significantly, as available information indicates. Indicators of compromise (IoC), for example, are growing. AlienVault's database, when searched with the keyword "Ukraine," results in almost 7,000 involved domain names, 340 URLs, 78 Hostnames, 33 files and file hashes, 28 IPv4 addresses, 12 email addresses, and 7 CVEs [30].

The cyberconflict in Ukraine, which had already been going on for a long time before the physical war, has strongly influenced cybersecurity technology, management, and processes. Incidents like the first successful attack on a power grid, the high-velocity spread of NotPetya, the evolution of related industrial control systems (ICS)-targeting malware, and weaponizing open software have exposed new attack vectors and demonstrated the feasibility and effectiveness of such attacks. Importantly, many threats against critical infrastructure, mobile devices and the cloud, news and social media, and supply chains have been combined or exploited in coordination, leading to effective attacks. The Ukrainian war shows once again that many technological advances are made and exploited during conflict.

As digitization across all domains progresses rapidly and decision-making at all levels becomes heavily dependent on automated data collection, the safety of government, civilian, and military operations depends heavily on secure systems and services at all levels, including information technology (IT) and operational technology (OT) technologies. The emerging cybersecurity technologies, for both attacks and defenses, as well as the incidents themselves, are critical to the progress of conflicts, as well as for political and military evaluations in the wider area and worldwide. Analogous cyberattacks appeared, for example, in Georgia in 2008 before open warfare took place that year between Russia and Georgia. Estonia has also been the target of significant cyberattacks, in April, 2007, when services by ministries, banks, and media were severely disrupted.

The types of cyberattacks initiated so far include distributed denial of service (DDoS), data corruption, and wiping malware with self-propagating capabilities, as well as misinformation campaigns. The increasing sophistication and complexity of the attacks require accelerated advances at all fronts of the cybersecurity process, ranging from technology and cybersecurity management and policy to education and awareness. Importantly, in addition to these attacks that are directly related to the Ukrainian conflict, there have been other incidents in different geographic areas, such as attacks on cryptocurrency and supply chain disruptions, where state actors are the suspected attackers. All these incidents provide a clear warning to governments and organizations—public and private—and to citizens worldwide of the need for coordinated actions to achieve resilience in infrastructures and services, from energy and the factory floors to web applications and government services.

Residents of countries engaged in cyberwarfare have experienced disruptions of commercial, business, and governmental services. Hacktivists and groups sympathetic to specific countries will continue to engage.

Governments increasingly realize that there is no safety without cybersecurity [31]. Resilient digital critical infrastructures and services, including OT and IT, are key to successful defense and safe operations, as the war in Ukraine demonstrates. This recent conflict is changing the way governments, organizations, and individuals build infrastructures, develop services, manage supply chains, and educate and raise awareness. Independently of the duration of the cyberwar in Ukraine, its effects will last for decades to come.

Bibliography

[1] "Known Exploited Vulnerabilities Catalog," Cybersecurity & Infrastructure Security Agency, 31 08 2022. [Online]. Available: www.cisa.gov/known-exploited-vulnerabilities-catalog. [Accessed 09 09 2022].

[2] "AlienVault Global Pulses," Alienvault, 09 09 2022. [Online]. Available: https://otx.alienvault.com/browse/global/pulses. [Accessed 09 09 2022].

[3] "Software tools," MITRE ATT&CK, 17 02 2022. [Online]. Available: https://attack.mitre.org/software/S0154/. [Accessed 12 09 2022].

[4] C. Stokel-Walker and D. Milmo, "'It's the Right Thing to Do': The 300,000 Volunteer Hackers Coming Together to FIGHT RUSSIA," The Gardian, 15 03 2022. [Online]. Available: www.theguardian.com/world/2022/mar/15/volunteer-hackers-fight-russia. [Accessed 14 09 2022].

[5] M. Srivastava, "Ukraine's Hackers: An Ex-Spook, a STARLINK and 'Owning' Russia," Financial Times, 04 09 2022. [Online]. Available: www.ft.com/content/f4d25ba0-545f-4fad-9d91-5564b4a31d77. [Accessed 09 09 2022].

[6] G. Tett, "Inside Ukraine's Open-Source War," Financial Times, 22 07 2022. [Online]. Available: www.ft.com/content/297d3300-1a65-4793-982b-1ba2372241a3. [Accessed 09 09 2022].

[7] P. Paganini, "BlackEnergy Used as a Cyber Weapon against Ukrainian Critical Infrastructure," Infosec, 12 01 2016. [Online]. Available: https://resources.infosecinstitute.com/topic/blackenergy-used-as-a-cyber-weapon-against-ukrainian-critical-infrastructure/. [Accessed 09 09 2022].

[8] A. Cherepanov and R. Lipovsky, "Industroyer: Biggest threat to industrial control systems since Stuxnet," ESET, 12 06 2017. [Online]. Available: www.welivesecurity.com/2017/06/12/industroyer-biggest-threat-industrial-control-systems-since-stuxnet/. [Accessed 09 09 2022].

[9] "W. House", "Statement from the Press Secretary," 15 02 2018. [Online]. Available: https://trumpwhitehouse.archives.gov/briefings-statements/statement-press-secretary-25/. [Accessed 20 04 2022].

[10] D. Swan, "Cyberwarfare: Russia vs Ukraine," CSCIS, 18 03 2022. [Online]. Available: https://cscis.org/2022/03/20/cyberwarfare-russia-vs-ukraine/. [Accessed 08 09 2022].

[11] "Destructive Malware Targeting Ukrainian Organizations," Microsoft Threat Intelligence Center (MSTIC), 15 01 2022. [Online]. Available: www.microsoft.com/security/blog/2022/01/15/destructive-malware-targeting-ukrainian-organizations/. [Accessed 08 09 2022].

[12] D. Kapellmann Zafra, R. Leong, C. Sistrunk, K. Proska, C. Hildebrandt, K. Lunden and N. Brubaker, "INDUSTROYER.V2: Old Malware Learns New Tricks," Mandiant, 25 04 2022. [Online]. Available: www.mandiant.com/resources/blog/industroyer-v2-old-malware-new-tricks. [Accessed 12 09 2022].

[13] Mandiant Threat Intelligence, "Evacuation and Humanitarian Documents Used to Spear Phish Ukrainian Entities [Online] [Accessed 12 10 2022].," Mandiant, 20 07 2022. [Online]. Available: www.mandiant.com/resources/blog/spear-phish-ukrainian-entities. [Accessed 10 2022].

[14] J. Wolfram, S. Hawley, T. McLellan, N. Simonian and A. Vejlby, "Trello From the Other Side: Tracking APT29 Phishing Campaigns," Mandiant, 28 04 2022. [Online]. Available: www.mandiant.com/resources/blog/tracking-apt29-phishing-campaigns. [Accessed 12 09 2022].

[15] Dragos, "Pipedream: Chernovite's Emerging Malware Targeting Industrial Control Systems," Dragos Inc., Hanover, MD, USA, 2022. [Online]. Available: https://hub.dragos.com/hubfs/116-Whitepapers/Dragos_ChernoviteWP_v2b.pdf?hsLang=en. [Accessed 27 03 2023].

[16] L. Abrams, "New Black Basta Ransomware Springs into Action with a Dozen Breaches," Bleeping Computer, 27 04 2022. [Online]. Available: www.bleepingcomputer.com/news/security/new-black-basta-ransomware-springs-into-action-with-a-dozen-breaches/. [Accessed 14 19 2022].

[17] M. Bagwe, "Update: What's BlackCat Ransomware Been Up to Recently?," Bankinfo security, 11 04 2022. [Online]. Available: www.bankinfosecurity.com/blackcat-attack-on-betting-company-disrupts-service-a-18886. [Accessed 14 09 2022].

[18] E. Pardo, "How Devastating Is a DDoS Cyberattack?," Deutsche Welle, 10 05 2022. [Online]. Available: www.dw.com/en/how-devastating-is-a-ddos-cyberattack/a-61748267. [Accessed 2022].

[19] J. Askew, "Eurovision 2022: Russian Hackers Targeted Contest, Say Italian Police," Euronews, 16 05 2022. [Online]. Available: www.euronews.com/culture/2022/05/16/eurovision-2022-russian-hackers-targeted-contest-say-italian-police. [Accessed 14 09 2022].

[20] A. Amante, "Pro-Russian Hackers Target Italy Institutional Websites-ANSA News Agency," Reuters, 11 05 2022. [Online]. Available: www.reuters.com/world/europe/pro-russian-hackers-target-italy-defence-ministry-senate-websites-ansa-news-2022–05–11/. [Accessed 09 2022].

[21] S. Treloar, "Russian Hackers Target Norway in Latest Volley of Cyber Attacks," Bloomberg, 30 06 2022. [Online]. Available: www.bloomberg.com/news/articles/2022-06-30/russian-hackers-target-norway-in-latest-volley-of-cyber-attacks?srnd=technology-vp. [Accessed 12 09 2022].

[22] P. Davies, "Estonia Hit by 'Most Extensive' Cyberattack Since 2007 Amid Tensions with Russia Over Ukraine war," Euronews, 19 08 2022. [Online]. Available: www.euronews.com/next/2022/08/18/estonia-hit-by-most-extensive-cyberattack-since-2007-amid-tensions-with-russia-over-ukrain. [Accessed 12 09 2022].

[23] "Global Cybersecurity Index 2020-Global Scores and Ranking of Countries," ITU-International Telecommunication Union, 2022. [Online]. Available: www.itu.int/epublications/publication/D-STR-GCI.01-2021-HTM-E. [Accessed 12 09 2022].

[24] "Putin's St Petersburg Speech Postponed," Yahoo!Finance, 17 06 2022. [Online]. Available: https://finance.yahoo.com/news/1-putins-st-petersburg-speech-111913097.html?guccounter=1. [Accessed 14 09 2022].

[25] K. Tishchenko, "Ukrainian Hackers Hacked Television in Crimea StratCom of the Armed Forces of Ukraine," Yahoo!News, 20 08 2022. [Online]. Available: https://news.yahoo.com/ukrainian-hackers-hacked-television-crimea-173439679.html?guccounter=1&guce_referrer=aHR0cHM6Ly93d3cuZ29vZ2xlLmNvbS8&guce_referrer_sig=AQAAAJsa-WkqNxB372pAi7Eic6gjVUGYfGRj6iq7EnilZ6_G0y2DznuVrgmA KoL2yp0Mq2VgWTqF444A2an69lc-C5DRun9g0. [Accessed 12 09 2022].

[26] D. Enerio, "Russia-Controlled 'Radio Crimea' Was Hacked, Ukraine Anthem Played On Air: Report," International Business Times, 31 08 2022. [Online]. Available: www.ibtimes.com/russia-controlled-radio-crimea-was-hacked-ukraine-anthem-played-air-report-3607677. [Accessed 12 09 2022].

[27] V. Petkauskas, "Hackers Created an Enormous Traffic Jam in Moscow," Cybernews, 06 09 2022. [Online]. Available: https://cybernews.com/cyber-war/hackers-created-an-enormous-traffic-jam-in-moscow/. [Accessed 12 09 2022].

[28] G. Carbonaro, "Hackers Honeytrap Russian Troops into Sharing Location, Base Bombed: Report," Newsweek, 22 06 2022. [Online]. Available: www.newsweek.com/hackers-honeytrap-russian-troops-sharing-location-base-bombed-report-1740070. [Accessed 09 09 2022].

[29] S. Mellor, "'You Have Blood on Your Hands': Russian Smart TVs and Online Platforms Hacked with Antiwar Messages on Victory Day," Fortune, 10 05 2022. [Online]. Available: https://fortune.com/2022/05/10/russia-smart-tvs-online-platforms-hacked-anti-war-messages-victory-day/. [Accessed 09 09 2022].

[30] A. Labs, "The World's First Truly Open Threat Intelligence Community," Alienvault inc, 20 04 2022. [Online]. Available: https://otx.alienvault.com/. [Accessed 20 04 2022].

[31]   D. Serpanos, "There is No Safety Without Security and Dependability," Computer, vol. 52, no. 6, pp. 78–81, June 2019.

[32]   M. Spring, "The Young Ukrainians Battling Pro-Russian Trolls," BBV News, 06 03 2022. [Online]. Available: www.bbc.com/news/blogs-trending-60596133. [Accessed 20 04 2022].

[33]   D. Gilbert, "Young Russian Tik Tok Influencers Appeared To be Following the Same Script When They Posted Videos Justifying the Invasion.," Vice News, 11 03 2022. [Online]. Available: www.vice.com/en/article/epxken/russian-tiktok-influencers-paid-propaganda. [Accessed 20 04 2022].

8

Cybersecurity Vulnerability and Risk of Industrial Control Systems

JOHN M.A. BOTHOS AND
VASILEIOS VLACHOS

8.1 Introduction

The First Industrial Revolution introduced the use of machinery in production through the general employment of steam energy. The Second Industrial Revolution focused on mass production employing electrical power. Then, the Third Industrial Revolution was characterised by its digital nature, with the use of information and communication technologies that increased the level of automation of production control. In the most recent years, the Fourth Industrial Revolution—known as Industry 4.0—integrates information and communication technologies (ICT) in the automation of production, improving and changing manufacturing processes.

Early industrial control systems (ICSs) operated in isolated industrial environments without being exposed either to connections with other systems via intranet networks or to the internet [1]. For this reason, the notion of protecting them against cyberthreats was not widely shared and not considered as a necessity, especially in the context of minimising production and operational costs. Even the wider adoption of the internet from the 1990s and into the early 21st century did not highlight the need for protecting ICSs, since they remained isolated to a great extent, operating in almost fully "sealed" modes inside production plants and factories. As a result, no relevant guidelines about their cybersecurity conditions and prerequisites were developed until very recently.

DOI: 10.1201/9781003314721-8

In recent years, there has been a significant conditional change, with ICSs being interconnected to each other through intranet networks or internet protocols. The modern era of Industry 4.0 is mainly characterised by the evolution of Industrial Internet of Things (IIoT), and its adoption mainly by the manufacturing and critical infrastructure sectors. In the framework of Industry 4.0, there is a merger of information technology (IT) and operational technology (OT) in the modern ICSs for the monitoring of industrial operational infrastructures [2]. ICSs are nowadays much more connected to the internet and the Internet of Things (IoT) via internet protocol systems (IPSs). That serves remote control purposes and better coordination of the production processes between different factories and production plants, in the context of networked manufacturing.

This digitalisation has brought a convergence of IT and OT connectivity, facilitating the flow of information from the industrial production field to control room engineers and providing insights to business analysts. But the legacy ICSs were not traditionally configurated for withstanding cyberattacks, and the operators of them did not have to bear considerable cybersecurity awareness and training. This evolution has raised the cybersecurity risk and the opportunity for potential cyberattacks at the ICSs of production plants and critical infrastructure by malicious entities [3]. Due to this enhanced connectivity, ICSs are vulnerable to network targeted cyberattacks, aiming to impact not only the IT procedures at the administrative layer, but also the OT processes at the physical production layer.

This is also pointed out in [4], where the continuous intertwining between the physical chain with the digital/virtual thread is characterised as a major vulnerability of an Industry 4.0 manufacturing system, which provides the potential for cyberattacks at different stages of the product development cycle. The possible targets compromise the integrity and confidentiality of the production processes, with IP thefts, industrial espionage, and sabotaging of hardware, production machinery, and power consumption metering infrastructure. All these affect the physical product development processes, resulting in low-quality production, industrial equipment failure and damage, production power line disruption, etc.

As more devices are interconnected, the more exposed the networks of interconnected production machinery or critical infrastructure become. This is because the cyberattack surface is extended [5]. It is much easier for an attacker to initially access and attack a single or a small number of systems/devices and then reach out to the other interconnected components. Such attacks are highly dangerous, since they may lead to serious malfunctioning of a considerable part of the ICSs in a very short period of time, resulting in disruptions of industrial production or in the normal provision of utility services.

8.2 Cybersecurity Vulnerabilities of Industrial Control Systems

Assessing the vulnerabilities of ICSs and their contribution in the exposure of ICSs to cyberattacks that aim to exploit them is critical for the effective protection and preservation of the smooth operation of production processes, without costly disruptions. These vulnerabilities stem from the interdependencies that modern technology evokes with the connection of different devices of production machinery and utility networks. There have been many attempts to categorise the vulnerabilities of ICSs in various taxonomies, according to the type of ICS and its operational-related features. Among them we can distinguish the following.

Durakovskiy et al. [6] describe how hackers exploit vulnerabilities of supervisory control and data acquisition (SCADA) systems. These vulnerabilities are most commonly associated with lack of secure connections between the interconnected system components, unreliable authentication processes for connection to all types of devices, inexistence of backup systems that can function individually and monitor the production processes independently of the main automated control system, and lack of cybersecurity awareness policies.

Ferrari et al. [7] also associate vulnerabilities of the real time ethernet (RTE) protocols in Industry 4.0 with the lack of cybersecurity mechanisms, such as the secure isolation of the industrial networks, the inadequate authentication and enciphering processes of RTE protocols, and the lack of cybersecurity awareness of industrial working personnel. They attribute this to the fast transformation of the RTE that provided inadequate time space for their design to incorporate cybersecurity properties as well.

Hu et al. [8] categorise vulnerabilities under five distinctive organisational sections, namely general cybersecurity policy and relevant software and hardware systems, organisation and resources for cyber-security, construction management, maintenance management, and cybersecurity-related computational capacity.

Mullet et al. [9] define vulnerabilities as weaknesses that might be exploited by hackers to compromise the system and can be either in the system, the security procedures, or the internal controls, such as remote access vulnerabilities, software vulnerabilities and LAN (local area network) or WLAN (wireless local area network) vulnerabilities.

Zhu and Liyanage [10] distinguish the cybersecurity vulnerabilities of the safety instrumented systems in the offshore oil and gas production sector in the following types: 1) governing standards and regulatory frameworks; 2) risk intelligence; 3) technical issues; and 4) operational issues—organisational and human issues.

Cormier and Ng [11] distinguish four categories of vulnerabilities of control systems, unsafe inputs, unsafe control algorithms, incorrect process models, and inadequate actuators and controlled processes.

Mosteiro-Sanchez et al. [2] characterise as vulnerabilities of IIoT systems in Industry 4.0, the lack of up-to-date software, the use of hardware with known vulnerabilities, the use of weak passwords and careless access control mechanisms, and the limited segmentation of the industrial production network.

Ur-Rehman et al. [12] distinguish the initial set up framework of IIoT networks as the main source of their vulnerabilities. Since they were originally designed to operate in isolated environments, and mainly targeting production performance, they were attributed with limited computing powers and storage capacity, and with little or any cybersecurity features like anti-virus software and intrusion detection systems. Also, these systems were designed to operate with specific network protocols with no adequate authentication and encryption commands, and hard-coded passwords. Furthermore, the management of patches to avoid unnecessary risks to the production line systems was kept at a minimum level, with no security data or low validity of related vulnerability models.

Wan et al. [13] classify the intrinsic vulnerabilities of the current networked ICSs as: 1) vulnerabilities related to the industrial plat-forms—such as operating system or database weaknesses, industrial application software bugs, and field control device flaws—which make industrial devices direct cyberattack targets; 2) vulnerabilities related to industrial networks, such as industrial communication protocol deficiencies that enable skilled cyberattackers to launch remote cyberattacks; and 3) vulnerabilities related to inadvertent cybersecurity policies and lack of cybersecurity awareness, such as lax authorisation, authentication, and access procedures; improper care for system updates; and negligent cybersecurity patching configuration. According to the authors, these vulnerabilities impose a two-dimensional cybersecurity challenge. At the edge node level, the unprecedented integration of IT and OT—in the framework of Industry4.0 IIoT with the direct connection of industrial field devices to the public information systems through the internet—creates potential cybersecurity risks and directly exposes them to cyberattacks. At network level, with the dynamic reconfiguration of various industrial network services through the internet, the passive static cybersecurity functions and strategies in traditional networked control systems could no longer be applied, making the cybersecurity of traditional fixed network structures unsustainable.

A taxonomy for classifying the vulnerabilities of ICSs should combine features of functionality and utility, as well, except of analytic recording of them according to their various types and origin. For this reason, we choose to categorise the vulnerabilities of ICSs in the framework of Industry 4.0 and IIoT, as shown in Table 8.1.

The given taxonomy provides an adequately clear picture of the degree of potential exposure of an organisation's ICS infrastructure to cyberthreats, covering all the fields where vulnerabilities can exist. From the literature review in this area, it emerges that all of these include serious vulnerabilities. The existence of vulnerabilities cannot be only attributed to the technical features of the IIoT devices and the ICS infrastructures or the interconnected networks of them. The role of humans in the loop—either as the employee operator of the systems or as the executive of the management team—is decisive for inducing or eliminating vulnerabilities.

With their actions or their omissions in their daily job routines, the operating and administrative personnel can activate or deactivate the potential for a cyberthreat to materialise and produce severe damages to the organisation's digital infrastructure. For this reason, cybersecurity awareness of every member of the organisation's personnel

Table 8.1   A Proposed Taxonomy of Industrial Control Systems' Vulnerabilities

FIELD OF VULNERABILITIES	TYPE OF VULNERABILITY
A. Vulnerabilities of the individual ICS components	1. Obsolete and legacy technologies and low cybersecurity protocols 2. Improper maintenance 3. Large number of interconnections with other devices 4. Mobility inside the production plant 5. Non-existence of cybersecurity software and irregularity of relevant updates [2, 3, 5–10, 12–28]
FIELD OF VULNERABILITIES	TYPE OF VULNERABILITY
B. Vulnerabilities of the ICS network	1. Industrial communication protocol inefficiencies 2. Network congestion 3. Lack of authorisation protocols for the interconnection with external networks 4. High degree of heterogeneity of the connected external networks 5. Low degree of potential isolation in terms of cyberattacks and relevant breaches in external interconnected networks [2, 3, 5–10, 9–23, 25, 29, 30]
FIELD OF VULNERABILITIES	TYPE OF VULNERABILITY
C. Vulnerabilities related to the human factor and the inconsistent cybersecurity management	1. Low cybersecurity awareness of personnel and executives 2. Limited interest to participate in cybersecurity training programmes 3. Lack of proper authentication, authorisation, and access procedures 4. Lack of safety and cybersecurity frameworks concerning operations, standards, prevention, mitigation, and resilience plans. 5. Dependency on external vendors and suppliers for cybersecurity issues. [2, 3, 5, 6, 8–10, 13, 15, 16, 20, 22, 23, 31–33]

becomes a necessity and the role of relevant training programmes is most significant, not only in terms of their content, but also as it concerns their frequency and repeatability, so that they can contribute to the Learning Curve of each one of the organisation's staff.

8.3 Cybersecurity Risk

The taxonomy described in Table 8.1 could serve very well also for providing numerous variables for the vulnerability factor needed for the estimation of the cybersecurity risk that an organisation faces. Cybersecurity can be regarded either as an element of the productive factor capital or as a component of production technology. So far, there has not been a lot of economic science–oriented research in this area. Most attempts have tried to elaborate mainly on the pioneering research of Gordon and Loeb [34] to model the investing behaviour of a firm seeking to maximise the expected benefit from investment for protecting information, but cybersecurity is heavily related to the productivity and the economic and technical efficiency of the production process, in the framework of Industry 4.0. The way in which cybersecurity is integrated into the production process entails certain technical modifications with specific economic consequences, such as productivity growth and economic and technical efficiency. The former concerns mainly the minimisation of production cost, while the latter is mainly about the optimisation of the usage of inputs and time in the production process. The relevant investments ensure the uninterrupted operation of industrial production, without breakdowns due to cyberattacks. For these reasons, there is much open space for novel research in this area that could exploit very interesting fields of economic science and computer science.

In this context, the role of cybersecurity risk becomes more and more significant, since it quantifies the event probability of the loss of functionality of production equipment due to operational damages caused by cyberattacks and affects the relevant investment costs for addressing potential cyberthreats and maintaining a minimum level of operational resilience. In addition, the estimation of the cybersecurity risk defines a threshold beyond which the relevant cybersecurity investments for preventing and/or addressing cyberthreats become unprofitable and it is preferable for industrial production enterprises to shift to the insurance against potential cyberattack incidents.

Furthermore, the study of the cybersecurity risk contributes to the evaluation of the economic moral hazard in coordinated cybersecurity investments concerning the issue of obtaining business benefits in interconnected computer networks and interdependent productive systems of cooperating firms, by underinvesting and exploiting other business partners' investments in joint cybersecurity schemes. The mismatch of investments addressing the cybersecurity risk provides disproportional benefits to the members of the network who do not participate in the spread of the costs of the relative investments, improving their competitiveness on the burden of the other members of the network.

Regarding the work in literature that has been done for modelling the concept of cybersecurity risk and its determinants, or the relevant cybersecurity investments, we can distinguish the following efforts.

Sawik [35] develops an efficient linear optimisation model for the mitigation of the impacts of both direct and indirect (propagated) cybersecurity risks in a multi-tier supply chain. The author attempts to determine the optimal cybersecurity investment under limited budget constraints and portfolio of cybersecurity controls to balance cybersecurity over the entire supply chain. Each supply chain node is characterised by the cost of loss caused by a cybersecurity breach and the intrinsic vulnerability, which is defined as the probability of an unsecured node being successfully attacked. For the exponential security breach function, the vulnerability of a node depends on the efficiency coefficient of security control. This is the vulnerability reduction factor for the specific node secured by a control implemented at a certain level. To reduce a node vulnerability, the cybersecurity investment is required to implement appropriate cybersecurity controls for preventing intrusions in information and control systems, and so provide protection against compromises and disruptions of confidentiality, control, integrity, authenticity, availability, and utility of supply chain nodes.

Also, in [36], Sawik presents a methodology for optimisation of cybersecurity investment in Industry 4.0 supply chains, introducing new efficiency measures such as the cybersecurity value, defined as the value gained by investing in a security safeguard portfolio and the cybersecurity ratio, defined as reduction of the cost of losses, per unit of cybersecurity investment. Sawik's methodology indicates the importance of intrinsic vulnerability in the cybersecurity design of the architecture of Industry 4.0 supply chain, even without taking into account the cyberattack probability and the potential losses from respective cybersecurity breaches. His work contributes to balancing the cybersecurity risks, due to vulnerabilities of the entire supply chain, and to the strengthening of the cybersecurity level of the weaker critical nodes of the supply chain.

Ani et al. [37] study the capability of personnel to appropriately address cyberattack incidents in an ICS environment. A statistical analysis is employed to identify the deficits of cybersecurity awareness that contribute to the increase of the likelihood of performed cyberattacks to be successful.

Sliwinski et al. [38] use a series of mathematical models for the quantitative estimation of the safety and security risk for ICSs of critical infrastructures. Their estimations are about the average probability of failure of the security design of the ICSs, based on the analysis of factors that can cause potential failures. The authors' work highlights the importance of integrating cybersecurity aspects in the design of systems operating in an industrial network.

Zarreh et al. [39] employ cost models to depict the financial losses from cyberattacks. Also, through a game theory model and statistical analysis, they attempt to predict the cyberattack probability, under different circumstances, in order to define the best cyberdefence strategy and evaluate the cybersecurity risks in manufacturing systems.

Also, Zarreh et al. [40] develop a game theory model to depict a cost function that incorporates defence strategies, production losses, and recovery from cyberattacks, as parts of the game payoff matrix. Once the cost function is developed to define the payoff matrix, the game is run for all possible combinations to find the best possible combination of the strategies and customise accordingly the manufacturing systems' utility function.

Zhu et al. [41] propose a multilevel flow model for the dynamic cybersecurity risk assessment of industrial production systems. The model describes the whole production process and the quantitative relationships among the devices and their functions, and a Bayesian network is employed to analyse the stages of the attack propagation over time and provide quantitative assessments about the consequences of the cyberattacks in the production process.

Miao et al. [42] develop a zero-sum, hybrid state stochastic game model against different types of attacks on cyber–physical systems. They assume optimality conditions for cost control and system dynamics, and attempt to estimate scalable and dynamic solutions for alternative equilibrium points, whereby the system's security and cost control are balanced.

Wang [43] presents economic models of cybersecurity investment for reducing relevant information gaps in the firms of a supply chain. Two types of cybersecurity investments are examined concerning the optimal allocation of cyberdefence measures and cyberattack detection tools. Wang tries to estimate the limits of a firm's knowledge as the cost–benefit frontier curve in the context of different classes of cybersecurity production functions and rates the perceived cybersecurity reliability as an incentive for the increase of cybersecurity investments.

Farrow [44] presents microeconomic models about the categories of cybersecurity costs and the associated financial losses. He then identifies these impacts as a set of partial derivatives that can be estimated with the use of statistical tools to study the behaviour of the firms.

A taxonomy for the work that has been done in relation to the cybersecurity risk subject areas, is presented in Table 8.2.

For the optimal estimation of the cybersecurity risk, the relevant econometric models need to incorporate as a determinant variable the cybersecurity-related vulnerabilities of an industrial production infrastructure. A first major distinction between them is among technical related vulnerabilities that involve the technical processes functioning in the production machinery and the associated technical equipment and ICSs, and behavioural-related vulnerabilities involving the operational security that incorporate the human element for monitoring the aforementioned technical processes, taking precautionary proactive measures and applying certain countermeasures in case of cyberattack.

Treating the cybersecurity risk of a system as a product derived by the multiplication of the probability of cyberattack against it, its exposure that is related to quantified technical damages and/or economic losses, and its vulnerability, expressed in lack of or inefficient cybersecurity technical processes of the systems' components and/or

Table 8.2   Fields of Cybersecurity-Related Research

AREAS OF RESEARCH	RELEVANT RESEARCH FRAMEWORK REFERENCES
A. Cybersecurity risk modelling	[30, 35, 38, 43–48]
B. Cyberattack detection	[36, 37, 39–42, 49–51]
C. Cybersecurity investments	[11, 52, 53]

behavioural procedures of the working personnel leads to the following equation.

$$R_{CS} = Prob_{CA} x\ E_{TD-FL} x\ V_{TP-BP} \tag{8.1}$$

where

R_{CS}: cybersecurity risk

E_{TD-FL}: exposure expressed either in technical damages or financial losses

V_{TP-BP}: vulnerabilities of technical processes and/or behavioural procedures

It can be assumed that the vulnerability influences both the other two factors. In this case, they can be expressed as stochastic functions of vulnerability among others, in the following forms:

$$Prob\ (cyber-attack)\ =\ f\ (vulnerability,\ ...)+\ u \tag{8.2}$$

$$Exposure\ (quantified\ technical\ damages\ /\ economic\ losses) \\ =\ f\ (vulnerability,\ ...)\ +\ u \tag{8.3}$$

with u being the stochastic error term, subject to certain statistical assumptions.

Regarding the functional form of the dependence of the probability of cyberattack on vulnerability, a logit probabilistic model can be employed in the form of

$$Prob_{CA} :\ P_i = 1\ /\ 1\ +\ e^{-\ (b1\ +\ b2\ *VTP-BP)} \tag{8.4}$$

or a probit probabilistic model in the form of

$$F^{-1}(P_i)\ =\ b_1 +\ b_2 *\ V_{TP-BP} \tag{8.5}$$

where F is the inverse of the normal cumulative distribution function

$$F(P_i)\ =\ 1\ /\ \sqrt{(2\pi)}\ *\ \int_{-\infty}^{b1\ +\ b2\ *\ VTP-BP} \left(e^{-\ (z2\ /\ 2)} \right)\ dz \tag{8.6}$$

The constant b_1 denotes the tendency for cyberattacks, which can be represented as the average number of cyberattacks in the firms of the relevant industry and sector per year during previous years. For more details regarding the structuring and the estimation of the aforementioned models, see Gujarati and Porter [54].

Concerning the functional form of the dependence of the exposure of a firm or an organisation on vulnerability, we can employ a lognormal model in the form of

$$E_{TD-FL} = A * V_{TP-BP}{}^{b1} * CSA^{b2} * CDF^{b3} \qquad (8.7)$$

The constant A denotes the tendency for cyberattacks, which can be represented as the average number of cyberattacks in the firms of the relevant industry and sector per year, in the previous years. CSA denotes the cybersecurity awareness of the management and the working personnel of the firms or the organisations, and CDF denotes the existence of precautionary mitigation policies—such as the existence of cyberthreat alert systems and reactive countermeasures for assuring the resilience of the operations of the firms or the organisations—in the relevant industry and sector. For more details regarding the structuring and the estimation of the aforementioned models, also see Gujarati and Porter [54].

Berndt [55] has also favoured relevant lognormal models for estimating hedonic price indexes for computers when incorporating the dimension of quality in the manufacturing of computer-related products (software, hardware, computer systems and networks, etc.). Also, Garvey [56] employs such models to provide estimations for cost of software development when there is uncertainty about the effort, the input prices, and the time schedule associated with software development projects.

With this transformation, we achieve to transform the estimation of cybersecurity as a product to a system of equations that can be estimated with various econometric methods. Depending on the actual mathematical forms of the given functions, and the availability and type of statistical data series, we can estimate each of these functions separately or as a system of stochastic equations, and check if we can derive statistically significant estimations regarding the influence of vulnerability in the other two factors shaping the product that depicts the cybersecurity risk of the organisation. Finally, after getting these estimations, we can proceed to provide estimation for the cybersecurity risk of the organisation.

The mathematical and econometric methodology toolbox for the estimation of systems of stochastic equations is rich. Gujarat and Porter [54] and Greene [57] provide detailed presentations about the structuring and estimation methods of simultaneous rquation models.

Furthermore, similar indicative theoretical frameworks can be found in Garvey [56], in which joint probability distribution models are utilised for modelling the estimation functions of system cost uncertainty and cost–schedule uncertainty. Systems engineering is associated with challenging schedules under limited funding frameworks. There is a continuous need for joint assessment solutions regarding the potential trade-offs between cost and time efficiency of the relevant work schedules, under given feasibility limits. Joint probability distribution models serve the validation of the mathematical integrity of the cost uncertainty analysis with key properties, since they capture the joint interactions between a system's cost and schedule, by directly incorporating correlations between variables on a given system, and their marginal distributions can receive various forms, either both normal or normal and lognormal or both lognormal, thus addressing adequately the complexity of the cost–schedule estimation relationships.

8.4 Conclusion

The present chapter presents the work that has been done to describe the cybersecurity-related vulnerabilities of industrial control systems (ICSs) in the framework of the Industrial Internet of Things (IIoT) and its incorporation in the production process and supply chain that characterises modern industry as Industry 4.0. The chapter reviews the work of several authors, presenting their efforts to categorise the cybersecurity vulnerabilities under several frameworks. It also attempts to provide an alternative taxonomy of vulnerabilities, according to their relation with on-site industrial devices, the other interconnected industrial networks, and the human factor that shapes the level of cybersecurity awareness.

Furthermore, the present chapter stresses the importance of cybersecurity as a factor that shapes productivity and efficiency of the modern industry in both technical and economic terms. It then proceeds to review the work that has been done in cybersecurity risk modelling and the associated fields of cyberattack vs. cyberdefence game modelling and relevant cybersecurity investment evaluation. Moreover, it presents a methodology for estimating the cybersecurity risk, based on theoretical frameworks of econometric analysis.

The aim of the chapter is to contribute to the scientific research in the wider field of cybersecurity, from an economic science–oriented perspective. So far, most research has been engineering-oriented works addressing the issue of modelling cybersecurity from a purely technical aspect from a computer science point of view. We aspire to contribute to this research through the employment of the theoretical framework and methodology toolbox of economic science, by juxtaposing the technical concepts of cybersecurity risk, vulnerability, and relevant damages with the economic concepts of cost and financial loss to try to find potential matching relationships.

References

1. Adam A. Creery, Eric J Byres, "Industrial cyber-security for power system and SCADA networks," Record of Conference Papers Industry Applications Society 52nd Annual Petroleum and Chemical Industry Conference, Denver, CO, 2005, pp. 303–309, DOI: 10.1109/PCICON.2005.1524567.
2. Mosteiro-Sanchez et al. "Securing IIoT using defence-in-depth: towards an end-to-end secure industry 4.0", (2020). Journal of Manufacturing Systems, Vol. 57, pp. 367–378, November 2020. DOI: 10.1016/j.jmsy.2020.10.011.
3. Corallo et al. "Cyber-security in the context of industry 4.0: A structured classification of critical assets and business impacts", (2020). Computers in Industry Vol. 114, January 2020. DOI: 10.1016/j.compind.2019.103165.
4. Babu et al. "Unauthorised usage and cyber-security risks in additively man-ufactured composites: Toolpath reconstruction using imaging and machine learning techniques", (2022). 2022 Advances in Science and Engineering Technology International Conferences (ASET), Dubai. DOI: 10.1109/ASET53988.2022.9734313.
5. Wu et al. "Cyber-security for digital manufacturing", (2018). Journal of Manufacturing Systems, Vol. 48, pp. 3–12, July 2018. DOI: 10.1016/j.jmsy.2018.03.006.
6. Durakovskiy et al. "About the cyber-security of automated process control systems", (2021). 2020 Annual International Conference on Brain-Inspired Cognitive Architectures for Artificial Intelligence (BICA*AI). 11th Annual Meeting of the BICA Society, October 10–11, November 10–15, 2020, Natal. DOI: 10.1016/j.procs.2021.06.027.
7. Ferrari et al. "Model-based stealth attack to networked control system based on real-time ethernet" (2021). IEEE Transactions on Industrial Electronics, Vol. 68, No. 8, August 2021.
8. Hu et al. "Research on cyber-security strategy and key technology of the wind farms' industrial control system", (2021). 2021 IEEE International Conference on Electrical Engineering and Mechatronics Technology (ICEEMT). DOI: 10.1109/ICEEMT52412.2021.9601591.

9. Mullet et al. "A review of cyber-security guidelines for manufacturing factories in industry 4.0", (2021). IEEE Access, Vol. 9, February 2021. DOI: 10.1109/ACCESS.2021.3056650.

10. Zhu and Liyanage "Cyber-security of offshore oil and gas production assets under trending asset digitalization contexts: A specific review of issues and challenges in safety instrumented systems", (2021). European Journal for Security Research, Vol. 6, pp. 125–149. DOI:10.1007/s41125-021-00076-2.

11. Cormier and Ng "Integrating cyber security in hazard and risk analysis", (2020). Journal of Loss Prevention in the Process Industries, Vol. 64, March 2020, DOI: 10.1016/j.jlp.2020.104044

12. Ur-Rehman et al. "Vulnerability modelling for hybrid industrial control system networks", (2020). Journal of Grid Computing, Vol. 18, pp. 863–878, July 2020. DOI:10.1007/s10723–020–09528-w

13. Wan et al. "Characteristic insights on industrial cyber security and popular defence mechanisms", (2021). China Communications Vol. 18, pp. 130–150, January 2021. DOI:10.23919/JCC.2021.01.012.

14. Stamatescu et al. "Cyber-security perspectives for smart building automation systems", (2020). 2020 12th International Conference on Electronics, Computers and Artificial Intelligence (ECAI), Bucharest, Romania, 25–27 June 2020, pp. 1–5. DOI: 10.1109/ECAI50035.2020.

15. Asghar et al. "Cyber-security in industrial control systems: issues, technologies, and challenges, (2019). Computer Networks, Vol. 165, December 2019. DOI: 10.1016/j.comnet.2019.106946.

16. Guttieres et al. "Cyberbiosecurity in advanced manufacturing models", (2019). Frontiers in Bioengineering and Biotechnology, Vol. 7, p. 210, September 2019. DOI: 10.3389/fbioe.2019.00210.

17. Kern et al. "A Cyber-security Risk Assessment Process for Model-Based Industry 4.0 Development", (2019). Proceedings of The 23rd World Multi-Conference on Systemics, Cybernetics and Informatics (WMSCI), July 6–9, 2019, Orlando, FL.

18. Leander et al. "Cyber-security challenges in large industrial IoT systems", (2019). IEEE International Conference on Emerging Technologies and Factory Automation (ETFA), Institute of Electrical and Electronics Engineers Inc., September 10–13, 2019, pp. 1035–1042. DOI: 10.1109/ ETFA.2019.8869162.

19. Li, Chen, "Challenging research for networked control systems: A survey", (2019). Transactions of the Institute of Measurement and Control, Vol. 41(9), pp. 2400–2418, June 2019. DOI: 10.1177/0142331218799818.

20. Redelinghuys et al. "Cyber-security Considerations for Industrie 4.0", (2019). 7th International Conference on Competitive Manufacturing (COMA'19), pp. 266–271, 30 Janary–1 February 2019, Stellenbosch, South Africa.

21. Abdo et al. "A safety/security risk analysis approach of Industrial Control Systems: A cyber bowtie—combining new version of attack tree with bowtie analysis", (2018). Computers & Security, Vol. 72, pp. 175–195, January 2018. DOI: 10.1016/j.cose.2017.09.004.

22. Lezzi et al. "Cyber-security for Industry 4.0 in the current literature: A reference framework", (2018). Computers in Industry, Vol. 103, pp. 97–110, December 2018. DOI: 10.1016/j.compind.2018.09.004.

23. Ani et al. "Review of cyber-security issues in industrial critical infrastructure: manufacturing in perspective", (2017). Journal of Cyber Security Technology, Vol. 1, pp. 32–74, November 2017. DOI: 10.1080/23742917.2016.1252211.

24. Cook et al. "The industrial control system cyber defence triage process", (2017). Computers & Security, Vol. 70, July 2017. DOI: 10.1016/j.cose.2017.07.009.

25. Cheminod et al. "Performance impact of commercial industrial firewalls on networked control systems," (2016). IEEE 21st International Conference on Emerging Technologies and Factory Automation (ETFA), Berlin, pp. 1–8, September 6–9, 2016, DOI: 10.1109/ETFA.2016.7733576.

26. DeSmit et al. "Cyber-physical vulnerability assessment in manufacturing systems", (2016). Procedia Manufacturing, Vol. 5, pp. 1060–1074, 44th North American Manufacturing Research Conference (NAMRC), June 27—July 1, 2016, Blacksburg, Virginia, United States. DOI: 10.1016/j.promfg.2016.08.075.

27. Cherdantseva et al. "A review of cyber security risk assessment methods for SCADA systems", (2016). Computers & Security, Vol. 56, pp. 1–27, February 2016. DOI: 10.1016/j.cose.2015.09.009.

28. Knowles et al. "A survey of cyber-security management in industrial control systems", (2015). International Journal of Critical Infrastructure Protection, Vol. 9, pp. 52–80, June 2015. DOI: 10.1016/j.ijcip.2015.02.002.

29. Kotzanikolaou et al. "Risk assessment of multi-order dependencies between critical information and communication infrastructures", (2013). Critical Information Infrastructure Protection and Resilience in the ICT Sector, pp. 153–172, January 2013. DOI: 10.4018/978-1-4666-2964-6.ch008.

30. Viduto et al. "A novel risk assessment and optimisation model for a multi-objective network security countermeasure selection problem", (2012). Decision Support Systems, Vol. 53, Issue 3, pp. 599–610, June 2012. DOI: 10.1016/j.dss.2012.04.001.

31. Karampidis et al. "Industrial cyber-security 4.0: Preparing the Operational technicians for industry 4.0," (2019). IEEE 24th International Workshop on Computer Aided Modeling and Design of Communication Links and Networks (CAMAD), Limassol, Cyprus, 2019, pp. 1–6. DOI: 10.1109/CAMAD.2019.8858454.

32. Zarreh et al. "Cyber-security concerns for total productive maintenance in smart manufacturing systems", (2019). Procedia Manufacturing, Vol. 38 pp. 532–539, 29th International Conference on Flexible Automation and Intelligent Manufacturing (FAIM2019), June 24–28, 2019, Limerick, Ireland. DOI: 10.1016/j.promfg.2020.01.067.

33. Ehrlich et al. "Modelling and automatic mapping of cyber security requirements for industrial applications: survey, problem exposition, and research focus", (2018). 14th IEEE International Workshop on Factory Communication Systems (WFCS), June 2018, Imperia. DOI: 10.1109/WFCS.2018.8402337.

34. Gordon and Loeb, "The economics of information security investment" (2002). ACM Transactions on Information and System Security, Vol. 5, No. 4, pp. 438–457, November 2002. DOI: 10.1145/581271.581274.

35. Sawik T. "Balancing cyber-security in a supply chain under direct and indirect cyber-risks", (2022). International Journal of Production Research, Vol. 60:2, 766–782, DOI: 10.1080/00207543.2021.1914356.

36. Sawik T. "A linear model for optimal cyber-security investment in Industry 4.0 supply chains", (2020). International Journal of Production Research, Vol. 60, No. 4, 1368–1385, December 2020, DOI: 10.1080/00207543.2020.1856442.

37. Ani et al. "Human factor security: evaluating the cyber-security capacity of the industrial workforce", (2018). Journal of Systems and Information Technology, Vol. 21, No. 9, November 2018. DOI: 10.1108/JSIT-02-2018-0028.

38. Śliwiński et al. "Integrated functional safety and cyber security analysis", (2018). IFAC—PapersOnLine, Vol. 51, Issue 24, pp. 1263–1270, August 2018.10th IFAC Symposium on Fault Detection, Supervision and Safety for Technical Processes (SAFEPROCESS), Warsaw, Poland, 29–31 August 2018. DOI: 10.1016/j.ifacol.2018.09.572.

39. Zarreh et al. "Cyber-security analysis of smart manufacturing system using game theory approach and quantal response equilibrium", (2018). Procedia Manufacturing, Vol. 17, pp. 1001–1008, July 2018.28th International Conference on Flexible Automation and Intelligent Manufacturing (FAIM), June 11–14, 2018, Columbus, OH, USA, Global Integration of Intelligent Manufacturing and Smart Industry for Good of Humanity. DOI: 10.1016/j.promfg.2018.10.087.

40. Zarreh et al. "A game theory-based cyber-security assessment model for advanced manufacturing systems", (2018). Procedia Manufacturing, Vol. 26, pp. 1255–1264, July 2018.46th SME North American Manufacturing Research Conference, (NAMRC), June 18–22, 2018, Texas, USA. DOI: 10.1016/j.promfg.2018.07.162.

41. Zhu et al. "Extended multilevel flow model-based dynamic risk assessment for cyber-security protection in industrial production systems", (2018). International Journal of Distributed Sensor Networks, Vol. 14, No. 6, September 2018. DOI:10.1177/1550147718779564

42. Miao et al. "A hybrid stochastic game for secure control of cyber-physical systems", (2017). Automatica, Vol. 93, pp. 55–63, July 2018. DOI: 10.1016/j.automatica.2018.03.012.

43. Wang "Knowledge set of attack surface and cyber-security rating for firms in a supply chain", 92017. SSRN, November 3, 2017. DOI: 10.2139/ssrn.3064533.

44. Farrow "Cyber-security: Integrating Information into the Microeconomics of the Consumer and the Firm", (2016). Journal of Information Security, Vol. 7, No. 5, pp. 281–290, October 2016. DOI: 10.4236/jis.2016.75023.

45. Sen and Song "An IIoT-based networked industrial control system architecture to secure industrial applications", (2021). 2021 IEEE Industrial Electronics and Applications Conference, 22–23 November 2021, DOI: 10.1109/IEACON51066.2021.9654520.

46. Sargolzaei et al. "Security challenges of networked control systems", (2018). In: Amini, M., Boroojeni, K., Iyengar, S., Pardalos, P., Blaabjerg, F., Madni, A. (eds) Sustainable Interdependent Networks. Studies in Systems, Decision and Control, Vol. 145. Springer, Cham. DOI: 10.1007/978-3-319-74412-4_6.

47. Mohamudally and Peermamode-Mohaboob "Building An Anomaly Detection Engine (ADE) For IoT Smart Applications", (2018). Procedia Computer Science, Vol. 134, pp. 10–17. The 13th International Conference on Future Networks and Communications (FNC-2018), July 13–15, 2018. The 15th International Conference on Mobile Systems and Pervasive Computing (MobiSPC), August 13–15, 2018, Gran Canaria, Spain.

48. Naghmouchi et al. "A new risk assessment framework using graph theory for complex ICT systems", (2016). MIST'16: Proceedings of the 8th ACM CCS International Workshop on Managing Insider Security Threats, pp. 97–100, October 2016. DOI: 10.1145/2995959.2995969.

49. Du et al. "Stability analysis of token-based wireless networked control systems under deception attacks", (2018). Information Sciences, Vol. 459, pp. 168–182, August 2018. DOI: 10.1016/j.ins.2018.04.085.

50. Sargolzaei et al. "Generalised attack model for networked control systems, evaluation of control methods", (2017). Intelligent Control and Automation, Vol. 8, No 3, pp. 164–174, August 2017. DOI: 10.4236/ica.2017.83013.

51. Zhang et al. "Multimodel-based incident prediction and risk assessment in dynamic cyber-security protection for industrial control systems", (2016). IEEE Transactions on Systems, Man, and Cybernetics: Systems, Vol. 46, No. 10, pp. 1429–1444, October 2016. DOI: 10.1109/TSMC.2015.2503399.

52. Li and Xu "Cyber-security investments in a two-echelon supply chain with third-party risk propagation", (2020). International Journal of Production Research, Vol. 59, No. 4, 1216–1238, February 2020, DOI: 10.1080/00207543.2020.1721591

53. Sargolzaei et al. "Resilient design of networked control systems under time delay switch attacks, application in smart grid," (2017). IEEE Access, Vol. 5, pp. 15901–15912, July 27, 2017. DOI: 10.1109/ACCESS.2017.2731780.

54. Gujarati and Porter (2008). Basic Econometrics, 5a Edição. McGraw-Hill/Irwin, New York.

55. Berndt (1996). The Practice of Econometrics: Classic and Contemporary. Har/Dis. Addison Wesley

56. Garvey, Book and Covert (2016). Probability Methods for Cost Uncertainty Analysis: A Systems Engineering Perspective. CRC press.

57. Greene "Econometric Analysis", (2003).

58. Zhang, Cheng, Shi and Chen "Optimal DoS attack scheduling in wireless networked control system", (2015). IEEE Transactions on Control Systems Technology, Vol. 24, No. 3, pp. 843–852, May 2016. DOI: 10.1109/TCST.2015.2462741.

Cyberwarfare and Cyberterrorism

What Is the Critical Difference?

PETE WILKINSON AND LEANDROS MAGLARAS

9.1 Introduction

When, if ever, does an act of cyberwarfare cross domains with that of cyberterrorism? As the well used quote goes, "One man's terrorist is another man's freedom fighter"—so how do we differentiate between the two?

The Cambridge dictionary definition of cyberterrorism is: "the use of the internet to damage or destroy computer systems for political or other reasons" [1].

The same source states the definition of cyberwarfare as: "the use of the internet to attack an enemy, by damaging things such as communication and transport systems or water and electricity supplies" [2].

The only difference of substance in the two definitions is the motivations behind the actions, but the second order effects of cyberwarfare and cyberterrorism have the same outcome, with the civilian population bearing the brunt of the impacts. The legal implications of cyberwarfare also appear to be a grey area of international law. In 2013, a group of experts wrote an academic, nonbinding study of how international law should apply to cyberwarfare. This was originally called the *Tallinn Manual on the International Law Applicable to Cyber Warfare* [3]. Its first iteration focused on large-scale cyberevents that could occur a part of a wider conflict, with the second edition updated to include the governance of cyberwarfare to peacetime legal regimes [4].

DOI: 10.1201/9781003314721-9

It must also be noted that there are many differing definitions of cyberwarfare, with no agreed-upon standard. There has been debate on whether the term 'cyberwarfare' is the correct descriptor. In 2012, Eugene Kaspersky, the founder of Kaspersky Labs, stated in a news article [5] that 'cyberterrorism' is a more accurate term than 'cyberwarfare'. He states that "with today's attacks, you are clueless about who did it or when they will strike again. It's not cyber-war, but cyberterrorism."

It is entirely possible that a nation-state has the capability to conduct both types of cyberactions, either by proxy in the form of a criminal group [6], or as part of a deliberate campaign [7]. The difficulty with attributing a cyberattack with a nation-state has always had its challenges. If one can narrow an attack down to an internet protocol (IP) address in a specific country, then the country will simply profess that the evidence has been manipulated to apportion blame in a false flag operation. Even if blame can be attributed, what consequences will befall those that are caught in cyberspace? Many countries believe they have been hacked by either Russia, China, or any number of states, but any repercussions seem to be either further retaliation within the cyberspace or financial sanctions in the real world, and certainly not with any kinetic military reprisals. North Korea is one of the most heavily sanctioned countries in the world, but this does not appear to curtail its criminal activity, so do the sanctions work effectively? A better term for the activities of North Korea is cybercriminality, as the main motivation for illegal activity seems to be purely financial, either by ransomware or the theft of intellectual property (IP) from technical companies. North Korea will not see its activity as criminal, rather that it is standing up to Western aggression and crippling sanctions, fighting back using all available resources. It is this blending of motivations and their definitions that will be explored within this chapter.

This chapter will seek to ascertain if the line between cyberterrorism and cyberwarfare has been blurred to such an extent that they are one and the same, or if there is still a delineation between the two.

9.2 Digitalisation and Cyberattacks

Technology has no doubt made the act of attribution of both cyberwarfare and terrorism more difficult. Before cyberwarfare was considered the fifth dimension of warfare [8], nation-states were waging proxy wars in countries where they wanted to affect influence. Great care and consideration had to be taken to ensure that any investigations into the activities would not lead back to an embarrassed government. If we use Russia's invasion of Afghanistan in 1979 and the resulting decade-long conflict [9] as an example, the United States supplied training and weapons to the Mujahedeen as a way of weakening Soviet power in the region, and by definition, on the world stage, affecting perceptions during the Cold War. This proxy war allowed the United States to gain a huge amount of intelligence about the Russian Army, including its doctrine and tactics, as well as how armoured vehicles and aircraft stood up to the latest Western materiel and munitions. All this was achieved with a relatively low chance of compromise, and certainly not risk of a nuclear war breaking out between East and West. More than 40 years later, proxy wars are still being waged, but now much of it takes place over the internet.

The ubiquitous element of technology now means that anyone with a laptop and a little knowledge can appear to be hosted in any country they want. In simple terms, the use of a virtual private network (VPN) to mask one's real location is not sufficient to hide from the attentions of a nation-state, but done correctly, it can deter a criminal investigation from crossing borders, incurring costs and generally making life very difficult for any investigators.

The rise of bulletproof hosting as a service means that attribution can almost be impossible by any investigating organisation [10]. It means that any group that wants to utilise the assets to host their malware can do so without the threat of being tracked by law enforcement. The physical hardware usually sits within a jurisdiction that cares little about legal standards and usually ignores complaints from any third parties. To combat these illegal assets, the IP address blocks of the servers can be blocked by other internet service providers (ISPs) so that their users cannot accidently visit the sites if they are sent any malicious links.

The use of affiliates within the criminal gangs also blurs the intelligence as to who is responsible for attacks, as they may use another level of deception to remove themselves from the criminal gang network. The ransomware groups effectively hire affiliates to hack into networks, which is arguably the most difficult part of the process and offers them a commission on any ransom paid by the organisation which they breached.

9.3 Threats and Vulnerabilities

Threats can and do come from many different groups involved in cyberwarfare. The threat of crippling communications systems or power grids in times of war is often the image one would expect to see manifested during open warfare, but what of the other threats?

Cyberespionage can be a precursor to open warfare, as countries look to exploit any technological advantages that their enemies may possess. IP within the defence industry is a secret that is guarded as closely as any physical asset. Country A will always try to see what country B is developing in regards to state-of-the-art technology and weapons—and cyberspace is just another avenue in which intelligence agencies will collect this data.

The weakening of technology-controlled infrastructure—such as the ability to cripple a power station, which would have required an air strike 30 years ago [11]—can now be achieved with non-kinetic measures [12]. We know that nation-states also collect unknown vulnerabilities in the form of zero-day exploits which are used in cyber-operations [13]. These exploits are purposely kept secret and hidden from the vendors, going against the responsible disclosure ethics by which most security researchers are bound. This means that these zero days can be used in the wild to exploit devices before the vendors are aware they exist [14]. In rare cases these zero-day exploits can be used together to construct a payload that can gain access to even the most secure of locations.

While nation-states have the resources to look for vulnerabilities to use for their own means, terrorist and/or criminal groups do not have the luxury of seemingly infinite resources. Instead, they tend to use known exploits and look for systems that have not been quick enough or diligent enough to patch the vulnerabilities. Even without the use of zero-day exploits, the sheer volume of exploits available on the internet mean that attacks are becoming more frequent.

A recent chart from Check Point, a U.S.-Israeli information technology (IT) security firm, shows the organisational breakdown of attacks for 2021 [15]. The education/research sector saw the greatest volume of attacks, followed by government/military. This evidence points towards the fact that concerted effort is paid by hackers to access secret data. It is also true that state-run entities do not always have the tightest security [16], mainly due to budget constraints, which can make them easier targets than commercial entities such as banks that have greater resources and are regulated to ensure conformity with the latest security requirements.

9.4 What Is Cyberwarfare?

One element that appears to be omitted from the Cambridge definition of cyberwarfare is the mention of nation-states. Britannica's definition states "war conducted in and from computers and the networks connecting them, waged by states or their proxies against other states" [17]. The definition by Britannica—that only nation-states can conduct cyberwarfare—is interesting and does raise the bar for entry into cyberwarfare activities.

An early indicator that warfare could be entering a new digital era may have taken place in 1982 when a U.S. satellite detected a large explosion in the Siberian area of Russia. A book released in 2004 has now described how the U.S. Central Intelligence Agency (CIA) had hidden code within software that was passed to a KGB agent whose mission was the theft of U.S. IP [18]. According to the author, the CIA had coded a logic bomb that would cause the software to malfunction after a number of months and cause catastrophic damage to the pipeline. Russian agents from the era have claimed the story as 'rubbish', stating it was a small incident, repaired within a day, and caused no casualties.

The validity of the story can not positively be confirmed, with many believing it to be a hoax, but the parallels with the Stuxnet attack cannot be ignored.

Perhaps the most famous case of cyberespionage is the attack on the Iranian plutonium processing plant by the malware known as Stuxnet. This attack on the Natanz nuclear plant was seen as a proportional attack on another nation-state that was trying to develop a nuclear capability. The reason for the apprehension was due to the threatening rhetoric used by Iran towards Israel, which came to the conclusion that Iran's possession of nuclear weapons could mean a frightening escalation between the two nations. The weight of evidence points towards a U.S.-Israeli collaboration with regards to attribution [19], but many questions still remain unanswered. Attribution aside, there was not much condemnation from the wider community of one nation-state attacking another, perhaps setting the scene that cyberwarfare is somehow more palatable than open warfare. If a nation-state had dropped a bomb on the nuclear plant, the consequences would be very different, probably causing a kinetic response by Iran, further desta-bilising the region.

The Stuxnet malware was a specific attack on Siemens PCS 7 con-trollers (PCS meaning process control system), which one can assume was a deliberate targeting of those used within the Natanz facility. The speculation around attribution was focussed on a number found within the code of the malware, 19790509. The numbers can be con-strued to read like a date and possibly represent May 9, 1979. A paper written by Armed Forces Communications & Electronics Association International (AFCEA) named "The History of Stuxnet" explains in detail how the attribution was driven by the media.

> The news media took the discovery of the date and credited it as a reference to the execution of Habib Elghanian who was a Jewish Iranian living in Tehran. The death of Habib Elghanian was one of the first civilian executions by the Islamic Iranian government following the 1979 Iranian revo-lution. Due to the execution, around 100,000 members of the Jewish community in Iran left the country. This led to the creation of theories and news articles that the numbers were left by an Israeli coder as a statement of revenge placed inside of Stuxnet [20].

Whether or not attribution can ever be correctly agreed upon, what is beyond doubt is that the attack on the Natanz plant was conducted by a nation-state. The number of resources used to carry out the attack precludes any terrorist or criminal organisation from being responsible.

One issue that the perpetrators of the Stuxnet malware probably never considered was how Iran may learn lessons from the incident. Reverse engineering malware gives researchers the ability to inves-tigate how it works—and more importantly, what exploits were used. The U.S. National Security Agency (NSA) was aware of Iran's growing capability of learning from attacks against it in 2012 [21]. If the Stuxnet worm deployment was seen as a just and measured response to progression of the Iranian nuclear programme, then it stands to reason that any condemnation of Iran repurposing the malware and using it to attack its enemies could be seen as hypocritical. This hypothesis leads back to the sentiment of one man's terrorist is another man's freedom fighter, and the idea that any distinction between cyberwarfare and terrorism is a distinction based merely on which side of the fence one sits on.

What descriptor is used if we look at a nation-state hacking a corporation, such as the case of North Korea hacking Sony in an attempt to stop the release of a film that considered disrespectful to its leader? [22]. Then-U.S. President Barack Obama suggested at the time it was not an act of cyberwarfare, but instead an act of cybervandalism, and that any response would be "proportionate" [23].

On the weight of evidence, it does appear that in order for a cyberattack to be deemed as cyberwarfare, it must be a state-on-state incident, with material damage being caused, either by the manipulation of critical national infrastructure (CNI) or by theft of sensitive data.

9.5 What Is Cyberterrorism?

There are many definitions of what constitutes cyberterrorism, with many early attempts being superseded by more recent ones that have been amended due to how the landscape has changed. An oft-cited definition by information security researcher Dorothy E. Denning made as part of a testimony in 2000 remains as a good example that has stood the test of time. In the testimony, she makes many points around the nuance of cyberterrorism but does attempt to define it: "It is generally understood to mean unlawful attacks and threats of attack against computers, networks, and the information stored therein when done to intimidate or coerce a government or its people in furtherance of political or social objectives" [24].

One of the most recent events that could be categorised as cyberterrorism was the attempt by Russia to influence the U.S. elections in 2016 [25]. Although this attack was not perpetrated by a terrorist group per se, the aim of the attack was definitely political. The aim of the attack was to weaken the position of Hilary Clinton in the eyes of the voters, therefore improving Donald Trump's chances of being elected. Whilst there is no evidence of actual vote tampering, there were significant email phishing campaigns that allowed the Russians to access the emails of members of staff and those email servers containing sensitive information [26]. The attribution aspect of this case appears to be conclusive, with the United States charging 12 individuals with hacking offences [27].

The reason for the interference, apart from the opportunity to undermine the U.S. democratic process, could be the destabilisation of continuity within the White House [28]. Clinton was coming from the role of U.S. Secretary of State, a role in which she had criticised Russian President Vladimir Putin in the aftermath of the Russian elections in 2011. Protests in Moscow followed Clinton's claims that the election was unfair [29].

In a somewhat turning of the tables, Russia has recently been subject to attacks from a group known as the IT Army of Ukraine [30]. This group was formed due to a request by the Ukrainian digital transformation manager, asking hackers around the world to come together and attack targets with links to Russia. From its formation, it now boasts a membership base of more than 280,000, with a list of successful operations that spanned the whole of the Russian government's digital infrastructure. In coordinated attacks, it managed to barrage the Kremlin website with a distributed denial of service (DDoS) attack, as well as a host of other governmental websites, also breaching a number of commercial entities from banks to gas companies, and stealing data.

The overall optics around the IT Army appear to be that of freedom fighters looking to take down the Russian dictators that invaded a sovereign country, at least from a Western perspective, but the Russian authorities probably view the group as terrorists. The motivations for the IT Army certainly meet the threshold for cyberterrorism, as they look to change Russian policy around the invasion.

Hacktivist organisations such as Anonymous could be considered modern-day terrorist organisations, using techniques such as denial of service (DoS) to take down websites of those who they consider to be the enemy. Much of their activity is based around disrupting autocratic regimes and perceived fascist and or greedy corporations around the world. Their cyberactivities are usually limited to DDoS and doxxing, but on occasions, they have shown the ability to coordinate more meaningful attacks. It has been estimated that during the first three months of the Russian invasion of Ukraine, some of the more invasive attacks from Anonymous have yielded almost six terabytes of information from Russian companies [31]. But what Anonymous appears to lack that precludes it as a true terrorist organisation is a unified purpose and the leadership to force any real change.

Denning's definition of cyberterrorism does appear to fit the actions of the IT Army of Ukraine, but if we follow the reasoning of the Britannica definition, the IT Army is actually just a proxy of the Ukrainian government, so it could also fall under the category of cyberwarfare. Herein lies the problem for anyone tasked with designating attacks in cyberspace. If one cannot even attribute an attack to a nation-state, then the attack cannot justifiably be denounced as either cyberwarfare or cyberterrorism.

9.6 Conclusions

The question posted at the beginning of this chapter—"Is there a difference between cyberwarfare and cyberterrorism?"—is nuanced, but under scrutiny, the evidence does not support the assertion that there is any actual difference other than who is committing the act. State-sponsored cyberactivity comes in many forms, from direct action of state-run intelligence services through to leveraging organised crime groups, or at the very least, turning a blind eye to their online criminality if it is aimed at the common enemy. Russia attempted to pervert the course of the U.S. elections, which would appear to fall into the terrorism bracket, and we can also assume it was an attack designed to weaken the democratic process in the United States. This attack on national infrastructure is also a tenet of cyberwarfare, and given that Russia has waged cyberwarfare on the United States in the past, one would be inclined to suggest that any actions taken by Russia in cyberspace should be classed as cyberwarfare, given Russia's status as a nation-state.

Whether or not the attribution can ever be 100% proven, there is still a definite disconnect in the actual consequences for a nation-state found to be conducting nefarious activities. It may well be the fact that a cyber 'bomb' is seen as a soft crime, similar to how espionage is viewed, that does not carry the same weight of an actual bomb, so any retribution must be measured to fit the crime. We could expect retribution to take place within cyberspace, with attacks on the networks of the instigators. This may happen more than we know, as both the United States and the UK often admit to being breached by suspected nation-state actors—but we rarely, if ever, hear the same from those states long suspected of either conducting cyberactivities or harbouring the criminals that perform complimentary actions.

The very definition of terrorism—be it cyber- or otherwise—is the use of force to leverage a particular political goal. There is currently no terrorist organisation that is conducting cyberoperations at scale in support of their political goals, so is there such a thing as cyberterrorism?

One could argue that cyberwarfare is only conducted by nation-states against other nation-states, with organised crime taking the mantle of what may be considered terrorism but is more akin to criminality, if the only motivation factor appears to be financial.

Bibliography

[1] Dictionary.cambridge.org., 2022. *Cyber Warfare.* [online] Available at: <https://dictionary.cambridge.org/dictionary/english/cyber-warfare> [Accessed 16 May 2022].

[2] Dictionary.cambridge.org., 2022. *Cyberterrorism.* [online] Available at: <https://dictionary.cambridge.org/dictionary/english/cyberterrorism> [Accessed 16 April 2022].

[3] Schmitt, M., 2022. *Tallinn Manual on the International Law Applicable to Cyber Warfare.* [online] Assets.cambridge.org. Available at: <https://assets.cambridge.org/97811070/24434/frontmatter/9781107024434_frontmatter.pdf> [Accessed 24 March 2022].

[4] Schmitt, M. and Vihul, L., 2017. *Tallinn Manual 2.0 on the International Law Applicable to Cyber Operations.* [online] Assets.cambridge.org. Available at: <https://assets.cambridge.org/97811071/77222/frontmatter/9781107177222_frontmatter.pdf> [Accessed 26 March 2022].

[5] Shamah, D., 2012. *Latest viruses Could Mean 'End of World as We Know It,' Says Man Who Discovered Flame.* [online] Timesofisrael.com. Available at: <www.timesofisrael.com/experts-we-lost-the-cyber-war-now-were-in-the-era-of-cyber-terror/> [Accessed 4 April 2022].

[6] CISA, 2022. *Russian State-Sponsored and Criminal Cyber Threats to Critical Infrastructure | CISA.* [online] Cisa.gov. Available at: <www.cisa.gov/uscert/ncas/alerts/aa22-110a> [Accessed 8 April 2022].

[7] Paul, K., 2022. *Russia's Slow Cyberwar in Ukraine Begins to Escalate, Experts Say.* [online] the Guardian. Available at: <www.theguardian.com/world/2022/apr/01/russia-ukraine-cyberwar> [Accessed 30 March 2022].

[8] Paganini, P., 2016. *NATO Officially Recognizes Cyberspace a Warfare Domain.* [online] Security Affairs. Available at: <https://securityaffairs. co/wordpress/48484/cyber-warfare-2/nato-cyberspace-warfare-domain. html> [Accessed 5 April 2022].

[9] Dormandy, X., 2007. *Afghanistan's Proxy War.* [online] Belfer Center for Science and International Affairs. Available at: <www.belfercenter.org/ publication/afghanistans-proxy-war> [Accessed 31 March 2022].

[10] Krebs, B., 2019. *Meet the World's Biggest 'Bulletproof' Hoster.* [online] Krebsonsecurity.com. Available at: <https://krebsonsecurity.com/2019/07/ meet-the-worlds-biggest-bulletproof-hoster/> [Accessed 6 May 2022].

[11] The Editors of Encyclopedia Britannica, 2022. *Strategic Bombing | Military Tactic.* [online] Encyclopedia Britannica. Available at: <www.britannica. com/topic/strategic-bombing> [Accessed 4 May 2022].

[12] Macola, I., 2020. *The Five Worst Cyberattacks against the Power Industry Since 2014.* [online] Power Technology. Available at: <www.power- technology.com/analysis/the-five-worst-cyberattacks-against-the-power- industry-since2014/> [Accessed 8 April 2022].

[13] Gaist, N., 2018. *To Stockpile or Not to Stockpile Zero-Days?.* [online] Dark Reading. Available at: <www.darkreading.com/threat-intelligence/to- stockpile-or-not-to-stockpile-zero-days-> [Accessed 10 April 2022].

[14] Sentinel One, 2019. *EternalBlue Exploit: What It Is and How It Works.* [online] Sentinel One. Available at: <www.sentinelone.com/blog/eternalblue- nsa-developed-exploit-just-wont-die/> [Accessed 2 April 2022].

[15] Check Point Blog, 2022. *Check Point Research: Cyber Attacks Increased 50% Year over Year—Check Point Software.* [online] Check Point Software. Available at: <https://blog.checkpoint.com/2022/01/10/check-point-research-cyber- attacks-increased-50-year-over-year/> [Accessed 12 April 2022].

[16] Hern, A., 2017. *NHS Could Have Avoided WannaCry Hack with 'Basic IT Security', says Report.* [online] the Guardian. Available at: <www.theguardian. com/technology/2017/oct/27/nhs-could-have-avoided-wannacry-hack- basic-it-security-national-audit-office> [Accessed 12 April 2022].

[17] Sheldon, J., 2022. *Cyberwar.* [online] Encyclopedia Britannica. Available at: <www.britannica.com/topic/cyberwar> [Accessed 17 May 2022].

[18] Hoffman, D., 2004. *Reagan Approved Plan-to Sabotage Soviets.* [online] the Washington post. Available at: <www.washingtonpost.com/archive/politics/ 2004/02/27/reagan-approved-plan-to-sabotage-soviets/a9184eff-47fd- 402e-beb2-63970851e130/> [Accessed 12 April 2022].

[19] Nakashima, E. and Warrick, J., 2012. *Stuxnet Was Work of U.S. and Israeli Experts, Officials Say.* [online] the Washington post. Available at: <www. washingtonpost.com/world/national-security/stuxnet-was-work-of-us- and-israeli-experts-officials-say/2012/06/01/gJQAlnEy6U_story.html> [Accessed 12 April 2022].

[20] Cyber Conflict Studies Association, 2012. *The History of Stuxnet: Key Takeaways for Cyber Decision Makers Military Category Cyber Conflict Studies Association -Call for Papers.* [online] Available at: www.afcea. org/committees/cyber/documents/thehistoryofstuxnet.pdf. [Accessed 12 April 2022].

[21] NSA, 2007. *Iran—Current Topics, Interaction with GCHQ—The Intercept.* [online] The Intercept. Available at: <https://theintercept.com/document/2015/02/10/iran-current-topics-interaction-gchq/> [Accessed 8 May 2022].

[22] BBC News. 2014. *The Interview: A Guide to the Cyber Attack on Hollywood.* [online] Available at: <www.bbc.co.uk/news/entertainment-arts-30512032> [Accessed 30 March 2022].

[23] Holland, S. and Chiacu, D., 2014. *Obama Says Sony Hack Not An Act of War.* [online] www.reuters.com. Available at: <www.reuters.com/article/us-sony-cybersecurity-usa-idUSKBN0JX1MH20141222> [Accessed 17 March 2022].

[24] Denning, D., 2000. *Cyberterrorism Testimony before the Special Oversight Panel on Terrorism Committee on Armed Services U.S. House of Representatives.* [online] Faculty.nps.edu. Available at: <http://faculty.nps.edu/dedennin/publications/Testimony-Cyberterrorism2000.htm> [Accessed 17 April 2022].

[25] Abrams, A., 2019. *Here's What We Know So Far about Russia's 2016 Meddling.* [online] Time. Available at: <https://time.com/5565991/russia-influence-2016-election/> [Accessed 10 May 2022].

[26] DHS Press Office, 2016. *Joint Statement from the Department of Homeland Security and Office of the Director of National Intelligence on Election Security.* [online] www.dhs.gov. Available at: <www.dhs.gov/news/2016/10/07/joint-statement-department-homeland-security-and-office-director-national> [Accessed 8 April 2022].

[27] BBC, 2018. *Twelve Russians Charged with US 2016 Election Hack.* [online] BBC News. Available at: <www.bbc.co.uk/news/world-us-canada-44825345> [Accessed 29 April 2022].

[28] McFaul, M., 2019. *Securing American Elections Prescriptions for Enhancing the Integrity and Independence of the 2020 U.S. Presidential Election and Beyond.* [ebook] p. 4. Available at: <https://fppc.ca.gov/content/dam/fppc/NS-Documents/DTTF/Stanford%20Cyber%20Policy%20Center%20-%20Securing%20American%20Elections%20-%20June%206%202019.pdf#page=11> [Accessed 2 May 2022].

[29] Elder, M., 2011. *Vladimir Putin Accuses Hillary Clinton of Encouraging Russian Protests.* [online] the Guardian. Available at: <www.theguardian.com/world/2011/dec/08/vladimir-putin-hillary-clinton-russia> [Accessed 5 May 2022].

[30] Shead, S., 2022. *We Want Them to Go to the Stone Age': Ukrainian Coders Are Splitting Their Time between Work and Cyber Warfare.* [online] www.cnbc.com. Available at: <www.cnbc.com/2022/03/23/ukrainian-coders-splitting-their-time-between-day-job-and-cyberwar.html> [Accessed 8 April 2022].

[31] Paganini, P., 2022. *Since Declaring Cyber War on Russia Anonymous Leaked 5.8 TB of Russian Data.* [online] Security Affairs. Available at: <https://securityaffairs.co/wordpress/130554/hacktivism/anonymous-leaked-5-8-tb-russian-data.html> [Accessed 17 May 2022].

Index

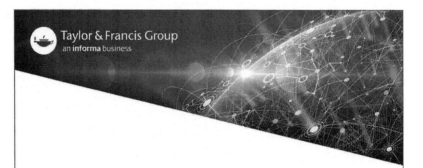

Printed and bound by CPI Group (UK) Ltd, Croydon, CR0 4YY

17/10/2024

01775681-0005